D0928163

THIS EARTHLY FRAME

THIS EARTHLY FRAME

The Making of American Secularism

DAVID SEHAT

Yale

UNIVERSITY PRESS

New Haven and London

Published with assistance from the foundation established in
memory of Amasa Stone Mather of the Class of 1907,
Yale College.

Yale University Press books may be purchased in quantity for
educational, business, or promotional use. For information, please
e-mail sales.press@yale.edu (U.S. office) or sales@yaleup.co.uk
(U.K. office).

Set in Janson type by IDS Infotech Ltd.
Printed in the United States of America.

Library of Congress Control Number: 2021941541
ISBN 978-0-300-24421-2 (hardcover : alk. paper)

A catalogue record for this book is available from the
British Library.

This paper meets the requirements of ANSI/NISO Z39.48-1992
(Permanence of Paper).

10 9 8 7 6 5 4 3 2 1

For
David A. Hollinger
and
Thomas L. Haskell, In Memoria

O thou, to whom all creatures bow within this earthly frame,

Through all the world how great art thou!

How glorious is thy name!

—PSALM 8:9, *Book of Common Prayer* (1818)

Contents

THIS EARTHLY FRAME

Introduction

In 1787, when former revolutionaries met in Philadelphia to draft the U.S. Constitution, they decided in defiance of all custom to make it a government without God. In spite of their decision the United States has never had an entirely secular arrangement. Christians of various stripes have long been leaders within American governance, holding office, directing institutions, dispersing funds, and setting the contours of debate. The religious cast to public life has pushed other groups into a series of difficult decisions, prompting them to criticism, accommodation, or cooperation depending on the issue. The tensions have made the United States one of the central sites in the wider disagreement about how religion and governance should be related.

This book traces the lineaments of the dispute. It shows how people conceptualized a nation based not, as the nineteenth-century agnostic Robert Ingersoll put it, "upon the rights of gods, but upon the rights of men." It also tracks how people resisted the secular idea, insisting that all liberties come from God so that religion ought to remain a central pillar of public life.[1]

To understand the historical debate we need to correct several assertions frequently made by contemporary writers. The first correction is straightforward. It is common to find in both contemporary and scholarly commentary the notion that the United States was born secular. The declaration has a far-reaching political implication. If the United States was set up to be secular, then any religious privilege in public life is both an aberration and a betrayal of founding intention.

There is, to be sure, a core truth in the claim. The godlessness of the Constitution was remarkable for its time. The unwillingness of the constitutional framers to use God for social stability suggests a desire on the part of at least some framers to limit religion's public role. But that founding desire did not translate into the secular political arrangement that some had hoped. Given the system of American federalism, states were free to support religion in any way they wished. Most early state governments sought to use the Christian religion to uphold social stability. They paid churches. They had religious tests for office. They maintained blasphemy laws, enforced Sabbath laws, and used religious ideas to prohibit divorce, obscenity, and vice. Even at the federal level religious ideas penetrated the government. It took time and effort before the secularist vision gained traction in American political culture. The United States, put simply, was not born secular. It has become more secular over time.[2]

Other commenters have gone in an alternate direction. They recognize the historic prominence of Christianity in American public life and assert that that prominence was modulated, even overcome, through the determined activities of nonbelievers. Again, there is a vital truth here. From the beginning of American history nonbelievers have grappled with the Christian strictures that defined and limited American life. They approached their position out of a variety of religious traditions, and their posture of dissent supported a remarkable number of political philosophies and persuasions. Regardless of their differences they came together to form a secularist class of activists and intellectuals who critiqued the dominant religious structures of American government.[3]

But the story of American secularism—and this cannot be stressed enough—is not merely a story of unbelief. Religious people had a central role to play in the history, and not just as antagonists. In a society with a high degree of religious adherence, a secular democracy requires religious support to have success and legitimacy. In the United States, secularism had that support in the past. Religious Jews, ecumenical Protestants, apocalyptic sects, and even Protestant missionaries joined heterodox and nonbelieving intellectuals to promote public secularism for their own reasons. The story of American secularism, in short, is one of religious and nonreligious alliance. Religious advocacy was vital to secularism's success.

A person might easily miss the religious component of American secularism, given the way that "secular" and its analogues are used in contemporary discussion. Many people tend to conceive of the secular or of secularism as a personal irreligious stance. It is in that sense that the atheist writer Susan Jacoby speaks of "Americans who adhere to no religious faith, whose outlook is predominantly secular, and who interpret history and tragedy as the work of man rather than God."[4]

Atheist or agnostic intellectuals who share Jacoby's sense have often engaged in a quasi-evangelistic endeavor. They have taken upon themselves the obligation to dispel illusion, to free others from the stranglehold of religion, and to counter a religious establishment that relies upon the simple credulity of the masses. The institutionalized version of secularism that they have supported is one of widespread irreligion, the social embrace of heterodoxy and antireligious opposition, what the intellectual historian Wilfred McClay has called " 'positive secularism,' the secularism of established unbelief."[5]

Other writers, more critical, have reinforced this notion. In the past twenty years a large, difficult body of literature has sought to interrogate secularism's supposed benefits. These writers contend that because the secular takes its meaning from an opposition to the religious, however defined, the secular project necessarily seeks to regulate religion, to define it, and to suppress it; in the process secularism takes aim squarely at the management of human difference. The People's Republic of China, Cuba, North Korea, the formerly communist countries of the Eastern bloc of Europe, autocratic countries like Egypt, and the long history of secularism in France, dating back to the French Revolution, serve as exemplars of secularism's oppressive tendencies. The resulting literature questions what the anthropologist Talal Asad has called "the triumphalist history of the secular." Imagine, if you will, a militant atheist as the head of a government agency tasked with deciding a religious exemption to federal law, and you get a sense of why, as Asad has put it, "a secular state does not guarantee toleration; it puts in place different structures of ambition and fear."[6]

Yet those who construe all forms of secularism as established unbelief are, in the American case, simply mistaken. In contrast to the secular arrangements in Egypt, Cuba, and even France, the secularism of the United States emerged out of a history of conflict and bargaining between religious and nonreligious groups. The result of their bargaining is a political arrangement in which exclusive religious ideas have, in theory, no authority outside an organized religious community but are not otherwise subject to state hostility. Wilfred McClay calls this " 'negative secularism,' the secularism of non-establishment." It requires a style of political discourse that in many cases has used the language of constitutional rights as a form of public reason. It includes an embrace of pluralism, of free exchange and disagreement on religious matters, of freedom of inquiry in public life, and of freedom from any official or established perspective, whether religious or nonreligious.[7]

The distinction between positive and negative secularism is crucial to understanding the particularities of the American experience. At bottom, negative secularism requires a separation between an individual's conception of metaphysical reality and the collective notions within the social and political order. The gap between the personal and the collective explains how religious intellectuals could make secular political arguments. Their public political reasoning involved a rhetorical conversion: from the language of the religious to that of the secular, from the private or communal stuff of one's religious identity to the public and therefore shared stuff of American civic and political ideals. Once converted, the language and the reasoning can be adopted by people with various commitments, whether they are conservative or liberal, religious or irreligious. A person who can speak only in the language of his or her faith is not likely to become a secularist, even of the negative kind. But for the religious people engaged in the secular project secularism did not demand the abandonment of belief. It needed only a commitment to mutual political exchange and, perhaps, to the privatization of religious ideas and rhetoric when they became unpersuasive to others in the debate.

This final obligation of religious privatization has led some writers and polemicists to allege that secularism is really a form of unacknowledged sectarianism. By conceiving of religion as a voluntaristic and easily privatized set of personal beliefs, these writers argue, the secular state defines religion in essentially Protestant terms. The result is a damning indictment of the secular project, if the argument holds up. Not only is secularism a new form of oppression, in this view, it is the worst kind of oppression, deriving from an essentially false consciousness. It purports to be neutral but actually promotes a specific religious ideology over others.[8]

There is much to say about the last contention, and in some sense the rest of the book is devoted to the task. But suffice it to say that even if the resulting system of secularism has occasionally taken on a Protestant cast, that does not make the system itself a form of Protestantism. If so, it would be difficult to understand how so many religious and nonreligious Jews became ardent supporters of the secular order. Nor would it explain why so many conservative Protestants were opposed to the growth of that order—hostile even to the idea of secularism—and remain so. Secularism is simply too complicated to see it as a form of Protestant sublimation.

This book, then, seeks to clarify the history of American secularism, to uncover its foundation and development, and to analyze its subsequent tensions and ambivalent results. There are many ways to go about the task, each of which might have merit. But in the main I tell the story of American secularism through its most prominent proponents and detractors, tracking its emergence as a political order through the social negotiation between groups. Put succinctly, I offer a story focused on the social history of secularist ideas within the American political tradition.

The attention to ideas requires some justification. As Walter Lippmann wrote in his classic 1914 book *Drift and Mastery*, "There is to-day a widespread attempt to show the futility of ideas." The same sentence would hold true over a hundred years later. Both then and now there are many who suspect that beliefs, arguments, and philosophies have little or no relevance to political life. What matters are not ideas but interests, the rational calculation of financial and personal gain in a complex system of winners and losers. Social scientists have spent the past seventy years building sophisticated models exploring the role of interests in politics. They have often simultaneously dismissed the notion that culture or ideas possess a motive political force in their own right.[9]

If correct, their claims would require an extensive shift in perspective. The interest-based conception of politics views public debate as froth churned up by deeper forces. Politician X says one thing to reporters. Politician Y criticizes her. Columnists and writers support or disavow the original statement. Individual citizens express their own thoughts. The conversation dies down or changes or produces some transitory political effect, and then it starts over. Proponents of an interest-based conception have asserted that ignoring the rhetorical foam produced by the convulsive concatenation of interests allows a person to understand the actual, deep workings of politics.

But the relevance of ideas to public life becomes more evident when the frame is longer than a news cycle or even an election cycle. Ideas are essential to the creation and maintenance of American public culture—the attitudes, beliefs, and categories that order the social and political process and that provide the primary assumptions or points of dispute within public debate. As the late intellectual historian Rush Welter put it, ideas have mattered in American politics precisely because they have the power to motivate people beyond their narrow interests and toward a collective aspiration. The creation of a collectivity and the engagements that call that collectivity forth are essential to the history of democratic governance.

"To the extent that the United States has been egalitarian in its social aspirations," Welter wrote, "to the extent that its educational institutions and media of information or persuasion have been popular rather than elite in their bias, to the extent that popular opinion (however misinformed) has been a given within which its political leaders were forced to work, the ideas current in the society at large have had more to do with how it conducted its affairs than have comparable ideas in other societies."[10]

In the United States the political culture has had long-standing keywords—liberty and equality foremost among them. Those consistent ideals emerge out of the peculiar fact that, with the critical exception of the American Civil War, American politics stretches back nearly unbroken to the formation of the Constitution in 1787, if not all the way back to the beginning of the Revolution. The United States is one of the world's oldest democracies still operating under the oldest Constitution. Within American political culture the Constitution operates as a kind of civic scripture.[11]

In that way the American political order shares characteristics of other creedal communities, with their discursive commitments and practices. A person cannot just invent a whole new way of conceiving of politics given the discursive parameters set by the foundational texts. He or she must work, to some extent, from within. It is not too much of a stretch to say that American politics reflects the philosopher Alasdair MacIntyre's definition of a tradition. It is, in his words, "an historically extended, socially embedded argument."[12]

The endeavor has been undertaken by people in disparate times and places who used the categories available to them for their own ends. The political concepts and the accreted volume of their past use have meant that the debate stayed remarkably stable. The available ideas have shaped outcomes in a variety of ways. Those who have sought to stray outside the tradition or to change it in some fundamental sense—radical socialists are one example—have labored to gain a consistent following in American public life partly because of the discursive limits they have encountered.

But the American political tradition is not singular, even if it has been consistent and long-standing. It involves, as MacIntyre says, an argument, which implies multiplicity and divergence. Like other traditions, it might be best characterized as "a family of disagreements," to borrow the phrasing of the historians David A. Hollinger and Charles Capper. The dispute was aired in a broader culture that sought to address the nation's collective experience.[13]

The public place of secularism was an essential part of the quarrel, which is not a surprise given the standing of Christianity within the United States. One's position on religion in American life inevitably became a key flash point in the wider dispute over the shape and texture of the nation's public culture. As the disagreement developed, the claims both invoked and pressed against other ideas within the political tradition—about liberalism, pluralism, legitimacy, authority, democracy, privacy, and governance.

To a considerable extent it fell to the legal system to work out the exact way that these terms fit together. American secularism is therefore inherently constitutionalized, drawing upon the First Amendment and elaborated through the courts. The U.S. Supreme

Court has been, until recently, an institutional medium of secularization, serving as a venue in which disparate groups could both
build out and contest the secular order.

American secularists turned to the courts to reject the often-
unequal distribution of privilege and power in society. They looked
with disdain at the Christian or sometimes theistic religious order
that got pride of place. They asked jurists to reorder the structures
of society to create a system of equality. And as they did so they ran
up against the partisans of entrenched Christian power who were
often unwilling to relinquish their hold on public life. The resulting
conflict was aggregate and layered, taking place at different points
in time and involving many people. Sometimes the participants
seemed ignorant of previous efforts and of others within the debate.
The disputes often turned multidirectional, working out of concert
to a variety of ends and frequently producing uneven effects. At any
given moment, it might have been difficult to determine any clear
vector of development. But gradually and fitfully the secularist efforts converged, decoupling American political culture from the notion of Christian civilization. By the end of the 1960s an informal
coalition of religious and nonreligious secularists had successfully
decentered the exclusive Christian assumptions of public life.

It is in that postsixties world of American secularism that we
still live. Because of the multiple efforts and unresolved disagreements, it is not an entirely coherent achievement. In spite of its
successes, American secularism remains beset by internal weakness.
The negative character of the secular order—its relative thinness
as a political and social ideal and its requirement of a careful division between shared political commitments and more substantively
personal ones—has resulted in a corresponding instability. The uncertainties have been magnified by the relatively archaic words and
categories that partisans use to state their case.

To make sense of where we are, we need to consider the terms
of debate, to understand how these terms came about, and to observe the suppleness, the malleability, and the resistances that these
terms generate in the formation of American social and political life.

And in order to do that, we have to go back to the beginning.

PART ONE

Foundations

CHAPTER ONE

An Enlightenment Settlement

Thomas Jefferson was a man of many obsessions, but none rose to the level of what he called "the holy cause of freedom." He believed freedom was the tendency of the age, or at least its logical endpoint, and that the United States was its natural locale. Americans breathed the fresh air of a new continent on which they could experiment with original ideas. The country had a material richness, a public-minded people, and a superior form of government that contrasted with the suffocating traditionalism of the Old World. Given the expansive advantages of the nation and its commitment to political liberty, he joined others in affirming that the national experiment, if properly shepherded, would result in a new order of the ages. It would be, in the Latin favored by the Great Seal, a Novus Ordo Seclorum.[1]

But Jefferson also had some concerns. As an enlightened man, he entertained a decided skepticism about organized religion, though it is difficult to say what precisely his religious sentiments were. He said very little about them in his letters. He left no diaries to which he revealed his innermost thoughts. He only occasionally pulled back the curtain to his belief. In 1801, the year he became president, he responded to a minister's query about his religious commitments. Jefferson told the minister that he had "ceased to read or to think" about what he called "the country of spirits." He had wrestled with the issue when he was younger. But in his maturity he had decided to lay his head on, in his words, "that pillow of ignorance which a benevolent creator has made so soft."[2]

One thing he was clear about: it was his decided opinion that religion was a private matter, of no consequence to either society or government. His position was, for the time, revolutionary, a stark rejection of the assumptions of the past. Religious and political authorities had been long connected, dating back to the beginning of European Christendom. Priest and Prince embodied hierarchical realms of rule. Religion supported the political order and vice versa. The arrangement had generated disagreements between rulers, and the Protestant Reformation had made the system fraught. But the presumption throughout the Christian world was always that religious and political authorities relied upon one another. Together they upheld the rule of God.[3]

Colonial America looked much like Europe. Historically, Christianity had supported the political order in the British colonies. Sometimes that Christianity was Puritan Congregationalism, as in the New England colonies. Other times it was Anglicanism, as in the southern ones. In the sole case of Maryland it was Catholicism. But in all cases the state looked to a religious order to promote societal cohesion.

The socio-religious arrangement often relied upon a series of exclusions. "Jews, Turks, and Infidels," a phrase that referred to followers of Judaism, Islam, and nontheistic religions, were forbidden from holding office. Officeholders had to swear oaths affirming their belief in the divine origin of the Old and New Testaments, the Christian doctrine of the Trinity, or the future state of rewards and punishments. Sometimes Catholics were excluded from office either explicitly or by adding an oath that renounced allegiance to a foreign ruler or prelate (that is, the pope).[4]

Citizenship and subjecthood drew upon these exclusions. Native peoples received a variety of appellations that testified to their place outside of Christian civilization: they were heathens, savages, and infidels who were ignorant, as the 1629 Charter of the Massachusetts Bay Company put it, of "the knowledge and obedience of the onlie [*sic*] true God and Saviour of mankinde." Christianity likewise supported African slavery. As one colonial court ruled in 1694, "[Negroes] are heathens, and therefore a man may have property in them." The exclusions turned out to be firm. Although both native Americans and African slaves began to convert to Christianity, white Christians often found their conversions suspect or shifted the justification for slave and Indian subordination to a racial order that they believed was ordained by God.[5]

The American Revolution was a challenge to the hierarchical world and to the system of governance that it supported. In proclaiming, as Jefferson put it in the Declaration of Independence, that "all men are created equal" and "endowed by their Creator with certain inalienable rights," the revolutionaries implicitly called into question the system of European Christendom they had inherited. After all, if the king no longer held sway over the political system, then what of the religious arrangements that supported the king?

Jefferson had no doubts. Once the American Revolution began, he thought that any connection of religion to the government was an anachronism. The past was illegitimate precisely because it tended to undercut liberty of mind. And to Jefferson the liberty to think was one of the deepest components of freedom, an outgrowth of the revolutionary commitments that required further elaboration. A person in the new political order ought to be able to work out his own beliefs free of exterior compulsion, Jefferson believed, and without any consequence to his participation in civic life.[6]

But many others in the new nation disagreed. Although the revolutionaries had rejected the king, they were not on the whole ready to renounce the elaborate system of Christian privileges that had existed up until that point. After the Revolution many of the arrangements stayed in place. Six of the thirteen states paid churches out of the public treasury. The great majority of states limited civil rights to Protestants, Christians, or theists. Some states continued requiring officeholders to swear belief in God and a future state of rewards and punishments. Others went so far as to limit office-holding to Christians or Protestants.[7]

In Virginia, Jefferson's home state, there was flat-out confusion. The 1776 Virginia Declaration of Rights avowed that because religion "can be directed only by reason and conviction, not by force or violence . . . all men are equally entitled to the free exercise of religion, according to the dictates of conscience." It was, on the surface, an expansive declaration that was modified in telling ways. It simultaneously defined religion as "the duty which we owe to our Creator," and it connected religious freedom with a corresponding obligation "to practise Christian forbearance, love, and charity toward each other." Conscience and religious duty still sat side by side, even if Christian obligation was tempered by a call to liberality.[8]

The language was the result of a bitter divide, what Jefferson characterized as one of "the severest contests" in which he had taken part. Jefferson wanted, in keeping with his political views, to eliminate any role for Christianity in the postrevolutionary state. During the debate over the 1776 Virginia Constitution he had sought to repeal all laws that interfered with religious worship. His efforts failed. He also sought to do away with the Anglican establishment, in which Virginia declared the Church of England the official religion of the state. His efforts failed there as well. Jefferson did persuade his colleagues to temporarily suspend state payments to Anglican clergy, since it seemed untoward to revolt against England while continuing to support its church. But he had been unable to go any further.[9]

The arrangement had detractors on all sides because it had no integrity as a political position. To uphold an official religion without paying the clergy seemed to undercut the legitimacy of an established church without repudiating it. The Virginia Assembly was bombarded with petitions either to do away with the established religion or to go back to paying the clergy. The sides were unable to break the impasse.

Jefferson monitored the situation, biding his time. Finally, in 1779, when he was elected governor of Virginia, he felt the moment was right. He pushed his allies in the legislature to introduce a measure that he had been working on for several years, a Bill for Establishing Religious Freedom. He sought to clarify the lingering uncertainties about religion and the state in Virginia. The bill's ultimate goal was a decoupling of religion from governance.

The central statement of the bill was clear in its intent. "[Because] our civil rights have no dependence on our religious opinions," the bill read, "all men shall be free to profess, and by argument to maintain, their opinions in matters of religion, and . . . the same shall in no wise diminish, enlarge, or affect their civil capacities."[10]

But Jefferson's idea in the bill was problematic to many legislators. They thought that religion was foundational in a political system that relied on popular consent. Religion upheld a public morality that, if degraded, would damage political life. The immoral masses, freed from religion, could vote into office immoral leaders. Those immoral leaders might lead the government astray. Many feared that the system was already failing. As the Virginia legislator Richard Henry Lee put it, "Refiners may weave as fine a web of reason as they please, but the experience of all times shows Religion to be the guardian of morals—and he must be a very inattentive observer of our Country, who does not see that avarice is accomplishing the destruction of religion."[11]

Given the anxiety, Jefferson's bill proved highly controversial. It made it through two readings, was postponed on the third, and from there was killed for the session. The factions were, it turned out, still deadlocked.

Meanwhile, the Revolutionary War continued. Everyone assumed that when it ended, a new arrangement would become possible. Jefferson's opponents, led by Patrick Henry, now took the lead in formulating a plan. Once peace was established in 1783 they announced that it was time to reconsider the place of churches in the state as an essential component of the postrevolutionary order.

But they did not call for a wholesale resumption of Anglican authority. The revolution had made that impossible. What they put forward instead was a "general assessment," or a tax, to support a variety of Christian institutions. In the words of one petition to the assembly that supported the measure, the religious assessment would uphold "the Broad Basis of Gospel Liberty & Christian Charity—Divested of Past Prejudices and Bigotry." The goal was to produce a broadly Christian establishment in Virginia that would support the teaching of the Christian religion in a postrevolutionary era.[12]

Their efforts looked promising at first, partly because their opponents were in transition. Jefferson, the natural opposition leader, was not going to be around for the debate. He had been appointed as the U.S. minister to France. Jefferson had a natural successor, though, in his friend and ally James Madison. Like Jefferson, Madison was an enlightened gentleman farmer who believed that religion ought to be an entirely private affair. He was also a sophisticated thinker and political theorist who systematized his ideas into a coherent whole. That ability would soon aid him in proposing the essential architecture of the U.S. Constitution, making him, as he is often called, the father of the Constitution.

But for reasons that are not entirely clear Madison failed to take the General Assessment bill seriously. Momentum built while he focused on other matters. Henry gained more and more adherents to his cause. Once Madison understood the situation, he scrambled to contain the damage. Trying to woo legislators back to his side, he put forward a variety of arguments against the assessment. In the process he offered a set of intellectual innovations that destabilized established categories and began to lay the foundations for a secular order.

Madison first seized upon language in the bill that referred to "teachers of the Christian religion." He asked the assembly, "What is Christianity?" From its beginning Christianity had been plagued by theological disputes. Christians disagreed about what parts of the Bible were inspired, about what its inspiration meant, about which doctrines within the scriptures were essential and which were peripheral. They even disagreed about the mechanism that could be used to adjudicate the disputes. Someone would have to decide between orthodoxy and heresy in order to ensure the bill's proper implementation. The task would inevitably fall to the courts of law, which Madison predicted would be a disaster. How, Madison asked, is a court to judge "whether any particular Society is a Christian Society?"[13]

Madison's second move was even more radical. Rather than arguing about the difficulties the state would face in determining the true Christian religion from a false one, he questioned how an established religion worked. Established religions, it seemed to him, required false adherence because people who were otherwise not inclined toward a religion or a sect would have to support it or conform to it on the outside while not believing it. But that was only one part of the problem. An established religion also created a class of religious leaders, supported by the state, who had financial incentives that might outweigh true religious devotion. You could never be sure what either the leaders or the people believed. Society would be suffused with deception. Taken as a whole the effect was the systematic cultivation of hypocrisy. If both religion and society were damaged, then the maintenance of a religious establishment, even of the broadest sort, would have the opposite effect that supporters of the bill had intended.[14]

These were, by the standards of the day, profoundly counterintuitive statements. They upended centuries-long ideas about how and why religion and the state ought to be related. They directly assaulted the assumptions of European Christendom. But their inventiveness did not persuade enough of his colleagues. Madison had to settle for a few parliamentary moves that allowed him to regroup. When it became apparent that the legislators were not quite ready to pass the bill but were also not ready to reject it, he used a Christmas Eve vote to postpone the final reading until the next legislative session.[15]

Shortly thereafter Madison wrote Jefferson to explain the situation. The bill, Madison said, rode an upwelling of *"pathetic zeal"* in favor of "reinstating discrimination." He was unsure whether it could be held back. "It is chiefly obnoxious," he said, "on account of its dishonorable principle and dangerous tendency."[16]

To resist the attempt Madison started work on an anonymous petition as soon as the legislature went into recess. His idea was simple and practical. He sought to gin up popular outrage by marshaling all the reasons he could think of against state support for religion. The result was his now-famous Memorial and Remonstrance Against Religious Assessments. It was, in many ways, even more radical than what he had offered the legislature. It constituted a genuine advance in American secular thought.[17]

He began by elaborating upon the themes that he first formulated during the assembly debate. But building on these themes, he made explicit what he had only implied before: that approval of the bill would result in religious coercion. To many people today his position seems like common sense. But it was not at all intuitively obvious back then. Partly the problem arose out of the political theory of the day. Many of the revolutionaries drew upon Whig political thought, an intellectual inclination that had developed in Great Britain in advance of the American Revolution. One of the central notions of Whig political theory was that liberty resided with the people. That was why so many revolutionaries referenced "the people" and demanded that they had the right of participation in government. If the people could petition the government in their own interests, Whigs believed, then that government would preserve freedom and a host of other rights.[18]

But when considering the religious assessment bill, Madison saw that the people's access to government could be used as a means of religious tyranny over a minority, as a means to the violation of rights rather than their preservation. So Madison took a step back by introducing a distinction. He created a class of rights in which the government was forbidden to do anything at all, regardless of the desire of a majority within society to petition the government for action. These rights were foundational and so fell into that category that could not be denied. Religious rights were part of the new class of rights. They existed prior to the formation of civil society and prior to the formation of government itself so they could not be abridged.[19]

The key to preventing tyranny was the scrupulous separation of government from religious life so that individuals could follow their conscience. In that way religious rights could be preserved. The separation—the stringent secularism—would preserve rights. The General Assessment bill, by contrast, did the exact opposite by blurring churches and government and thereby violating, in his words, "that equality which ought to be the basis of every law . . . by subjecting some to peculiar burdens . . . [and] by granting to others peculiar exemptions."[20]

But Madison went still further. Because he was writing not merely a political treatise but also a petition to the assembly that had to generate popular support, he needed to appeal to the many dissenting Christians—Baptists and Methodists above all—who objected to state support for churches. From the Memorial's opening passages, Madison defended an essentially religious proposition. He said that an established religion created a hypocritical regime that was displeasing to the Creator. He ended the Memorial by "praying . . . that the Supreme Lawgiver of the Universe" would illuminate the legislators in the assembly so that they could recognize the true religion. When properly illumined, he wrote, they would step back from trampling God's "holy prerogative" and instead "establish more firmly the liberties, the prosperity, and the happiness of the Commonwealth."[21]

The somewhat mixed message ran throughout the Memorial. He alternated between rights-based arguments and expansive religious justifications for rejecting the establishment, sometimes giving voice to an enlightened rationalism, sometimes speaking for the many dissenting Christians opposed to the establishment, but in either case winding up in the same place: in support of public secularism.

Once he put the finishing touches on his petition, Madison leaped into action. He had decided to circulate the Memorial around the state to gather signatures. But he also encouraged others to do so as well, thinking that the more petitions there were, the more difficult it would be to pass the bill. Other petitions sprang up, though none as theoretically rich as his.

When the new legislative session opened, as Madison reported to Jefferson, "the table was loaded with petitions & remonstrances from all parts against the interposition of the Legislature in matters of Religion." Faced with an organized and vocal opposition, the proponents of a general assessment retreated. The bill went down in defeat.[22]

But Madison was not content to leave it there. He sensed that the victory had, as he later told Jefferson, "produced all the effect that could have been wished." He seized the moment and put forward Jefferson's Bill for Establishing Religious Freedom. Opponents still objected to parts of the bill that smacked of deism and heresy, especially Jefferson's pronouncement that "the opinions of men are not the object of civil government, nor under its jurisdiction." But the momentum had shifted in Madison's favor. Once he acceded to a few changes, the opposition caved. The religious freedom bill became law.[23]

The episode was a first step. Madison had articulated a compelling justification for the divorce of religious sentiment from the operations of government. And he had proven that such a justification could motivate many groups—from dissenting Christians to enlightened rationalists—within the state. But the Virginia debate left several issues unaddressed. If religion was wholly exempt from interference by the state, did that mean religion was irrelevant to the state? Could the state survive if a large portion of the people did not believe in anything?

The next year, as the delegates gathered at the U.S. Constitutional Convention, those questions were unresolved. Madison, again, proved crucial to laying out the issues by articulating a subtle skepticism toward a public role for religion. In spite of his defense of Christianity in the Memorial, he did not see it as something that could be counted upon to prevent social and political pathology. Prior to the convention, as he was formulating his constitutional theory, Madison noted that religion too often served as "a motive to oppression" rather than the preservation of rights.[24]

The Constitution followed the basic idea. It barely referenced God apart from a passing mention of "the year of our Lord" in Article VII. It forbade a religious test for office on the federal level. Otherwise it had nothing to say on the subject of religion at all.

The Constitution's lack of an explicit Christian foundation caused many people discomfort. Thomas Wilson of Virginia was not alone in complaining: "The Constitution is de[i]stical in principle, and in all probability the composers had no thought of God in the consultations."[25]

The lack of a religious test for office was troubling. As one critic put it, in an article reprinted all over New England, the Constitution's indifference to promoting the right religion would allow into office "1st. Quakers, who will make the blacks saucy, and at the same time deprive us of the means of defence—2ndly. Mahometans [Muslims], who ridicule the doctrine of the Trinity—3rdly. Deists, abominable wretches—4thly. Negroes, the seed of Cain—5thly. Beggars, who when set on horseback will ride to the devil—6thly. Jews etc. etc."[26]

The solution to the godless Constitution, its critics concluded, was simple. It required an amendment to protect religious rights and to promote Christian religious priorities. Only then would Christian groups be secure in their belief against the hostility of a nonbelieving state.

Madison initially opposed amendments, possibly for obvious reasons. He distrusted who was calling for them. As he explained to Jefferson—who was still in France and not involved in the debate—the amending process was too likely to have a bad outcome given the religious bigotry on display. Those desirous of establishing religion in the new government objected, in Madison's words, that

"Jews Turks & infidels" could take part in governance. The critics came from the New England states, with their Christian religious establishments. Given their motivation, any amendment addressing religion that was supported by New England would narrow, not broaden, the secularism that had already been achieved by not mentioning God at all.[27]

But as the controversy over amendments continued, Madison started to think he might be able to use the process to his advantage. Even though the Constitution was godless, some states still paid churches out of the public treasury. And almost all religious questions were still decided on the state level. If the Constitution was changed so that federal law became controlling over the states, true church–state separation might spread throughout the land, and a genuine secular order might be achieved. So once Madison was elected to the House of Representatives he began to craft language that would work out his vision.[28]

Madison proposed two amendments to that end. His first, which he wanted to insert between the third and fourth clauses of Article I, section 9, read, "The civil rights of none shall be abridged on account of religious belief or worship, nor shall any national religion be established, nor shall the full and equal rights of conscience be in any manner, or on any pretext, infringed." The amendment would have made it difficult to discriminate against anyone for his belief or nonbelief.[29]

Madison's second amendment went further. He wanted to insert it between the first and second clauses of Article I, section 10. It read, "No State shall violate the equal rights of conscience, or the freedom of the press, or the trial by jury in criminal cases." This amendment would have potentially invalidated all state religious establishments and forbidden any state from declaring an official religion.[30]

But because Madison's amendments did not protect the social role of Christianity in government, as many people had wanted, his fellow legislators resisted his formulations. Once his proposals were referred to committee, they began to make changes. His first amendment was modified to read more simply, "No religion shall be established by law, nor shall the equal rights of conscience be infringed."[31]

When the modified amendment came up for debate on the floor even the less expansive wording proved controversial. Elbridge

Gerry, a representative from Massachusetts, fretted that the amendment could prohibit the rights of states to have a state religion (as Massachusetts did until 1833). Peter Sylvester of New York, which did not have a state establishment but still discriminated against non-Protestants, fretted that the amendment would "have a tendency to abolish religion altogether." Benjamin Huntington of Connecticut, which had a Congregationalist establishment, wanted the amendment "to secure the rights of conscience, and a free exercise of the rights of religion," while not protecting "those who professed no religion at all."[32]

To answer the objections, the House changed the wording again. This time the representatives went with the following: "Congress shall make no law establishing religion, or to prevent the free exercise thereof, or to infringe the rights of conscience." That wording became the final version from the House.[33]

The Senate was working on another track entirely. The senators did not share Madison's impulse to guard the individual. They wanted to protect religious groups. Unfortunately, there is no record of the Senate debate until 1794, so we do not know exactly how they got to their version. But when the religion amendment emerged from the upper house, it read, "Congress shall make no law establishing articles of faith, or a mode of worship, or prohibiting the free exercise of religion." The wording would have allowed Congress to pay churches on a nondiscriminatory basis. It did not in any explicit way protect the rights of conscience. It did not offer any protection to nonbelief. Its main purpose seemed to be to prevent Congress from supporting one religious group over another. At the same time, the Senate rejected Madison's second amendment that sought to regulate the states. Madison was unable to get them to consider it.[34]

During the conference between the House and Senate to resolve the disagreements in their bills, the committee dispensed with the Senate version and focused instead on the House's, changing it to make it closer to the Senate's. The committee struck off the clause "or to infringe the rights of conscience," which could have been used to affirm nontraditional or even nonreligious rights. It rewrote the rest of the amendment in order to finesse the remaining disagreements between the two chambers. The rewritten, final version read, "Congress shall make no law respecting an establishment of religion, or prohibiting the free exercise thereof." That version became the first part of the First Amendment to the U.S. Constitution.[35]

But what did it mean?

Take the first clause, the establishment clause. The committee used the gerundial construction "respecting an establishment of religion," presumably to maintain parallelism with the second clause, "prohibiting the free exercise thereof." The phrasing raised questions. How would Congress respect an establishment? Did it mean that Congress should make no law holding an establishment in esteem? Did it signify that Congress should not make a law touching upon any facet of an establishment (in the same way that we might use the phrase "in respect to")? Did it primarily indicate that Congress should not interfere with state-level establishments that might exist then or in the future? It was unclear.

Or take the second clause, the free-exercise clause. Whose rights were being protected? Madison had wanted to protect the individual rights of conscience. Did this amendment protect individual rights? Or did it guard the right of religious groups, as the Senate seemed to desire? Or did it uphold the right of states? Again, it was unclear.

The amendment meant too much; it had a plenitude of meanings. The committee of people who designed it had wanted incompatible things. Madison's original proposal was changed and reduced, but still they were unable to agree. So the legislators resorted to what the historian Sidney Mead has described as the amendment's "laconic brevity and consequent vagueness." Far from solving the debate, the passage of the First Amendment revealed how little clarity had been achieved.[36]

But events soon overtook the legislators. By the end of 1791, when the First Amendment was ratified, those paying attention would have noticed signs of change all across the religious landscape that would upend the debate. The fervent Baptists and Methodists, already multiplying after the American Revolution, would soon explode in numbers. Itinerant preachers and enthusiasts began moving throughout Appalachia, the southeastern seaboard, Pennsylvania, New York, and eventually the Deep South of Alabama and Mississippi. Urban church construction began rapidly accelerating. In both city and country religious teachers brought a new brand of Christianity that stressed individual conversion in response to God, deep feeling as a test of sincerity, and strict attention to a moral code that governed all aspects of life.[37]

The expansion of what became known as evangelicalism was a profound social development in the new nation. Historians now see this movement as the beginning of the Second Great Awakening. Evangelical groups overran the more established Anglican, Congregationalist, and Presbyterian churches. The number of churches, ministers, and members grew at several times the rate of the population. The evangelicals were organizationally creative, direct in their approach, and relentless in their drive to convert the nation. Their massive mobilization and their exponential growth over a short period of time made them into a powerful political force in the United States.[38]

And yet calculating their exact political significance is not straightforward. The early effects of the evangelical expansion look, at first blush, to be an advance in public secularism of the sort that Madison and Jefferson promoted. Even as they expanded, evangelicals remained hostile to supporting churches out of the public treasury or to declaring an official state religion. Such arrangements had often been used against them. One of their earliest labors was to overthrow religious establishments in state after state. By 1833, when Massachusetts became the last state to end its institutional establishment, evangelicals had helped achieve, in part, the kind of church–state separation that Madison and Jefferson supported.[39]

Jefferson had noticed early on the hostility that evangelicals bore toward state payments for churches, which is why he began to cultivate an alliance with them in the 1790s as he worked toward higher office. It became clear to him that the best way forward might be to unite Enlightenment rationalists like himself with the Baptists and Methodists who had worked with Madison. He eventually rode the coalition into victory, winning the election of 1800 to become the third president of the United States.[40]

But their support for his candidacy and their hostility to religious establishments perhaps deluded him about the true nature of their goals. In 1802, when the Danbury Baptist Association of Connecticut sent Jefferson a letter commending him for his work, Jefferson responded with an enormous compliment. He saw in the Baptists exactly the kind of political outlook that had led to the creation of the First Amendment. They shared with him, he thought, the belief that religion is a private matter between a man and his God. The First Amendment was, in his view, the expression of that idea. It built out, he wrote in response to their letter, "a wall of separation between Church & State." As the First Amendment idea spread, he told the Danbury Baptists, he looked forward to an expansion of the wall and a corresponding restoration of natural rights to mankind.[41]

But evangelicals did not share his view that religion was a matter between a man and his God. Evangelical expansion involved an enlargement of the role of religion in public life. Almost immediately with the start of the Second Great Awakening, evangelicals began to form voluntary associations -what we would today call civil society groups—to impose Christian moral authority on American culture and government. The American Board of Commissioners for Foreign Missions (founded in 1810), the American Bible Society (founded in 1816), and the American Sunday School Union (founded in 1824), to name some of the largest associations, connected large groups of evangelicals and leveraged their organizational power to access the machinery of governance.[42]

In making their way into the public realm, evangelicals had a clear sense of political mission. As the evangelical preacher Lyman Beecher put it, they sought to create a moral reformation and political reconstruction all at the same time. In their public efforts a voluntary association served an indispensable function. It allowed large groups of people to band together across denominations to combat what evangelicals considered the atheistic tendencies within American life. Church and state might be formally separate, but through organized pressure Christian religious norms could become dominant. As Beecher put it, once properly developed a voluntary association would act as a "sort of disciplined moral militia" that would "repel every encroachment upon the liberties and morals of the state."[43]

Evangelical associations soon became the central vehicle for the official Christian tone of public life. A few years after Jefferson's letter to the Danbury Baptists, they could be found in nearly every state of the union working toward a characteristic set of moral interests: the prohibition of alcohol, the suppression of vice and obscenity, the promotion of Christian Sabbath enforcement, and so on. What the historian Charles I. Foster has called "the Evangelical United Front" used its organizational power to order the nation within a fundamentally religious framework. Evangelicals infused their values into American culture so thoroughly that their vision of Christianity created a conceptual and normative structure that operated in the background for much of the nineteenth century. Those who opposed that structure—and there were many—had to work around it or through it. The result was not a wall of separation between church and government, as Jefferson understood it, but its opposite, a mutual penetration between religion and governing authority in a way that made the state a mechanism of religious power.[44]

Although Jefferson was slow to recognize what was happening, by 1809 when James Madison became president evangelicals had begun to use their newfound sway. Madison was unable to hold back the religious energies. He even acceded to the wishes of Congress and proclaimed "a day of public humiliation and prayer" at the start of the War of 1812. George Washington and John Adams had issued such proclamations with regularity. Jefferson had not. Madison's proclamation accepted the new political realities. A set-aside day would invite denominations to ask God, in Madison's words, to "take the American people under His peculiar care and protection."[45]

Christian sentiments also began to pervade judicial rulings. Religious judges started declaring that Christianity was part of the law of the United States. Blasphemy against God and taking the Lord's name in vain were now prosecutable, even if a state had not passed an actual statute prohibiting either offense. Other judges upheld Sunday laws against the objections of Jewish and non-Christian business owners. As the Pennsylvania Supreme Court put it in 1817, the Christian Sabbath was enforceable so that people would "be reminded of their religious duties at stated periods."[46]

Jefferson, who finally awoke to the dynamic, could only fulminate against the usurpation of the Founders' intentions. To no avail.

Soon Jefferson and Madison were dead, and the trend intensified. By 1845, with the Second Great Awakening reaching saturation point, the U.S. Supreme Court declared that the First Amendment (like the entire Bill of Rights) did not apply to states. That meant that the amendment, regardless of its vagueness, could not be used to protect the rights of citizens within the states, which were free to have whatever religious arrangements they wished.[47]

The result was obvious and predictable. For much of the nineteenth century, state laws recognized the Christian religion in a variety of ways. They favored churches by not requiring them to pay taxes, which created in effect a quasi-establishment because the tax burden was shifted to everyone else. Some states made it difficult to create charitable organizations separate from a religious body, if not a Christian one. Protestant religious groups had a dominant place in American schools, often creating the first schools and then controlling the common school system (or as we would say today, the public-school system) thereafter.[48]

The treatment of churches reinforced a comprehensive public favoritism in defense of Christian morals. Every state had blue laws, which restricted what business or recreational activities could take place on Sunday. Statutory laws drew upon Christian and often Protestant ideas about public morality, marriage, race, and sex. The Anglo-American ideal of coverture, in which a married woman's public existence was suspended after marriage and the husband represented her before the state, drew upon the patriarchy of the Christian scriptures. In the South proslavery advocates invoked the Bible to justify the slave institution, just as some antislavery activists quoted the Bible to oppose it. Both sides marched to war in 1861 laying claim to Christianity and God for their side alone.[49]

Christian religious ceremonies honeycombed American government. State executives tended to call for days of prayer and fasting. Religious oaths were required for officeholders. There was an almost universal reliance on theistic oaths in courts and in other places where citizens encountered the state. Many laws required a witness to swear that he or she believed in God and a future state of rewards and punishments. The agnostic Robert Ingersoll pointed out, bitterly, that even though he was a lawyer admitted to the bar in both Illinois and New York, in many states he could not give testimony because his agnosticism (and his integrity) prevented him from swearing by a god whose existence he questioned.[50]

State and municipal courts were especially solicitous to Christian prerogatives and Christian normative demands, though without ever acknowledging the quasi-Christian establishment that the laws upheld. In a blasphemy law case in 1824, the Pennsylvania Supreme Court upheld that state's blasphemy laws because a person's criticism of God undermined the foundation of morals, which was Christianity. That logic meant that nearly any dispute over morality became, by default, a religious issue, and in those contests Christianity usually came out on top.[51]

The First Amendment constrained none of these things.

As Lyman Beecher had predicted, the power of evangelical voluntary associations meant that a biblical ethos soon pervaded American society and government, in spite of the godless Constitution. The Protestant Christian Establishment, operating through a myriad of moral laws on the state level, remained firmly in place for much of the nineteenth century. For secularists, the political moment had closed.

CHAPTER TWO

The Sociology of Law

The secularist moment would not open again until the 1880s. And to a remarkable extent that new moment can be traced through a friendship. One of the friends was Louis Brandeis, a crusading lawyer, a social reformer, and an inveterate optimist. The other, Oliver Wendell Holmes Jr., was not the reforming type.

It was an unlikely pairing.

Of the two, Brandeis did not seem to be well-positioned to lead a secular movement in law. As a boy growing up in Louisville, Kentucky, he occupied a margin within a margin within a margin. His family was abolitionist in a slaveholding state that stayed with the Union. He was a Jewish child in a largely Christian southern city. And although he never denied his Jewishness, he had no real interest in Judaism as such.

His parents came to the United States after the revolutions of 1848 in Europe, a series of liberal uprisings that were eventually crushed. In Prague, where his father and mother lived, anti-Semitic reactions convinced them to flee. After considering the options, his father, Adolph Brandeis, toured the American Midwest and found it congenial. He wrote his wife, Frederika Dembitz Brandeis, to extol the new land in a way that gestured toward his wider political sympathies. America's progress, he told her, "is the triumph of the rights of man."[1]

Once settled in the United States, the Brandeises lived in relative comfort and at a distinct remove from the Reformed synagogue in town. Frederika later explained that she raised Louis and his siblings without religion because of the tenuousness of religious commitments in the modern world. "Love, virtue, and truth are the foundation upon which the education of the child must be based," she said. "They endure forever. . . . And this is my justification for bringing up my children without any definite religious belief: I wanted to give them something that neither could be argued away nor would have to be given up as untenable, namely a pure spirit and the highest ideals as to morals and love." She added without irony, "God has blessed my endeavors."[2]

The Brandeises initially seemed to be prospering, but the Civil War proved problematic. Their business suffered. And their abolitionism was not welcome. A few years after the conclusion of hostilities, about the time that Louis reached high school age, the family went abroad. In Dresden, Germany, Louis gained entrance into a *Realschule*, a type of high school that allows for maximum flexibility to move to higher levels of education for those who are academically successful or, for less academically inclined students, to move into a craft apprenticeship. It was not the most rigorous of German schools, but it offered much more than he had been given in Louisville.

Brandeis arrived at the *Realschule* at an opportune moment, just as a new form of social theory emerged in Europe. In the years since the American Revolution, much about Western societies had changed. The urban–industrial transformation, which began at the end of the eighteenth century, had reordered human social relations on a scale not seen since human beings adopted agriculture in the Neolithic period. The increasing complexity of human societies, their interdependence through vast technical systems, and the layers of bureaucratic management necessary to achieve collective aims raised fresh social questions. Social theorists, who soon called themselves social scientists, began to take up these questions, asking how societies promoted stability, what sources of authority were possible within the vast urban spaces, and what the best structure for human societies was in the aftermath of industrial capitalism.

The outlook of the new social sciences was distinctly modern and often secularist. In almost every case the core of the social–scientific project involved a rejection of the explanatory power and authority of traditional faith. The bourgeois life of the city, the new industrialized forms of capitalist exchange, and the place of the individual in the social whole could not, social scientists believed, be understood in the old terms. It was not that all social theorists agreed on the solutions to modern problems. But they all agreed that only new, modern forms of knowledge—empirical in orientation, free of moralism or preformed normative commitments, unbound by dogma—would suffice to deliver a solution. They offered up their theories to critique waves of resurgent religiosity, which worked against their secularizing impulse, through the latter part of the nineteenth century and the first half of the twentieth.[3]

Brandeis reached Dresden as all this was taking shape. He imbibed the protosocial scientific spirit at his German school and attributed his ability to think and his orientation to facts and to data—what he thereafter considered his social scientific inclinations—to his time in Germany. He later told his law clerk Paul Freund that the Dresden experience gave him a sense that empirical study could by itself yield a normative perspective. "It was not until he went to Dresden that he really learned to think," Freund said of Brandeis. "In preparing an essay on a subject about which he had known nothing," Freund continued, "it dawned on him that ideas could be evolved by reflecting on your material. This was a new discovery for him."[4]

From that point forward Brandeis privileged knowledge of facts and empirical testing over dogmatic maxims. As he put it later to another interviewer, "It has been one of the rules of my life that no one shall ever trip me on a question of fact."[5]

Dresden also influenced Brandeis's perception of the role of religion in society. His time there came at an opportune moment for European Jews. Parts of Europe began to eliminate civil disabilities to allow Jewish citizens access to public life. With the advance of political movements like the Revolutions of 1848, which had originally driven the Brandeises from Europe, assimilated and emancipated Jews became one of the central agents of political liberalization on the continent. Their cultural modernity and their traditional exclusion from public life prompted many Jews to emphasize neutral public spaces in which citizens could meet and confer about matters of public import regardless of their ethnic or religious identification. In many cases the emergence of Jews into European public life and the embrace of modern, liberal cultural forms were one and the same process. As the historian Yuri Slezkine explains, "The universities, 'free' professions, salons, coffeehouses, concert halls, and art galleries in Berlin, Vienna, and Budapest became so heavily Jewish that liberalism and Jewishness became almost indistinguishable." Although Dresden was not necessarily at the center of the process, it still bore on Brandeis's experience and conferred upon him a lasting skepticism toward the place of Christianity in public life.[6]

But Germany was, in another way, not where he wanted to be. "German paternalism got on my nerves," he later explained. He decided that he wanted to come home and that, like his abolitionist uncle, he wanted to be a lawyer. So Brandeis returned to the United States and enrolled in Harvard Law School. His timing was, again, impeccable. Harvard was just then being transformed in a way that fed into Brandeis's emergent secularist thinking.[7]

The change had to do with religion. Harvard and other institutions of higher education, up until that point, were led by clergymen. The college as a whole reflected its religious leadership. Students entered college as a cohort, taking all the same classes in a coherent curriculum that terminated in a capstone course in moral philosophy, taught by the college's president. The entire course of study portrayed a settled, coherent body of knowledge that grew out of the singular mind of God.[8]

But a variety of discoveries had begun to challenge the Christian character of the college. Geologists were uncovering a past history of the earth that stretched back through millions of years. Biologists encountered species in the fossil record that no longer seemed to exist. Charles Darwin's 1859 publication of *On the Origin of Species* put forward a biological explanation for life that seemingly did not require a deity and that clashed at many points with the Christian creation narrative. Biblical scholars began to show that the cosmological, social, and political beliefs of the ancient Near East were fully expressed in the Christian scriptures. The more biblical scholars worked, the more it became clear that the Bible itself had a social and textual history that bound it to specific times and places. The flood of scientific and academic knowledge made God an unnecessary postulate to explain the world and its operations.[9]

The college began to change accordingly, as the Christian system of higher learning came apart. In 1869, six years before Brandeis matriculated to Harvard, Charles W. Eliot published an essay in *Atlantic Monthly* lamenting the state of higher education. It was, Eliot thought, outmoded. He proposed in its place a "New Education," a reordering of the curriculum to allow for choice among the disciplines. This was the so-called elective system of higher education that looks, roughly, like what we have today. Soon he became president of Harvard College and began to institute his reform program. His curricular modifications did away with the idea that truth existed as a seamless robe, that all branches of knowledge reinforced one another, and that together they revealed the mind of God. Instead, education became an exercise in choice, which involved self-knowledge, self-development, and self-actualization into a branch of inquiry rather than a fitting of oneself into the plan of creation that God had handed down and that the curriculum revealed.[10]

President Eliot was interested in reforming the professional schools, which is why he invited Christopher Columbus Langdell to become the Dane Professor of Law and the dean of Harvard Law School in 1870. Langdell's subsequent innovations furthered the secularist spirit that Brandeis would imbibe.

Prior to Langdell's efforts, legal education often involved lecturing on the rules of law. Students listened to lectures, mastered the rules, and then were expected to apply those rules to specific cases. Legal education was, in that way, like theological education. Its desired goal was the acceptance of a coherent and largely unchanging intellectual system elaborated in lecture form. The educational model was an extended catechesis. To the extent that it invited thought, it emphasized deduction rather than inquiry. But Langdell had come to believe that the study of law needed to follow the path of the rest of the university. Law in his view was a science that, like other sciences, needed to be learned inductively through specific facts and experience. The only way to do that was to return to the original sources, using cases to teach students legal principles by working through actual problems. In that way the Langdellian revolution in legal education marked a challenge to religious influence within law.[11]

The challenge had fundamentally to do with the pattern of thought required of a legal thinker. There had long been a bias among lawyers toward axiomatic thinking, a tendency to reason from prior rules that the system of legal education had inculcated. Law, as a result, often partook of a spirit of conservatism, a backward-looking orientation that reinforced existing social structures. The conservative impulse was especially clear when it came to the place of religion in American society. Judges presumed and often announced the special place of Christianity in the United States. They did not always articulate what they meant, and they often did not concede that their statements were in any way controversial. But having categorically stated that the United States was a Christian nation, judges would work deductively to apply that rule in many areas of life to sustain Christian privilege.[12]

Such affirmations were common in state courts but were also present in federal rulings. In 1844, in a dispute over a will that the Supreme Court heard because one of the plaintiffs was a foreign national, the court ruled that Pennsylvania's law protected Christianity. The government acknowledged, the court said, Christianity's "divine origin and truth."[13]

By the time Langdell began to reform the Harvard Law School, the tendency of jurists to make such statements was waning though still frequent. In 1890 the U.S. Supreme Court upheld legislation that stripped the Mormon church of its incorporation because the church refused to renounce polygamy. In explaining its decision, the court said that polygamy was "contrary to the spirit of Christianity." Since the United States was a Christian nation, polygamy must be forbidden. Two years later the court exempted religious institutions from otherwise neutral employment laws that prohibited the importation of labor from abroad. It did so because it was inconceivable, the court explained, that the Congress of a "Christian nation" would have limited the importation of ministers. Four years later the court upheld a Georgia law that prohibited running freight trains on the Christian Sabbath (Sunday). It reasoned that such a law did not interfere with interstate commerce, which would have made it a federal matter and would have required the law to be struck down, primarily because the law honored a day "kept by many under a sense of religious duty," which made it simply a local or state regulation. All the rulings presumed or proclaimed the basic Christian orientation of American public life.[14]

Inasmuch as Langdell thought that legal education should result in the acquisition of legal rules, he personally did not challenge such thinking. Oliver Wendell Holmes Jr. criticized Langdell on this point. Law, in Langdell's estimation, had a logic that could be discerned by encountering cases so that the unity of the field came into view. The inductive process still sought to unveil a coherent system. That made Langdell himself, in Holmes's estimate, a "legal theologian" precisely because he looked to logic, rules, and internal consistency as the animating principle of law. Although he preached an inductive process, he still treated law as a kind of religious creed. In legal circles his orientation became known as legal formalism. It involved a focus on the specific forms of law without any sociological attention—that is, without considering the context of a dispute, the relative social power of the litigants, the political and social effects of a legal judgment, and the outcomes that a case might take for a variety of ends.[15]

But the Langdellian revolution in pedagogy did not necessarily terminate in formalism. Brandeis found the approach entirely congenial to an encounter with facts, data, and the grubby and contradictory realities of the world. He later wrote that the law school introduced him to legal reasoning "as an integral part of the drama of life" that worked with his social scientific orientation. Brandeis found at Harvard a secularized legal education that offered him the ability to build out the house of law by considering not what law is but what it might be, given social needs and social conflict.[16]

Brandeis, in fact, thrived in the setting. He graduated first in his class. It was a remarkable accomplishment, even in the more relaxed educational world of the nineteenth century. His future seemed wide open. After considering his possibilities, Brandeis decided to set up a legal practice with his friend Samuel Warren, who graduated second in the class.

On the night Brandeis was admitted to the bar they got together in Warren's room. But in a fateful turn of events, Warren invited Oliver Wendell Holmes Jr., whom he met while working in Holmes's law firm. The three men drank a mixture of champagne and beer. Warren and Holmes told jokes and talked. Brandeis listened, while lying on the couch. In spite of the celebration in his honor, he did not say much.[17]

The evening might not have seemed a momentous occasion, though it turned out to be. At the time of their meeting the men had little in common other than an interest in law, which only went so far. Even at a young age Brandeis had a desire to use law as a mechanism for social betterment, a goal that Holmes did not necessarily share. They also differed in disposition. Brandeis's quiet conviction and his ethical sensitivity separated him from Holmes, who was a decade and a half older but who had a weary cynicism that intimated a bigger gulf still.[18]

Their dissimilarity was partly one of experience. Unlike Brandeis, Holmes had been old enough to fight in the Civil War. He was wounded three times, including a shot through the neck at Antietam. He emerged from the war with a grim view of human beings, a skeptical orientation toward platitudes and certainties, and a disdain for any kind of religious conviction. "When I say that a thing is true," Holmes later explained, "I mean that I cannot help believing it. . . . I therefore define the truth as the system of my limitations and leave absolute truth for those who are better equipped."[19]

That perspectival notion of truth characterized all of Holmes's thought. The war had shown him that life was marked by conflict and struggle. Provisionality marred all human endeavors. Individuals were thrown about by forces that they could neither understand nor control, so it was no use making axiomatic pronouncements that would have to be later retracted.

His skeptical sensibility extended to law, particularly the body of evolving precedent known as the common law that dated back to when the North American colonies were part of England. Many commentators spoke of it as though it had the characteristics of God. It was rational, omnipresent, and existed through a set of rules that regulated human experience. And because Christianity had shaped Anglo-American law, many judges saw the common law as expressive of Christian norms and values in the regulation of society. England had a Christian religious establishment, they reasoned. The assumptions of that establishment were written into the legal arrangement of the English system and then continued in American law after the Revolution. The Christian orientation of the common law acted as a foundation for the Christian character of the American people and the justification for their regulation.[20]

Holmes rejected the traditional conception because it sought to connect law to religion or to God. As he later complained, "The common law is not a brooding omnipresence in the sky."[21]

He had his own secular conception. Two years after Brandeis met him, Holmes articulated his ideas in a landmark treatise on the common law that is still cited today. From the first sentence of the book, he renounced any attempt to look to God or tradition or logic as the animating impulse within law. "The life of the law has not been logic," he wrote, "it has been experience."[22]

What he meant is that law, like people, responded to changes in circumstance and condition. The sociological maxim that one must understand external pressures on individuals to account for their behavior was equally true of the development of law. "The felt necessities of the time, the prevalent moral and political theories, intuitions of public policy, avowed or unconscious, even the prejudices which judges share with their fellow-men," Holmes wrote, "have a good deal more to do than the syllogism in determining the rules by which men should be governed. The law embodies the story of a nation's development through many centuries, and it cannot be dealt with as if it contained only the axioms and corollaries of a book of mathematics."[23]

From that historical starting point, Holmes sketched the centuries-long development of law as a product of social forces. He would later point out that his historical approach was just a prelude to a more wholesale reconsideration. It was designed to lead to "an enlightened scepticism" of the law as it then existed, because the historical approach required asking why the law was as it was in the first place. The question led to the realization of how much law was simply a holdover from the past, which was not a compelling basis for much of anything. "It is revolting to have no better reason for a rule of law than that so it was laid down in the time of Henry IV," he said. "It is still more revolting if the grounds upon which it was laid down have vanished long since, and the rule simply persists from blind imitation of the past." Studying history, in Holmes's conception, was an invitation to consider whether "the social end" of existing law was adequate to the present day.[24]

The answer, he implied, was that often it was not. He wanted something else, something more attuned to the realities of the late nineteenth century. Human social knowledge needed to move beyond the unconscious, the inarticulate, and the customary. The blind guesses of the past would need to be replaced. "For the rational study of law ... the man of the future is the man of statistics and the master of economics," he said.[25]

Holmes was, in effect, offering one of the first articulations of the sociological perspective on law. The social scientific disciplines, with their testable hypotheses and their accumulation of empirical knowledge rather than tradition or social convention or religious rationale, could guide legislatures and judges toward a better formulation. Law could meet social conditions. "I look forward to a time when the part played by history in the explanation of dogma shall be very small," he concluded, "and instead of ingenious [historical] research we shall spend our energy on a study of the ends sought to be attained and the reasons for desiring them." For someone with a developing sense of social mission like Brandeis, Holmes contributed a bracing view of the possibilities of law.[26]

Brandeis soon joined Holmes's project in a way that would yield an opening for American secularism. In 1890, shortly after Warren left their practice to work in the family business, the two former partners sought to apply Holmes's theories in one field. At the time, Warren had just married a society darling named Mabel Bayard. The Warren–Bayard wedding was the high event of the season, covered in all the papers. The massive press coverage continued even after the nuptials, as the yellow press sought intimate details of the couple's life. Mabel Warren fiercely objected to the constant scrutiny, which led her husband to consider whether there might be something like a "right to privacy" in American law.[27]

The resulting essay was a remarkably wide-ranging reconsideration that destabilized the system of individual rights and social responsibilities. Its effect was so far-reaching because, as the intellectual historian Sarah E. Igo has suggested, to call something private was "to make an argument about the proper relationship among citizen, state, and society." In the early debate over secularism, the notion that one's religion was personal and therefore private had been essential to the notion that religion ought to be decoupled from governance. Madison and Jefferson contended that religious power could be neutralized and religious disagreements could be overcome through religion's partial privatization. By 1890, when Warren and Brandeis published their article, social relations were in flux with the rapid changes of the era. Their theoretical efforts raised a whole new set of issues, questions, and policy considerations to which jurists and legal theorists had to respond.[28]

The essay opened with a remarkable statement of legal modernism in the development of law. "Political, social, and economic changes," Warren and Brandeis wrote, "entail the recognition of new rights, and the common law, in its eternal youth, grows to meet the demands of society." In their view the extraordinary development of the past one hundred years had generated many novel rights. None was more foundational in contemporary civilization than the right to privacy, the right to be let alone.[29]

The task of the essay was to elaborate this right, to account for its rise, and to sketch its implications. But explaining where it came from was a little tricky. Within law, one could not just state that rights existed. They had to be related to what came before. To get around the problem, Warren and Brandeis reasoned from the common law maxim that personal papers and other writings were shielded from external intrusion. The rule seemed to recognize that each individual, because of the deeply personal nature of writing, had the right to what Warren and Brandeis called "an inviolate personality."[30]

Their affirmation was, in itself, an innovation. Up until their essay, to invoke the concept of privacy within law was inevitably to invoke the idea of property. The economic marketplace presented the framework within which the law sought to protect individual liberties, so much so that for much of the nineteenth century personal liberties meant primarily the ability to enter into contracts and to establish a private order through one's own property. Rights were in that way intrinsically bound to the status of a piece of property. A private domicile was different than a public house, with distinct rights and responsibilities. A person's property was his private domain because it was his alone and not therefore answerable to the public.[31]

But Warren and Brandeis took the idea of privacy in a new direction, conceiving of it not as a characteristic of property but as one of personality. A person's private life was an interior domain, not just what occurred in the four walls of a house but what occurred inside a mind. The ability to think, to reason, to speak candidly, and to feel emotions or to experience the world in one's own way, rather than having society dictate and surveil a person's thoughts and behavior, were requirements of modern life. The right to privacy was part of a wider solicitude for the rights of individuals that Warren and Brandeis thought they saw in the development of American law.[32]

A careful reader would have noticed a fundamental tension in their reasoning. Between the remarkable expressions of legal modernism were extended episodes of pearl clutching. The essay featured a moralistic critique of the supposedly immoral press, and its conception of the right to privacy ran counter to press freedom. The point, as they understood it, was to bind the press from the kind of intrusion into private life that the Warrens were experiencing. But what would prevent the right to privacy from muzzling the press on topics of public interest?

Warren and Brandeis acknowledged the problem, but they thought it could be minimized so long as the courts understood the distinction between public and private persons—another conceptual innovation—or between persons in their public capacity and persons in their private capacity. The press could publish what was in the public interest so long as it remained within the bounds of propriety, however understood. That would allow public matters to be discussed, while private interests would be shielded.

There is some evidence that Brandeis was not entirely persuaded by his own article. Shortly after it appeared, he wrote his then-fiancée, Alice Goldmark, to say that he had thought about writing another article entitled, "The Duty of Publicity"—"a sort of companion piece to the last one," he said, "that would really interest me more." Publicity, more than privacy, was closer to Brandeis's concerns.[33]

But Brandeis did not immediately get around to that second article. Meanwhile, the right-to-privacy essay became enormously generative for subsequent legal thought. It was the most cited article in American legal scholarship until 1947. Its power came from its engagement with established legal standards. The legal system possessed an internal elaboration that was self-reinforcing. Current opinions made reference to past opinions in a giant web of precedent. As Roscoe Pound, another formulator of sociological jurisprudence and soon-to-be dean of Harvard Law School, explained, "Every rule is so related to and articulated with every other that any local disturbance in the system has many wholly collateral results, often entirely unexpected." The notion of privacy destabilized the system. As people engaged with the essay, they encountered new conundrums. The act of response created fresh legal thought in order to apply the law to new situations, which set the foundation for other conceptual innovations that tended toward secularism.[34]

Warren and Brandeis's article also inaugurated a wider reconsideration—not just of law and its purposes but of American liberalism as well. In some sense the article expressed a new conception of liberalism that had been a long time in coming. Dating back to the Age of Revolution liberals had united around several key propositions—that humans were free and equal in a natural state, that they possessed inviolable rights, and that they offered up some rights, but not all, to a government in return for protection. Liberals presumed that at some point in the past the arrangement had become perverted, that the rights of man became overwhelmed through a despotic coalition of priests and kings. The classically liberal proposal to fix the problem was to remove the coalition of priests and kings—that is, to remove the institutions of involuntary restraint—and then individual people would be free. Madison and Jefferson had articulated parts, though not all, of this liberal package as they promoted secularism. And for much of the nineteenth century liberals built upon the foundational stance. If human beings were granted political rights and freed from customary social forms such as the religious, the tribal, or the kinship networks that limited individual development, then, liberals reasoned, social harmony and individual flourishing would inevitably follow.[35]

But the emergence of new social forms in the latter part of the nineteenth century—the growth of the modern corporation, the creation of vast new institutions of finance, new markets, and new modes of exchange, and the development of an empowered federal government after the Civil War—convinced liberal thinkers that individuals could not just be freed from customary restraints and thereby properly emancipated. Once freed, that person would simply be swallowed up by other corporate forms that left them no less able to pursue their own ends. To account for the new social realities, liberals drew upon social science to construct a more substantive commitment to freedom, a positive reformulation of governance that looked to a strong state in order to protect the individual.[36]

The new commitment could be seen in a variety of organizations and institutions that were created in the period to articulate and to defend rights. In 1909, a group of liberal Protestants, atheists, and agnostics, many of whom were committed to some form of socialism, founded the National Association for the Advancement of Colored People (NAACP). It was not an accident that the organization invited the black agnostic social scientist W. E. B. Du Bois to direct publicity and to create the organization's magazine, *The Crisis*. Du Bois had come to national prominence a few years earlier with the publication of his book *The Souls of Black Folk* and had since been languishing in Atlanta while he watched, powerless, as the Jim Crow regime was constructed around him. He accepted the chance to articulate his vision outside the South, moving from Atlanta University to New York City in 1910.

From his new perch as magazine editor and NAACP organizational officer, Du Bois routinely assailed American Christianity as an institution that had long been on the side of the oppressor rather than the oppressed. He invited prominent humanists and freethinkers such as John Dewey, Franz Boas, and Clarence Darrow to contribute to the magazine. The result was a consistent message. *The Crisis* and by extension the NAACP targeted southern white evangelicalism as the root of racial exclusion and confronted the theologies of segregation as an inappropriate civic stance in a secular republic. The organization, in a characteristic move, looked to the federal state as the guarantor of black rights against white Christian racists.[37]

Others began to undertake a more theoretical reappraisal of the relationship between individual rights and social responsibilities. At the head of the reconsideration was a new class of intellectuals that began to come of age in the first decade of the twentieth century. The group included people like the young Walter Lippmann, a precocious thinker who would become an influential journalist for the next forty years; Walter Weyl, an economist with two degrees from Wharton Business School who was close to Lippmann; and Horace Kallen, a philosopher from Harvard whom Woodrow Wilson hired to teach at Princeton, becoming the first Jew to join the faculty. The intellectuals were connected to a bohemian class that gathered in the downtrodden quarters of American cities—archetypally in the West Village of Manhattan—and that included activists like the anarchist Emma Goldman. The young intellectuals were opposed to what they saw as the stifling provincialism of American life and the widespread commitment to a cultural and religious past that no longer made sense.[38]

The young intellectuals were disproportionally Jewish. They came from the second or third generation to have immigrated to the United States, and they were especially critical of the Christian assumptions that tended to be dominant within American public culture. Jews had been at the forefront of American radicalism dating back to the 1880s. Although there were many orthodox and conservative Jews among the new immigrants that began flocking to the United States in the late nineteenth century, the vocal minority who were influenced by European Marxist or anarchist thought far outnumbered the orthodox in public political agitation. These free-thinking Jews often combined their political radicalism with religious agnosticism. By the early twentieth century, as the young intellectuals began to organize, freethinking and radical Jews had begun to profess, in the historian Paul Buhle's words, "a sense of exile from the Judeo-Christian promised land [of the United States] and an inner determination to regain their legacy."[39]

The rise of an alienated class of freethinking Jewish intellectuals created the opportunity for an alliance with post-Protestant thinkers who were then assuming a more prominent place in social affairs. The post-Protestants of the era are now equally well-known figures: the social critic Randolph Bourne, the bohemian journalist

John Reed, the political philosopher and essayist Herbert Croly, and, a little later, the black and closeted gay philosopher Alain Locke, who would become the herald of the Harlem Renaissance.[40]

Together, the young intellectuals began interrogating many aspects of American life. In their gatherings they digested and debated the social thought that was emerging out of the new academic disciplines. Lippmann turned to Freudian ideas throughout his classic 1913 book *A Preface to Politics* in order to show the psychological and social damage that occurred when trying to use old beliefs as a guide in the political world. Nearly everyone in bohemia took for granted that new ideas were the only ones worth considering. As Weyl put it in his 1912 book *The New Democracy*, "America to-day is in a somber, soul-questioning mood. We are in a period of clamor, of bewilderment, of an almost tremulous unrest. We are hastily revising all our social conceptions." Or as the critic and editor Floyd Dell later said, looking back on his younger days, "We were of the present. And, though we did not realize it, what we wanted was an interpretation of our own time—an interpretation which would make us feel its significance, and the significance of our own part in it."[41]

The urgent task, according to the young intellectuals, was the reformation of American institutions to bring them into concert with the currents of the age. According to Lippmann, that reformulation began with an emotional and mental reconciliation to the loss of transcendence. God did not ordain all the rules of life because there was no God. The recognition of loss allowed for the acknowledgment of other possibilities. People responded in a myriad of ways to the vicissitudes of modern life, based on their values, their temperaments, and their other commitments. Only "a pluralistic philosophy," in Lippmann's words, adopted by those "strong enough to do without an absolute faith" would allow American society to become properly liberal.[42]

Lippmann's invocation of a pluralistic philosophy was a widely shared motif among the new intellectuals and an essential component of their liberalism. The concept came not from Lippmann himself but from the pragmatic philosophers with whom he had studied, chiefly William James but also John Dewey and Charles Peirce. All of the pragmatists emphasized, like Holmes, the perspectival character of knowledge and the social necessity of plural perspectives in order to arrive at a working approximation of truth. Their relativistic sensibility tended toward secularism in that it destabilized a single public perspective that established an orthodox position in society, which meant that it tended to destabilize the Protestant Christian authority that had been so dominant in American life.[43]

Other liberal-progressive intellectuals expanded upon the pluralistic notion. In an attempt to address the exploding population of immigrants, American policy makers had long pursued a forthright strategy of Americanization. The goal was to assimilate newly immigrated protocitizens in a way that erased or at least minimized their cultural separation from dominant Anglo-Protestant ideals. But the newly forming intelligentsia did not share that goal of Americanization. Though the precise formulations differed, the new intellectuals rejected national, ethnic, and religious chauvinism as the beginning of their theorizing. What Horace Kallen called "cultural pluralism," what Randolph Bourne called "trans-national America," and what Alain Locke called "race pride"—all affirmations of diversity as something to be nurtured in order to promote equality—became the intelligentsia's guiding concepts.[44]

These affirmations had a dual vision that changed liberalism's characteristic commitments. Rather than focusing merely on the individual, as nineteenth-century liberalism had done, without much success, and rather than offering up political theories that addressed only the social whole, as nineteenth-century socialism tended to do, also without much success, liberal-progressivism of the early twentieth century sought to recalibrate individual rights within social responsibilities, to develop the social matrix in such a way that the individual would achieve some kind of substantive personal freedom through social programs administered by the state. Here was an example of social thought that drew upon the new social scientific formulations in order to arrive at a fresh political perspective.[45]

Brandeis had started down this same path with his right-to-privacy essay—he began to clear that path with his essay—but he had been otherwise occupied for much of the next twenty years. His own reconsideration of liberalism snapped back into focus in 1910, when he became involved in the Zionist movement. Up until that point he had been a cultural assimilationist, seeing the necessity of comporting to dominant standards in order to get ahead. But he had become convinced that Jewish emancipation, under the old ideas, was always partial and subject to revocation. His apprehension grew by 1914 with the beginning of the First World War, as he watched the dark forces of ethnic nationalism gather within the United States under the banner of a muscular Anglo-Saxon Protestantism. By 1915 he was fully into his reassessment when a lynching occurred that shook him.[46]

The events are now well known. In Atlanta, Georgia, a working girl named Mary Phagan had been found murdered on the factory floor. The superintendent, a Jewish man named Leo Frank, was eventually convicted of the murder. The evidence against him was slim to nonexistent. There were irregularities in the trial, and a definite tone of mass hysteria surrounded the legal proceedings. All of it indicated to many impartial observers that Frank had been wrongly convicted. Frank himself loudly stated his innocence and appealed his conviction all the way to the Supreme Court. He argued that anti-Semitic public sentiment had put the jury against him. He asked the court for a new trial.

The court turned down his petition. Oliver Wendell Holmes Jr., who had earlier joined the court, chastised his colleagues for their formalistic obtuseness. "We must look facts in the face," he said. In the Frank trial the forms of law had been observed in the sense that there was a judge and a jury and a conviction. But all the evidence pointed to a judge and a jury terrified to do anything but convict because of the anti-Semitic animus toward Frank. "It is our duty," Holmes said, "to declare lynch law as little valid when practised by a regularly drawn jury as when administered by one elected by a mob intent on death."[47]

Holmes's warning went unheeded, but it was prescient. Soon a group calling itself the Knights of Mary Phagan broke into the jail, removed Frank from his cell, took him to Marietta, Georgia, Phagan's hometown just outside of Atlanta, and there lynched him. The extrajudicial killing turned out to be a beginning of sorts. A few months later another group of men came together on Stone Mountain in Georgia, where they burned a cross and announced the rebirth of the Ku Klux Klan (KKK).[48]

Brandeis watched all this with alarm. The second Klan was led by conservative Protestant ministers who were anti-immigrant, anti-Semitic, and anti-Catholic. It promoted a commitment to white supremacy, a persistent xenophobia, and a virulent form of Protestant moralism that it thought would protect white Christian America. Although the organization's real successes would come in the 1920s, even in 1915 the development was ominous.[49]

The Frank trial and its aftermath led Brandeis more fully into the thinking of the young intellectuals, notably that of Horace Kallen. He imbibed from Kallen and other theorists the connections they drew between liberalism, modernism, and cosmopolitan individualism to aid his own thinking. "The Jewish Problem," as Brandeis termed it, became a catalyst for his intense reconsideration of individual rights in a secular political system.[50]

Around the time that Leo Frank was murdered Brandeis published an essay that outlined the beginnings of his theoretical pivot. The fundamental dilemma of the period, he noted, was liberalism's somewhat complacent assumption of equality and progress. "Half a century ago," Brandeis said, "the belief was still general that Jewish disabilities would disappear before growing liberalism. When religious toleration was proclaimed [in Europe], the solution of the Jewish Problem seemed in sight. When the so-called rights of man became widely recognized, and the equal right of all citizens to life, liberty, and the pursuit of happiness began to be enacted into positive law, the complete emancipation of the Jews seemed at hand." But emancipation had not arrived. Anti-Semitism still persisted. The proclamation of tolerance did not involve the positive embrace of difference.[51]

The acceptance of alternative mores and peoples was at the heart of Brandeis's Zionism. It involved the divorce of ethnicity and religion from nationalism—which is ironic given the subsequent development of Zionism via the state of Israel—and a reenvisioning of the United States as a nation united around secular, pluralistic ideals. As Brandeis put it a few months later, on July 4, true Americanism was embodied in the motto E Pluribus Unum, out of the many one. He reinterpreted the motto to mean not the unity created out of different states but the unity created out of diverse intellectual, cultural, and ethnic developments in American life. True American ideals, he said, were "the development of the individual for his own and the common good; the development of the individual through liberty, and the attainment of the common good through democracy and social justice." "Not until these principles of nationalism, like those of democracy, are generally accepted," he continued, "will liberty be fully attained and minorities be secure in their rights."[52]

Not all secularists in the period agreed with Brandeis and the young intellectuals. Some who might earlier have been attracted to social Darwinism had moved into a more managed response to what they saw as the problem of undesirable populations. Eugenics and other forms of racial engineering gave them a mechanism to solve social conflict in a secular society, though even among eugenicists there was disagreement. Some looked to the active management of populations by the state. Others, such as the birth control activist and eugenicist Margaret Sanger, saw eugenics as something to be practiced as the outgrowth of individual fertility management.[53]

But Brandeis's position—his conception of the relationship between individual rights, cultural pluralism, and political economy— would be foundational to the American secular order, unlike eugenics, which would soon be discredited. By the beginning of the twentieth century Brandeis had become a prominent public thinker and an influential political actor in his own right. After 1912, when he participated in Woodrow Wilson's successful presidential campaign, there had been talk of a cabinet appointment in reward for his efforts. It never materialized because of opposition from Boston business leaders that many people had attributed to anti-Semitic prejudice. By 1915, when he began to speak on the Jewish Problem, there was not a more prominent legal personality in the United States.

Finally, in early 1916, when a spot opened on the U.S. Supreme Court, Wilson reached out to Brandeis to gauge his interest in the position. When Brandeis responded positively, his acceptance set off a nasty confirmation battle. Conservative senators immediately launched a campaign against the nomination. Brandeis worked behind the scenes to coordinate his defense through press proxies. Croly, Lippmann, and one of Brandeis's protégés, Felix Frankfurter, then a professor of law at Harvard, took to the press to defend him.

The debate was caustic, bruising, and entirely out of line with historical precedent.[54]

In the end, his opponents could find nothing that would stick. Brandeis made it through the nomination and took his seat on the court right as world events would make his perspective most relevant. The global order was about to encounter, in Frankfurter's later assessment, "economic and social forces far more upsetting to the preëxisting equilibrium than the changes wrought by the French Revolution and the Napoleonic Wars." It was in the context of global breakdown and nationalist uprising that Brandeis's sociological jurisprudence, now informed by a reinvigorated sense of rights and responsibilities, would lay the foundations for a secular political order.[55]

CHAPTER THREE

Piers of American Secularism

On the morning of October 2, 1914, Charles Taze Russell, the founder and leader of a group of apocalyptic Christians, came down to breakfast in a large, old Brooklyn house. He and his followers had bought the residence as a base to preach the end times and to wait for the coming apocalypse. The Bible Students, or the Jehovah's Witnesses as they are called today, had been proclaiming that the world was coming to an end sometime in the first week of October 1914.

"Good morning, all," he said to those gathered around the table. Then he began to clap his hands and declaimed, "The Gentile times have ended; their kings have had their day."[1]

Russell's announcement was pregnant and fraught. It implied that the Students' expectations of an imminent demise were perhaps not quite on point. But no one knew exactly what that meant for sure. A month later, when war broke out in Europe, Russell decided that the commencement of hostilities marked the end of the world system and that 1914 was not the absolute end but the beginning of the end.

"Millions now living will never die," the Bible Students began to declare. Their preaching became more urgent and aggressive, as befitting the final, unexpected dispensation before the coming fiery destruction of the world. They were still at it a couple of years later when Russell himself died. He was replaced by the group's former legal counsel, Joseph F. Rutherford, a combative man who thought the urgency of the situation required an even more aggressive response. But Rutherford's election as president of the Watchtower Tract and Bible Society would put the Bible Students in direct conflict with the U.S. government, challenging the religious structures of American political culture and promoting, somewhat contrary to their intentions, an American secularism. The confrontation was related to the war, though the dynamics were not entirely apparent at the time Rutherford was elected.[2]

The United States had originally sought to stay out of the European feud, a reflection of its historical dislike of foreign entanglements that did not have to do with the Western Hemisphere. But a series of incidents had made neutrality impossible for American leaders. In 1915 the Germans sank the passenger liner *Lusitania*, en route to Great Britain from New York, killing nearly twelve hundred people. A couple of years later British intelligence intercepted the Zimmermann telegram, a secret communiqué between the German Foreign Office and the Mexican government that sought to bring Mexico into the war. Germany promised Mexico that if it entered on the German side, at the war's successful conclusion Mexico would receive Texas, Arizona, and New Mexico back as Mexican territory. The twin episodes inflamed American sentiment against the Central Powers.[3]

In April 1917, a little over three months after Rutherford was elected as head of the Bible Society, President Woodrow Wilson went before Congress to ask for a declaration of war. His War Message was a remarkable turnaround for someone who had promised to keep the United States neutral. But having made the turn, he embraced the effort with a missionary zeal in keeping with his brand of Christianity. Standing before Congress in an evening address, he justified the fight in terms that made the United States into the world's messiah. "We have no selfish ends to serve," he said. "We desire no conquest, no dominion. We seek no indemnities for ourselves, no material compensation for the sacrifices we shall freely make. We are but one of the champions of the rights of mankind."[4]

His speech was perfectly pitched to appeal to a wide range of people, from liberal rationalists, who heard their own commitments in his rhetoric, to Christian groups, who warmed to what they saw as the calculatedly Christian terms of the American mobilization. Christian bodies began to amplify his message, as they understood it. The Federal Council of Churches immediately embraced his vision because, in its view, American democracy was "the expression of Christianity" and so needed to be spread abroad. The Reverend Austen K. De Blois of the First Baptist Church in Boston avowed that the coming conflict was "America's Holy War" and "a grand campaign for righteousness." Liberal Christians and conservative Christians both found a way to support mobilization, liberals emphasizing the goodness of humanity that needed military support and conservatives emphasizing the God-given power and destiny of the United States. The administration, seeing the Christian enthusiasm, used churches to create and distribute propaganda materials, to recruit soldiers, and to raise funds.[5]

But the Bible Students were having none of it. Under Russell, the group's first leader, the Watchtower Society had already rejected any and all forms of nationalism. Existing governmental systems, even the U.S. political order, were irretrievably unjust, vehicles of Satan marked for destruction at the end of days. No patriotic allegiance to any such system could be countenanced. Under Rutherford, the new leader, their posture became more rigid as the United States began the march toward battle. [6]

The war and its impulse toward religious patriotism brought into crisp focus several long-standing tendencies in American life. Christian leaders, or sometimes just Protestant leaders, set the parameters of political debate so that there was, in effect, a political orthodoxy. The true doctrines changed over time but they established a fuzzy yet existent set of boundaries about what could be discussed in public. Blasphemy charges, obscenity convictions, vice campaigns, birth control suppression—the entire panoply of Christian moral regulation—had existed going back to the founding era. But the war heightened the tendency of religious bodies to use coercive suppression, especially after the Bolsheviks in Russia seized power in 1917, a revolution that the journalist John Reed described as "ten days that shook the world." The formation of the first communist state shocked global leaders, and the avowed atheism of the Bolsheviks was one of the main causes for alarm. The Russian leader Vladimir Lenin, following Karl Marx, denounced religion as an opiate of the people or, as he put it, "a sort of spiritual booze, in which the slaves of capital drown their human image."[7]

For American political authorities and American religious leaders alike the revolution was a terrifying development that they sought to contain. There had been a long-standing anxiety among American leaders about what they saw as the godless political ideologies among the American Left—chiefly Marxism but also anarchism, socialism, and anarcho-syndicalism. In labor disputes dating back to the nineteenth century, in which laborers often marched under the leadership of leftist organizers, many churches and church leaders supported the owners over the workers. Christian ministers frequently called on the state to intervene on the owners' side. Apprehensions about secularism often overlaid the labor dispute, and the fight over workers' rights frequently became a proxy battle about the role of religious belief in American society.[8]

The Russian Revolution both realized and amplified the anxieties many Christian leaders had. Authorities began to fear that communism would radicalize American laborers, who were needed to work in factories and to fight as soldiers. They worried also about the protection of property. And they fretted that the Christian religion would be undermined if the leftist ideology spread. All three anxieties were connected. Many American leaders thought that Christianity was inseparable from American economics, which was itself inseparable from American institutions, so that criticizing any component would undermine the entire structure. The U.S. government became especially disturbed as American leftists and radical leaders moved to align themselves with the Russians, denouncing the war effort as a capitalist–imperialist venture that could not be supported.[9]

In response the U.S. government created new ways to suppress dissent. A couple of months after the U.S. entered the war, Congress passed the Espionage Act of 1917. It promised fines and imprisonment for interfering with the recruitment of soldiers or for mailing newspapers or magazines that had the same effect. Congress later added an amendment known as the Sedition Act of 1918, which prohibited speech criticizing the government, casting the war effort in a negative light, or interfering with the sale of war bonds.[10]

Looked at in one way, these laws could be considered an attempt to defend the secular ideal of national unity in wartime. There was not anything explicitly religious about the Espionage and Sedition Acts. But given the overwhelmingly Christian tone of the war effort, in which churches became vehicles of state propaganda and portrayed the war in the Christian terms generated by government leaders, the Espionage and Sedition Acts look less like a secular effort and more like acts designed by a Christian establishment to suppress anything that they labeled as antireligious dissent. Both acts were instantly used to reinforce mainstream Christian power in public life against those who challenged it.

Not surprisingly, the Bible Students soon came under the government's watch. In February 1918 Rutherford traveled to Los Angeles, where he delivered a lecture denouncing the military effort. His denunciation came packaged in a comprehensive theological critique of the existing connections between church and state. To Rutherford and the Bible Students the war was but the latest instance of the religious usurpation of government for selfish ends. For fifteen hundred years, he said, the clergy had taught that kings ruled by divine right. Catholics still tended to speak in such terms. Even Protestants, Rutherford said, "mixed politics and religion, church and state" in an attempt to increase their power. It was clear to him that all the existing religious leaders were corrupt, implicated as they were in the wider violence of American life. The clergy's fundamental problem, he said, was an allegiance to the nation rather than to the coming order of God. To Rutherford, their allegiance was simple idolatry that, in the context of armed hostilities, was a justification for murder. It could not under any circumstances be tolerated.[11]

His themes had an obvious resonance. Although he spoke in the tones of theology, Rutherford's criticism dovetailed with the leftist critique of the war. The similarity was perhaps inevitable, given that many of the people attracted to Rutherford's message came from the same down-and-out classes that socialists, communists, and anarchists drew upon. Those who were feeling crushed by the system were inevitably those likely to be responsive to an ideology of fundamental critique.[12]

Clergymen were outraged. When a full-page report of the lecture was printed in the *Los Angeles Morning Tribune*, the local ministerial association quickly sent an emissary to speak to the paper's editor. They objected that so much of the lecture had been published, which tended to spread the message to far broader audiences than it would have otherwise reached. The authorities also took note of Rutherford's comments and responded accordingly. Three days after the speech the U.S. Army Intelligence Bureau raided the Los Angeles headquarters of the society and gathered up its publications. Two months later the Department of Justice raided Bethel, the Brooklyn headquarters, and took the society's officers into custody. They were soon indicted for having violated the Espionage and Sedition Acts and made to stand trial.[13]

The Watchtower leaders faced a conundrum in mounting their defense. They did not see the court as legitimate, since it was a vehicle of Satan, but neither did they wish to go to jail. So they tried various arguments in spite of their fundamental belief in the illegitimacy of the proceedings. Their strongest was that the Watchtower Society was a wholly religious organization and that their work was wholly religious as well, not political. But the government blew past that contention, pointing to society publications that clearly rejected patriotism, war, and the widespread Christian connection with the state. Whatever the Bible Students claimed, their teaching had political import that undermined a core component of American government and ran against the teaching of the other churches that did, appropriately, support that government. The Bible Students countered that the specific publications entered into evidence were published before the United States joined the war and before the Espionage and Sedition Acts were passed. Criminal laws cannot be applied retroactively so their prosecution was entirely inappropriate. That fact in another context might have led to their acquittal. But to the jury it did not matter. They were convicted on all counts.[14]

It was, to the Bible Students, a trying but instructive experience. The result tended to confirm what they already thought. Rutherford and the other leaders were convinced that their legal prosecution was essentially a religious persecution, an expression of Christian religious bigotry that sought to use the government for chauvinistic religious ends. In that way, according to the Watchtower leaders, they had been arrested on false pretenses, or at least on a partial pretense. They were convicted not because they criticized the war, the Bible Students believed, but because they criticized the clergy and the clergy's association with state power. Their suspicions were confirmed when U.S. district judge Harlan B. Howe announced their sentences.

"The religious propaganda in which these men are engaged is more harmful than a division of German soldiers," Howe said. "They have not only called in question the law officers of the Government and the army intelligence bureau but have denounced all the ministers of the churches. Their punishment should be severe." He handed down twenty years for each of the four counts, to be served concurrently.[15]

Immediately after their sentencing, the Bible Students asked to be released on bail while they pursued their appeals. Judge Howe denied their request. They were sent instead to the Atlanta Federal Penitentiary.

The government was moving against other critics as well. Hundreds of leftists, many of them Jewish, were arrested for violating the Espionage and Sedition Acts. The constriction of national political debate would have, it turned out, a long tail. It persisted through the fighting and, once the war ended, in many ways it intensified. American policy makers, who were terrified of the power of international communism, soon launched a Red Scare that sought to root out communists from their place in American life. Left-leaning and anti-religious activists protested, often to little avail, as the government sought to eliminate dissent even in peacetime.

It was in that context of political and religious persecution that the court was finally pulled into the conflict. Cases on appeal slowly began to make their way through the court system. In early 1919 the Supreme Court heard a case challenging the constitutionality of the prosecutions under the Espionage Act. It would invite Louis Brandeis to apply his thinking on individual rights to a new, potentially explosive situation. It began, as a result, the long reformulation of American law that would culminate in a new secular order.

The case was not complex. The appellant, Charles Schenck, was a secretary of the Socialist Party in the United States. During a raid on Socialist Party headquarters authorities found leaflets that criticized the war effort. On one side of the pamphlet Schenck had printed the Thirteenth Amendment, which forbade slavery in the United States. On the other side he described the draft as a form of slavery supported by the capitalist class. The pamphlet urged citizens to lay claim to their rights in defiance of political repression and in resistance to capitalist rule.[16]

Writing for a unanimous court that included Brandeis, Oliver Wendell Holmes upheld the constitutionality both of the Espionage and Sedition Acts and of Schenck's conviction. Holmes acknowledged that there were free-speech issues raised by Schenck, but he thought that they did not apply in the case. There were, he said, limits to speech that everyone recognized. A man could not falsely shout "Fire!" in a crowded theater, for example, as that would likely cause panic and endanger others.

"The question in every case," Holmes wrote, "is whether the words used are used in such circumstances and are of such a nature as to create a clear and present danger that they will bring about the substantive evils that Congress has a right to prevent." During wartime, it was obvious to Holmes that statements normally permitted could be curtailed, that the substantive evils to be prevented were more expansive. The hindrance of the war effort was one such evil that Congress had the power, even the duty, to prevent.[17]

A week later the court handed down another decision, this time involving the five-time Socialist Party presidential candidate Eugene Debs. A couple of years earlier Debs had given a speech that explained socialism, recounted its history, and predicted its success. He had been careful throughout not to run afoul of the law. He praised socialist comrades who, though he did not say it, had been arrested for obstructing the draft. He hinted to the crowd that he wanted to say more, but he could not do so because he did not want to get into trouble with the authorities. He declined to go any further. But it turned out that he had said enough to be arrested.

During his trial Debs contended that his speech did not warrant charges against him because it was about socialism, not the war. But then he did not do much to dissuade the court from convicting him. Addressing the jury directly, he said, "I admit it. Gentlemen, I abhor war. I would oppose the war if I stood alone." Still, he said, that did not mean he had violated the Espionage and Sedition Acts.[18]

The jury disagreed. It convicted him. Prior to his sentencing Debs addressed the court. He could have pled for leniency, but he did not. He did the opposite. He reiterated everything he said in his original speech but with more eloquence. His commitment to articulating socialism was unswerving, even in the face of war, because, as he put it, "in this high noon of our twentieth-century Christian civilization" money still trumped every humane consideration. "Your Honor, years ago I recognized my kinship with all living beings, and I made up my mind that I was not one bit better than the meanest on earth," he told the court. "I said then, and I say now, that while there is a lower class, I am in it, and while there is a criminal element, I am of it, and while there is a soul in prison, I am not free."[19]

The judge sentenced him to ten years in prison. Debs appealed his conviction all the way to the U.S. Supreme Court. But in another unanimous decision written by Holmes, the court upheld his conviction and cited its prior case involving Schenck. Debs was sent to the Atlanta Federal Penitentiary, where he ran for president while still in prison in 1920.[20]

With the possibility of national political debate tightening, liberals who had been seduced into supporting the war began to reconsider. Up to that point they had had the somewhat complacent assumption that a modernizing spirit was inevitably opening American political culture. But the persecution of war critics demonstrated that the right of dissent and the right of conscience itself were far more precarious than they had thought. The rulings by Holmes, whom many people considered, inaccurately, an extravagant liberal, were even more disturbing. John Dewey, the philosopher and public intellectual whose essays had done much to make militarism respectable among the liberal intellectual class, complained about "the conscription of mind" in national debate. "The increase of intolerance of discussion to the point of religious bigotry has been so rapid," he lamented.[21]

In some sense Dewey and others ought not to have been surprised. Radical war critics certainly were not. The cracking down on dissent was in keeping with campaigns against anti-Christian labor leaders going back to the nineteenth century. And the curtailment of speech, which Holmes's opinion had supported, simply reinforced a conception of law that had been used to suppress working-class activism for some time. Jurists had relied upon what was known as the bad tendency test, put forward by William Blackstone in the eighteenth century, to determine the limits of speech. The test was fairly straightforward. If speech was likely to produce behavior prohibited by a statute, it could be punished. Because the test was broad, speech was often curtailed. The government could prosecute pretty much any speech if it judged that an utterance had the tendency to lead to unlawful action. Holmes was simply applying the test. His basic idea in both cases was that free speech was not an absolute right, that it was limited to prevent bad outcomes, and that that limitation had been a long-standing facet of American law. [22]

But writing in the *New Republic*, Ernst Freund, a prominent exponent of sociological jurisprudence, attacked Holmes's opinions as a failing to consider wider implications of the law and its social effects, the very thing that Holmes urged in his earlier writing. "To know what you may do and what you may not do, and how far you may go in criticism, is the first condition of political liberty," Freund wrote. "To be permitted to agitate at your peril, subject to a jury's guessing at motive, tendency and possible effect, makes the right of free speech a precarious gift." [23]

Brandeis, who had joined the opinions, was bothered by the criticism. Given his commitment to cultural pluralism, he should have been more alive to the issues than he was. It seems, retrospectively, that his earlier deliberations might have had bearing on the issue of free speech. But his thinking, it was now clear, had a giant lacuna. He was somewhat blind or at least insensitive to the curtailment of leftist speech, and he had no wider theoretical lens through which to view the issue. He later confessed to Felix Frankfurter, "I have never been quite happy about my concurrence in [the] Debs and Schenck cases. I had not then thought the issues of freedom of speech out." [24]

The problem was that when Brandeis considered individual rights, he conceptualized the issues in terms of private ordering and private rights. The state needed to protect an individual's ability to order his or her life, he thought, free from governmental interference. But the right of free speech was not a private right and did not protect, necessarily, an individual's ability to pursue self-fulfillment in a context of personal freedom. Free speech, as Freund pointed out, preserved a public freedom, the ability of an individual to participate in public life and to speak on matters of general interest. Brandeis did not have the right categories to understand the topic.[25]

A couple of months after the *Debs* decision, Brandeis began to see how the problem of speech could radiate to other substantive issues as well. He received an appeal from the Bible Students. They had had a hard time of it, even by the standards of wartime dissenters. After Judge Howe had sent them to the Atlanta Penitentiary, they asked for bail from the Second Circuit Court of Appeals while they pursued their case. Their requests were summarily denied. They tried a third time, in this instance appealing to Brandeis, who oversaw the Second Circuit.[26]

Their petition arrived on Brandeis's desk a couple of weeks after the court handed down the *Debs* decision, as he was growing uneasy with its reasoning. He took the opportunity to rethink his position. Here was a case of overt religious discrimination in addition to political suppression. He sent the case back to the appeals court for reconsideration. The Bible Students were released on bail. Soon the appeals court vacated the convictions because of the many irregularities during trial. In the end, the government abandoned the case.[27]

Other critics continued to pound away at the court's free-speech stance, which further unnerved Brandeis. A couple of months after the *Debs* opinion, Zechariah Chafee, another exponent of sociological jurisprudence, published an essay that was directly aimed at the emergent liberal wing of the court. It was a masterful dismantling of many of the court's key assumptions from the perspective of someone who had thought through the social implications of law.

Chafee began by noting the importance of the free-speech issue to the current moment. There had been over two hundred espionage and sedition prosecutions during the war, a situation that called for a careful appraisal of the purposes of speech in a free society. In that assessment, Chafee contended, one needed to take care to frame the issues in the correct way. The usual liberal approach began by considering free speech as a right. Chafee disagreed. "It is useless to de-fine free speech by talk about rights," Chafee insisted. Rights often conflicted. The individual had a right to speak. The government had a right to wage war. The rights opposed one another. Deadlock ensued.[28]

To break the impasse one must go behind the talk of rights to understand the interests at stake. The individual sought to speak. Society wanted the successful prosecution of the war. Those interests were relative, not absolute. "Individual interests and social interests ... must be balanced against each other, if they conflict," Chafee wrote, "in order to determine which interest shall be sacrificed under the circumstances and which shall be protected and become the foundation of a legal right." The balancing procedure was essentially a policy-oriented endeavor, an expression of sociological jurisprudence in the modern world. One must consider what Holmes had earlier called "the social end" of a regulation in the development of law.[29]

In the case of speech, the social function of free expression was much more capacious than the court seemed to acknowledge. "One of the most important purposes of society and government is the discovery and spread of truth on subjects of general concern," Chafee wrote. In order to promote free inquiry the First Amendment was prejudiced toward, in Chafee's words, a "national policy in favor of public discussion of all public questions." Free speech was simply and obviously a prerequisite for having a full public debate.[30]

If Chafee had stopped there, he already would have been saying a lot. In cases that involved the regulation of speech, he removed the burden from those who wanted to speak and placed it upon those who wanted to curtail speech. Those who wished to limit speech had to prove decisively that the prevention of substantive evil would more than compensate the obvious costs to public discussion.

But Chafee went beyond his own formulations by arguing that Holmes had, in fact, already recognized the social purpose of freedom of speech. Holmes had noted in the *Schenck* opinion that the First Amendment allowed for the regulation of speech only when it caused "clear and present danger" to some vital social interest. Holmes had simply employed the old bad tendency test using a new turn of phrase. But Chafee reinterpreted Holmes as proposing a new, more stringent standard for the regulation of speech that could be useful in the future.

In Chafee's construal, Holmes had limited the government's ability to regulate speech to those few cases in which speaking caused an immediate danger to others. The clear and present danger test affirmed that all citizens could express their opinions free of governmental interference. It was obvious to Chafee, on that standard, that the court had wrongly decided the Debs case because Debs's speech held no danger to any vital interest. Debs was simply expressing an unpopular opinion that ran against the political orthodoxy that the government was trying to protect.[31]

Chafee's creative misconstrual of the court's opinion was enormously useful to both Holmes and Brandeis. It offered "intellectual cover," as the legal scholar David Rabban has put it, for changing their minds without repudiating their prior positions. The new direction allowed for a new jurisprudential orientation to enter law.[32]

Six months after the *Schenck* and *Debs* decisions, they were able to acknowledge their partial volte-face. The case, *Abrams v. United States*, involved five Russian-born radicals convicted for their role in distributing two circulars, one in English and one in Yiddish, that spoke favorably of the Russian Revolution. The appellants maintained that they were within their rights to publish and distribute the flyers. The Espionage Act was unconstitutional, they said, on the grounds of freedom of speech and freedom of the press.[33]

The court, in a 7–2 opinion, disagreed. "Even if their primary purpose and intent was to aid the cause of the Russian Revolution," the court said, "the plan of action which they adopted necessarily involved, before it could be realized, defeat of the war program of the United States." To justify its finding, the court cited its own prior rulings written by Holmes.[34]

But Holmes did not vote with the majority. In his dissent, which Brandeis joined, Holmes insisted that he never had occasion to doubt the earlier speech opinions he had written. His clear and present danger test had disposed of the cases accurately, while also proposing a new rule. But the court in this case had incorrectly followed his guidance by not understanding that the new test had a prejudice toward free speech. It required that an actual threat be shown before speech could be curtailed. In the current case, no threat had been shown.

"Nobody can suppose," Holmes wrote, "that the surreptitious publishing of a silly leaflet by an unknown man, without more, would present any immediate danger that its opinions would hinder the success of the government arms or have any appreciable tendency to do so."[35]

That seemed, to his mind, to dispose of the case. But he was not content to leave it there. Holmes offered, in a not-quite-apology for his past opinions, a stirring articulation of why he thought free speech merited protection and why the court had gotten the issues wrong.

"Persecution for the expression of opinion seems to me perfectly logical," he wrote. "If you have no doubt of your premises or your power, and want a certain result with all your heart, you naturally express your wishes in law and sweep away all opposition." But, he continued, dogmatism did not afford an adequate social justification for belief in the modern world. The better approach was to allow "free trade in ideas," he advised, because "the best test of truth is the power of the thought to get itself accepted in the competition of the market, and that truth is the only ground upon which their wishes safely can be carried out." This was the pluralistic idea that liberal intellectuals had been advancing for two decades.[36]

The opposite impulse was on display in the current case. "I think that we should be eternally vigilant against attempts to check the expression of opinions that we loathe and believe to be fraught with death," Holmes wrote, "unless they so imminently threaten interference with the lawful and pressing purposes of the law that an immediate check is required to save the country."[37]

His dissent was a remarkable reconsideration, though he did not acknowledge it as such. There is some evidence that Brandeis had pushed him into it. A month and a half after Holmes's *Schenck* and *Debs* decisions Brandeis wrote him with a chastisement. "You, who have pried open the legal door to effort," Brandeis said, "should not close it to hope." Holmes was, in this case, persuaded.[38]

But disagreements remained. Holmes continued to exhibit a cynicism about individual human beings and their experiences in society. His view was rooted in the notion that life is struggle and that competition is one of its dominant impulses. His metaphor of the free market of ideas had vaguely social Darwinist overtones, which was in keeping with his form of nonbelief. An idea that survived through exertion and rivalry, Holmes contended, was more likely to be correct.

Brandeis was moving in the opposite direction. As a believer in social reform, he had begun to embrace free speech as a necessary component of democratic deliberation and as a prerequisite by which human beings could use intelligence to shape their destiny. Brandeis was able to articulate his own point of view in a case argued the same day as *Abrams* but not decided until four months later. *Schaefer v. United States* was yet another wartime case involving political leftists. The five appellants all took part in running a pro-German and Leftist newspaper and were convicted of violating the Espionage Act. In a 6–3 opinion the court upheld the conviction of three of the appellants, while dismissing the conviction of the other two for lack of evidence.[39]

Brandeis wrote in dissent, with Holmes joining. He was not satisfied that the newspaper constituted a clear and present danger to the war effort. But rather than leave it there Brandeis expounded upon the wider threat within the court's jurisprudence that he saw developing. The issue of the case was not merely one of speech in wartime, he said, since the right of free speech was the same in peace and war (this, in itself, rejected Holmes's claim in *Schenck*). The wider issue of the case was that some powerful people in government had decided to regulate the opinion of individuals with whom they disagreed. "Convictions such as these, besides abridging freedom of speech," he wrote, "threaten freedom of thought and belief."[40]

A week later Brandeis went further still. In *Pierce v. United States* several men were convicted for distributing flyers and making speeches against the war. The defendants admitted their intention to make converts to socialism but not to interfere with the war. The court upheld their conviction. Brandeis, with Holmes concurring, complained that the court was constricting the democratic process. "The fundamental right of free men to strive for better conditions through new legislation and new institutions will not be preserved," he wrote, "if efforts to secure it by argument to fellow citizens may be construed as criminal incitement."[41]

Still the cases kept coming. A few months later the court heard an appeal challenging a Minnesota law that made it illegal to discourage enlistment in the military. The convicted man, Joseph Gilbert, was a socialist and a lawyer who was convicted under the law. The case posed novel issues because the law in question was passed by a state, while the free-speech clause of the First Amendment, like the rest of the Bill of Rights, applied only to the federal government. The majority ruled that Gilbert had improperly criticized national policy and had advocated, in effect, a policy of anarchy. It was within the state's power to enact a law that established order and preserved peace.[42]

Brandeis's dissent was restrained but moving, and it obviously sought to appeal to Holmes. "Like the course of the heavenly bodies," Brandeis wrote, "harmony in national life is a resultant of the struggle between contending forces. In frank expression of conflicting opinion lies the greatest promise of wisdom in governmental action, and in suppression lies ordinarily the greatest peril."[43]

The problem the court faced, one which would be central to the development of secularism, was just how far the state could go in promoting a political orthodoxy, how intensely it could regulate individual belief. This was the underlying current in all of these cases. But after *Gilbert v. Minnesota* (1920) the court took a breather and decided no other free-speech case of import for five years. In the meantime the national political environment continued to constrict. The diminished room for debate, in turn, led political dissidents to seek new alliances that further developed the institutional matrix of American secularism.

In January 1920, a coalition of liberal Protestants, post-Protestants, and liberal Jews came together to form the American Civil Liberties Union (ACLU). The founders hailed from a variety of organizations formed during the war—the Bureau of Legal First Aid, the Legal Defense League, the Liberty Defense Union, and, especially, the National Civil Liberties Bureau (NCLB). The smaller organizations had proven to be too fragmented. By contrast, the ACLU immediately became a nexus through which all the groups interested in civil liberties could come together.[44]

It occupied such a central place largely through the dynamism of its leader, Roger Baldwin, whose wartime experience transformed his perspective. Like many moderate liberals prior to the war, Baldwin had not much initial interest in free speech. He taught sociology and worked at a settlement house in St. Louis, where he had moved on the advice of Louis Brandeis after Baldwin graduated from Harvard. But after a few years in St. Louis he went by chance to hear the anarchist Emma Goldman speak. The encounter was the beginning of a political awakening, and from that point forward he became both a philosophical anarchist and a pacifist.[45]

His new politics became a problem once the United States entered the war. Determined to live out his convictions, Baldwin made his way into the American Union against Militarism, which in July 1917 created the Civil Liberties Bureau to advocate for conscientious objectors to the war effort. A couple of months later the Civil Liberties Bureau broke off to become the NCLB, with Baldwin at its head.[46]

In spite of his radical turn, Baldwin had a somewhat naïve trust in the American government and in the good intentions of the governmental elite. As the Department of Justice began to crack down on dissenters Baldwin continued to believe he could work within the system. When the government asked for information about his clients, he willingly handed it over. Soon government lawyers began to suspect that the NCLB itself was guilty of criminal activity. It opened an investigation into the organization, pressured the NCLB's landlord into issuing an eviction, and eventually conducted a raid to cart off the bureau's legal files en masse. The Department of Justice declined ultimately to prosecute the NCLB, but the legal files became very useful in its other prosecutions.[47]

Baldwin himself became the next object of scrutiny. Because of his pacifism he declined to enroll in the draft. The U.S. government indicted him as a draft dodger. At trial he engaged in a long philosophical exchange with the judge about the rights of conscience and the theory of American government that, in his view, protected his actions. But his efforts failed. The judge found him guilty. There was still some hope that he might have a lenient punishment. But the judge told Baldwin, "A Republic can last only so long as its laws are obeyed," before he sentenced him to a maximum of eleven months and ten days in federal prison.[48]

Baldwin's imprisonment shattered whatever faith he had in government. He served his time and emerged from the pen just as the Supreme Court began to hear cases on appeal that dealt with free speech. Each negative decision from the court reinforced his conviction that litigation was a waste of time, that the government was no more likely to acknowledge rights than the judge was in his own case. To persuade, to litigate was to presume that the government would grant rights. Experience had proven otherwise. So instead of litigating, Baldwin began to favor direct action by aligning his efforts with those of other leftist resistance movements, especially the labor movement, that fought for rights via strikes and protests. This posture of resistance to state authority became a pillar of ACLU thought. But other civil rights organizations disagreed.[49]

When the ACLU was organized, it joined an increasingly crowded civil rights landscape that included the NAACP, the Anti-Defamation League (formed in 1913), and the American Jewish Congress (AJC, formed in 1918). Unlike the ACLU, each of these organizations viewed the federal government as a positive protector of rights, at least potentially. Even within the ACLU there were those who favored patient litigation in an attempt to bring the government around to their position.[50]

For the most part Baldwin tolerated other approaches and sought to create a big tent for civil liberties cooperation. Shortly after the ACLU was formed, Baldwin invited James Weldon Johnson, the NAACP's executive secretary, to sit on the ACLU's executive committee. That started a long-standing organizational connection between the two bodies.[51]

But given their divergent views about the role of government in protecting civil liberties, tension was inevitable. In 1920, after Protestant fundamentalist ministers revived and revitalized the KKK, the NAACP sought some way to counter its growth. As KKK membership swelled, the NAACP asked the postal service to ban Klan literature. In doing so, it presumed that the distribution of Klan material led to violence against black Americans, so the literature itself could be deemed a form of incitement.[52]

The ACLU thought otherwise. Albert DeSilver, a cofounder of the organization, wrote to Johnson explaining their opposition.

"We do not think it is ever a good policy for an organization interested in human liberty to invoke repressive measures against any of its antagonists," DeSilver said. "By doing so it creates a danger of making a precedent against itself."[53]

A few years later the city of Boston banned public meetings of the KKK. Tension flared again. The Boston ACLU protested the rule as an unacceptable limitation on speech. If left intact and adopted elsewhere, the ban would have far-ranging consequences. "There would be considerable parts of this country in which religious intolerance would prohibit Catholics, Jews, and indeed, the representatives of some Protestant sects, from holding meetings or speaking at all," the ACLU declared. The silencing of offensive sentiment required someone to determine when speech crossed the line into the unacceptable, which was a problematic endeavor and which inevitably created a new orthodoxy. The line that should be drawn, the ACLU held, was "between word and deed," not between "one kind of speech and another."[54]

In effect, the two organizations had rival goals. The ACLU wanted to reject the reigning orthodoxy by creating an official agnosticism—a form of negative secularism—about political and religious matters. Free speech was a way to support that agnosticism. Individuals or groups might have whatever substantive positions they wanted—however noxious they might be to other people—but the government, the law, and the political process ought to support a freewheeling pluralism in American public life by remaining studiously noncommittal to any substantive position. The rights of conscience would be thereby guaranteed, and the rights of free speech, public deliberation, and political participation for all would be protected.

The NAACP agreed with the vision up to a point. It wanted to reject the reigning orthodoxy, in its case the white Christian order that supported inequality. But it wanted to substitute that orthodoxy with a new one that limited public debate and that inculcated a more substantive political commitment to equal protection. It was, in essence, a new secular civic orthodoxy that the NAACP sought to endorse.

But if the ACLU's stance blocked full cooperation with some groups, it opened paths to coordination with others. It was especially attractive to Joseph Rutherford and his followers. The Bible Students had emerged from prison at about the same time as Baldwin, and, like Baldwin, their time in the federal pen made them even more fervent in their opposition to state authority. They also shared his deep skepticism toward curtailments of free speech, since they thought any limitation was likely to be used against them.

Their wartime experience had changed them in a more fundamental way. The conflict had come and gone without the apocalyptic fulfillment of prophesy. They recognized that even if the world was slated to end, it might not necessarily be imminent. The postponement of God's kingdom meant that they had still more preaching to do, so they committed themselves to building out their organization in order to stay on message while scaling their efforts.

It started at the top, with Joseph Rutherford, who began to make phonographs of his sermons that could be played by his followers on a portable player. The society also expanded its printing efforts, putting out tracts in the hundreds of thousands and, soon, the millions. Within a few years their operations had expanded so much that the society built an eight-story printing plant to support its endeavors.[55]

The organizational efforts fed into a vastly expanded program of evangelism. On Sundays the devout would load into cars and travel to a neighborhood. From there they would fan out to knock on doors or to approach people in the streets. The Bible Students' standard procedure was to ask potential converts whether they would be willing to listen to a phonograph of Rutherford's message. Whether or not the person said yes, the evangelists offered a variety of pamphlets or tracts for a donation. If the person declined to offer a contribution but promised to read the pamphlet, the Bible Students would give it away for free. Soon they were also using sound trucks—vehicles with speakers mounted on all sides—that broadcast Rutherford's sermons while slowly circling through a neighborhood or while standing next to a park.[56]

Challenges began immediately. The obnoxious nature of the message was the chief source of conflict. The Bible Students rejected pretty much every existing power structure within American society. They thought that clergy, politicians, and businessmen— what the Watchtower Society called an unholy trinity—had banded together to do the work of Satan. Existing religious organizations, especially the Roman Catholic Church, were rackets designed to enrich the clergy and protect their power while suppressing the true message of the scriptures. All was corrupt in the current order, the Students believed, and all must be opposed.[57]

Their preaching was, accordingly, harsh. The Bible Students denounced any and all connections between religion and the government as the work of the unholy trinity. They rejected Prohibition as a "scheme of the Devil," even though they personally did not drink, because they regarded the effort as a nakedly religious attempt to coerce people into good behavior. They objected to blue laws and other laws that compelled religious observance for the same reason. They renounced religious instruction in the schools as an impermissible attempt to use public institutions to indoctrinate the American citizenry. Like the ACLU, the Bible Students criticized laws—which existed in a majority of states—that suppressed the advocacy of political and economic beliefs that undermined the social order and general welfare. They thought, rightly, that the authorities often used those laws against religious minorities.[58]

The government responded to the Watchtower Society much as it did to the labor movement. Many clergymen wrote government officials to request an investigation into Watchtower practices. Agents from the Federal Bureau of Investigation placed Rutherford under surveillance. The Watchtower Society was considered an incipiently communist organization. The Bible Students also faced difficulties on the local and state levels. When they showed up in a neighborhood, offended citizens, many of them Catholic, would call the cops to come arrest the proselytizers or they would take matters into their own hands. It was not uncommon for Bible Students to go proselytizing with their toothbrushes, expecting to end the day in jail.[59]

As Bible Students ran into trouble, the ACLU stepped in to defend them. The organization's justification was as unbending as always. Regardless of the offensive nature of their speech, the ACLU said, the First Amendment permitted it.

Soon Rutherford began to hear about the ACLU's efforts on behalf of his movement. One day he decided to pay Baldwin a visit. He asked one of his colleagues to arrange a meeting. When he arrived at Baldwin's office with a large retinue of female followers, he settled into a chair like he owned the place and got down to business.

"I have to come to see you to express our appreciation of what you are doing to help our people," Rutherford told Baldwin. "I want you to be able to continue it without cost, and so would like to make a contribution for that purpose."

Baldwin tried to assure him that that was unnecessary. "Our business [is] to help anyone get civil rights," Baldwin replied. The ACLU's existing contributors already gave so that the organization could offer services for free. It did not need payment after the fact.

"No, no," Rutherford responded. "I don't want you to tax them for us."

He asked his secretary whether they had money in the bank. The secretary responded that they did.

"Well, in that case," Rutherford told the secretary, "write out a check for a thousand dollars for Mr. Baldwin, and send him another when he asks for it."[60]

Baldwin later recounted, "I was somewhat taken aback." A thousand dollars was a lot of money back then. "But," he said, "not being in the habit of refusing honest money for the cause, I accepted it."[61]

It was the beginning of a long association that would, in time, bear secular fruit.

While their partnership was developing, others within the ACLU were looking for test cases to change the law. They did not have much reason to be optimistic. The Supreme Court had spoken clearly, with Holmes and Brandeis in dissent, often by themselves. The law seemed settled.

But their plan was to pursue appeals that would allow Brandeis and Holmes to continue to critique the direction of the court. An alternative vision of the law, they hoped, might grow in influence over time.

The first big breakthrough happened in 1925, when the court heard the case *Gitlow v. New York*. Benjamin Gitlow was a Jewish communist who, along with other communists following the Russian Revolution, had broken with the Socialist Party. The socialists thought that they could work toward their goal through existing political channels. The communists accepted the Soviet contention that socialist revolution required the overthrow of existing governments. As a member of what became known as the Left Wing Socialists (i.e., communists), Gitlow had printed, published, and distributed a magazine, *The Revolutionary Age.*[62]

In one issue of the magazine he included the Left Wing Manifesto. "The world is in crisis," it announced. "Capitalism, the prevailing system of society, is in the process of disintegration and collapse. . . . Humanity can be saved from its last excesses only by the Communist Revolution."[63]

For printing and circulating the manifesto, Gitlow was arrested along with several colleagues under a New York law that made it a crime to advocate criminal anarchy or, in the words of the law, "the doctrine that organized government should be overthrown by force, or violence, or by assassination of the executive head or of any of the executive officials of government, or by any unlawful means."[64]

Gitlow was happy to be arrested. It was all part of the plan. As he later recounted, "We were in the best of spirits. We were, after all, revolutionists, ready to sacrifice all for the revolution, so that a mere arrest and a ride in a patrol wagon was a trifling incident."[65]

But in spite of his optimism, his trial went badly. He was convicted. After the jury delivered the verdict, the presiding judge thanked them for their service and opined that the problem with political radicalism was that it led men to hope for heaven on earth. "So long as we are on this mundane sphere, the only way that we can stand firm and erect in the sight of God is to keep our feet on the ground, only allowing our own heads to be in the clouds." He commended the jury for saving the country from "misguided idealists."[66]

Gitlow appealed his conviction to the circuit court. He lost again. In upholding his conviction, the court wrote that Gitlow's case revealed the importance of immigration restriction. If the flow of foreign people and ideas were blocked, the court wrote, "the God-fearing, liberty-loving Americans" would make sure that "these pernicious doctrines are not permitted to take root in America."[67]

Undeterred, Gitlow appealed to the Supreme Court. The ACLU got involved. Gitlow lost yet again. In a 7–2 opinion the court ruled that the Left Wing Manifesto was an incitement to overthrow the government. The state was permitted to punish those who abused freedom of speech "by utterances inimical to the public welfare, tending to corrupt public morals, incite crime, or disturb the public peace."[68]

If that was all the opinion said, it would have been just like all the rest. But the remarkable part of the decision was its somewhat casual assumption that the First Amendment applied to the states, which would have enormous consequences for the secularization of law. Because the First Amendment begins, "Congress shall make no law," the courts had long held that it applied only to the federal government. But legal doctrine had begun to change after the Civil War when Congress passed the Fourteenth Amendment to protect former slaves from state abuse. It forbade states from infringing upon the rights of U.S. citizens. And it allowed the federal government to protect U.S. citizens from curtailment of their liberties. But the amendment had left the rights of citizenship undefined. By the end of the nineteenth century, some legal thinkers were inclined to say that the rights of U.S. citizenship could be found in the Bill of Rights and, especially, in the First Amendment.[69]

In Brandeis's dissent five years earlier in *Gilbert v. Minnesota* (1920), he had asserted that the free-speech protection of the First Amendment was part of or, in technical legal jargon, was incorporated into the due process provisions of the Fourteenth Amendment. The rest of the court refused to affirm Brandeis's position at the time.

Yet five years later, in the *Gitlow* case, the majority opinion simply accepted that First Amendment free-speech protection was incorporated into the Fourteenth. That part of the First Amendment then applied to the states, and states could no longer violate free speech without the federal government getting involved. The majority still thought that in this specific case the regulation of speech was justified. But by applying free-speech protection to the states, the conservative majority had made an enormous concession. Chafee called it "a victory out of defeat."[70]

The *Gitlow* decision showed the power of Brandeis's and Holmes's strategic approach. On the surface the case simply continued the trend of Holmes and Brandeis in lonely dissent from the rest of the court. But a wider perspective revealed how far they had come. The majority on the court had accepted in principle, though not in practice, the clear and present danger standard as the essential test for regulating speech. The prejudice of the clear and present danger test in Chafee's construal was toward freedom of speech, not its regulation, which required the court to use the test while working around its implications. The court likewise accepted that all levels of government were bound to honor free speech by applying the First Amendment to the states.

The *Gitlow* case also uncovered the underlying issue, which was that the majority seemed to desire an intellectual homogeneity through the regulation of belief. Freedom of conscience was necessarily suspect. The more time that elapsed after the First World War, the more obvious it became that this was the real issue facing the court when free-speech appeals came before it.

Two years later, for example, the court heard a case involving Anita Whitney, a well-to-do woman from California. She was an unlikely revolutionary, born two years after the Civil War to a wealthy family whose ancestry included five people who came over on the *Mayflower* and a governor of the Massachusetts Bay Colony. She was closely related to David Josiah Brewer, a late-nineteenth-century Supreme Court jurist who widely proclaimed that the United States was a Christian nation. Whitney had begun her political work as a clubwoman, which was respectable, before moving into social work, which was less so, and then into political radicalism.[71]

Her journey from that point was pretty typical. When the communists split from the socialists, she went with the communists and gave speeches throughout California to drum up support for the Communist Labor Party of America. As part of that effort she gave a speech in Oakland condemning the wave of lynching that had spread across the nation after the First World War. She urged Congress to pass an antilynching law to protect equal rights for all. At a time when communists were at the forefront of civil rights activism for black Americans, the sentiment was again fairly standard for a Communist Party event. But shortly after the speech Whitney was arrested, charged, and convicted of violating the California Criminal Syndicalism Act.[72]

By the time her case made it to the High Court, the fissures were well known. Holmes and Brandeis had become, in the words of the *St. Louis Post-Dispatch*, "a separate liberal chamber of the Supreme Court." "On the great issues that go down to the fundamental differences in the philosophy of government," the paper continued, "these two are nearly always together; often they are together against the rest of the court."[73]

Their estrangement was true even when the decision was unanimous, as it was in *Whitney v. California* (1927). The majority opinion, joined by seven justices, upheld Whitney's conviction by saying, yet again, that freedom of speech did not eliminate the police power of the states. The law against criminal syndicalism was an expression of police power. Because Whitney's speech tended toward lawbreaking, the majority held, she was rightly convicted.[74]

In a concurring opinion joined by Holmes, Brandeis critiqued the court's reasoning. The problem with California's criminal syndicalism law was not what it forbade—support for criminal acts in the attempt to bring about political, social, or economic change. The problem was that it extended guilt to anyone who associated with organizations preaching criminal syndicalism. The prosecution had alleged that the Communist Labor Party of America, which Whitney supported and which did not explicitly support criminal behavior, was a front for the more radical International Workers of the World, which did endorse violence to achieve political aims. Brandeis worried that such associative concern led to hysterical forms of abuse. "Men feared witches and burnt women," he pointed out, and some version of the dynamic seemed to be what was happening in the present case.[75]

Brandeis's comparison to the witch trials was useful and telling. It implied a reactionary and superstitious response to political radicals by those who wished to regulate speech. But the power of speech, Brandeis wrote, was that it freed people from irrational fears by promoting "the discovery and spread of political truth." "To courageous, self-reliant men, with confidence in the power of free and fearless reasoning applied through the process of popular government," Brandeis continued, "no danger flowing from speech can be deemed clear and present unless the incidence of evil apprehended is so imminent that it may befall before there is opportunity for full discussion."[76]

Brandeis, though, stopped short of saying that Whitney had been wrongly convicted. There was some evidence of conspiracy to commit a criminal act, he said, although what the evidence was he did not elaborate. Because it was not possible to retry the case on appeal, he swerved at the end to agree with the majority in upholding the verdict, though it seemed to pain him.

So what was the point of writing the opinion? As was true of many of his dissents, Brandeis was able to use the case to elaborate his conception of political rights and social purposes. He showed how the protection of individual liberties nourished social goals—in this case, the maintenance of democratically supported truth—and vice versa. By contrast, the suppression of free speech yielded irrationality and superstition that used the powers of the state, which was also on display in the court's reasoning.

It was an argument that did not try to persuade the court but sought instead to persuade the public and others who joined the court in the future. And it appeared to be working the next year when the court heard *Olmstead v. United States.* The case involved Roy Olmstead, a bootlegger who ran an alcohol smuggling ring in the Pacific Northwest. His activities had been of interest to the cops for some time, but he had not been caught. To gather evidence the authorities wiretapped his house, without court approval, and then used the evidence to convict him of violating the National Prohibition Act, which forbade the manufacture and sale of intoxicating beverages except under certain, limited conditions. Olmstead stressed that the wiretapping, which was conducted by federal Prohibition officers without a warrant, violated his Fourth Amendment protection against illegal search and seizure. The decision to use that evidence in court violated his Fifth Amendment rights to the due process of law. In a 5–4 decision the majority upheld the conviction and ruled that Olmstead's rights had not been violated.[77]

The minority opinions were fractured, which demonstrated a wider disarray of reasoning. Holmes held that it was obviously illegal to wiretap without a warrant and that the government ought not violate the law in the interest of catching others who violate it.

Pierce Butler, ordinarily a reliably conservative vote, announced that the court was bound by the intent and principles articulated in the Constitution rather than merely the literal meaning of the words. Those principles would seem to have protected Olmstead from unfettered surveillance.

Brandeis went the farthest. The Olmstead prosecution demonstrated to Brandeis why the court needed to recognize a right to privacy. His reasoning was not, at first, entirely obvious. In the case of other dissenters who were engaging in political activity, the court's desire to regulate opinion was clear. Left-wing activists sought to articulate their ideas in a public forum in order to win supporters to their side. The government opposed their ability to do so, and the court had upheld the government's actions. Brandeis's opposition made sense from the facts of each case. But in *Olmstead* government agents were not regulating opinion. They were simply trying to enforce the law against an obvious and egregious lawbreaker.

And yet there were wider implications in that surveillance. To Brandeis, the government's actions revealed a darker possibility that needed to be protected against. If a person could be illegally surveilled to prevent bootlegging, who was to say that a person would not be surveilled because he was a political radical or a religious zealot or some other yet-to-be-named social problem?

"The makers of our Constitution undertook to secure conditions favorable to the pursuit of happiness," Brandeis wrote. "They recognized the significance of man's spiritual nature, of his feelings, and of his intellect. They knew that only part of the pain, pleasure, and satisfactions of life are to be found in material things. They sought to protect Americans in their beliefs, their thoughts, their emotions and their sensations. They conferred, as against the Government, the right to be let alone—the most comprehensive of rights, and the right most valued by civilized men." The government's violation of Olmstead's right to privacy and its use of evidence wrongly gathered in a criminal proceeding ought to have invalidated the conviction. But, more broadly, Brandeis thought the government ought not be able to surveil its citizens so that they could be free to develop themselves as they wished. This was an update on Brandeis's right-to-privacy notion, and the update showed why the notion was so foundational in the first place. The right to privacy ramified outward from the First Amendment to the Fourth and Fifth Amendments and, potentially, beyond.[78]

With this opinion Brandeis completed his intellectual transformation in a way that would have powerful import in the future. When he first defended the right to privacy with Samuel Warren, his conception of the right was a threat to freedom of speech and freedom of the press. Over the next forty years he reconfigured his ideas about rights and responsibilities, eventually coming to affirm the importance of public political reasoning and the right of free speech. In his *Olmstead* dissent he came full circle by reconceiving the right to privacy from one that threatened freedom of speech into one that honored intellectual independence, personal difference, and the right of conscience. That reconfiguration would soon be picked up by the court.[79]

One might wonder about Brandeis's optimism in these opinions. Would he have expressed his views on speech in the way he did if the defendants were Nazis after the Second World War? There is a confidence here about free speech and the rational progress of humankind that not everyone can share. That optimism led to a kind of free-speech absolutism, a belief in the sanctity of personal convictions and their ability to be expressed publicly, that would become especially vexing in the future as the court built out the structures of American secularism.

His free-speech doctrine also contained an ambiguity. What was the relationship between the public rights of free speech to the private rights of religion or free association or other instances of private ordering? Brandeis had not entirely worked it out, which would also vex the court in the future.

But he was soon joined by someone who would attempt to work it out or at least work out one solution. The fourth dissenter in the *Olmstead* case was a newcomer to the Supreme Court, a liberal Protestant named Harlan Stone. During the First World War Stone served on a War Department Board of Inquiry that reviewed cases in which lower-level draft boards had rejected claims of conscientious objection. By 1919, as the free-speech cases began to make their way to the court, Stone started to express sympathy for the dissenters. "The Army was not a bed of roses for the conscientious objector," he later wrote in the *Columbia University Quarterly*,

"and the normal man who was not supported in his stand by profound moral conviction might well have chosen active duty at the
front as the easier lot." Their courage to stand by their convictions
won him over to their side and began to change his perspective
more generally. Soon he was defending socialists and others who
faced prosecution on free-speech grounds.[80]

By the time Stone joined the court, he had become a proponent
of sociological jurisprudence. That position aligned him immediately with Holmes and Brandeis. In the *Olmstead* case he joined
both Holmes's and Brandeis's dissents. He also joined Butler's insofar as it dealt with the merits of the case, but he did not endorse
Butler's constitutional theories. Butler's jurisprudence had no sociological sense and usually upheld positions that a liberal progressive
would consider bad policy. Stone's vote indicated his basic orientation in the future.[81]

The *Olmstead* case marked a turn, not because of an immediate
change in the dynamics of the court but because American society
was about to go through a fundamental upheaval that finally created
an opening for the court's liberal jurisprudence. Not long after the
court handed down the *Olmstead* ruling, the United States went into
a profound economic slump that soon became a depression. It is difficult to communicate how jarring the downward turn was after the
roaring economy of the 1920s. Whole industries ceased to function.
Communities were devastated. For workers who lost their jobs, the
depression called into question the desirability of capitalism itself.

Brandeis watched the situation with dismay, disturbed that
President Herbert Hoover seemed unwilling to use the full force
of the federal government to address the misery. "The widespread
suffering, the economic helplessness, and the general dejection are
appalling," Brandeis confessed to Harold Laski, an economist and
sociologist of law at the London School of Economics. But in spite
of the suffering, nothing much was being done. American businessmen and their enablers in government had no sense that they
needed to reconsider their theories in light of market paralysis.
"The process of debunking continues," Brandeis wrote, "and if the
depression is long continued—which seems likely—America will
gain much from her sad experience."[82]

On the court there were changes but little progress that Brandeis would recognize, at least at first. On the eve of his ninetieth birthday Oliver Wendell Holmes decided to, in his words, "bow to the inevitable" by retiring. Hoover nominated a secularist Jewish appeals court judge, Benjamin Cardozo, as Holmes's replacement. Cardozo was in many ways the perfect substitution. His judicial philosophy comported with Brandeis's sensibilities, and he was committed to the use of law for progressive political ends.[83]

"As we lose Holmes," Brandeis wrote to one correspondent, "the appointment of judge Cardozo gives joy."[84]

Other developments also gave Brandeis ballast. By 1932 Hoover had lost all legitimacy, and the Democratic candidate, Franklin Delano Roosevelt, put forward a vision of wholesale political renovation that Brandeis could embrace. Roosevelt was a thoroughgoing progressive. He thought the times demanded what Walter Lippmann had called "a new sense of political values." His basic posture, and the rhetorical burden of his presidential campaign, was to offer a vision of governmental reconstruction in order to meet the challenge of human suffering that the Great Depression was causing.[85]

Roosevelt's campaign message was, accordingly, simple and focused. At the Democratic National Convention he demanded "a new deal for the American people" that would create an invigorated relationship between the government and its citizens. He was not, he told the crowd, one of those "who squint at the future with their faces turned toward the past, and who feel no responsibility to the demands of the new time." The crisis of the Depression had shown the folly of that historical posture because the governmental practices of the past had become obsolete in the light of industrial civilization. The breakdown of order and the depression itself now required the Democrats to embrace their transformative mission, to become, as Roosevelt put it, "prophets of a new order."[86]

Brandeis was delighted, telling his niece that Roosevelt had been "much underrated by the Liberals."[87]

Once Roosevelt entered office he set about bringing the new political order into effect. What the New Deal required was an expanded role for the federal government in regulating the nation's economic life. As Congress responded with a flurry of legislation that built out the administrative capacities of the executive and created what became known as the New Deal state, businessmen and their allies on the court moved into opposition. In response to cases brought by business leaders, lower courts and then the Supreme Court began striking down key components of New Deal legislation, sometimes in 6–3 decisions with Brandeis, Cardozo, and Stone in dissent and sometimes in 5–4 decisions with Chief Justice Charles Evans Hughes joining the liberal justices.[88]

The judicial impasse had an important effect. The election of 1936 became a straightforward referendum on the constitutionality of the New Deal, which is another way of saying that it became a plebiscite on the desirability of the liberal–progressive vision that Roosevelt articulated. It was a make-or-break opportunity. And in an indication of how expansive the public's appetite for political change was, Roosevelt demolished his Republican opponent by one of the widest margins in a presidential election.

But his victory did not solve the problem of the court. In an effort to deal with judicial recalcitrance, Roosevelt put forward a proposal to reorganize the judiciary. He sought, in effect, to pack the court with new justices so that he could have his way. Associate Justice Robert H. Jackson later remarked that the scheme was "the political manifestation of a long-smouldering intellectual revolt." When Roosevelt tried to add judges to the court in order to compel its acquiescence, he sought in effect to bring it into line with the other modernizing currents in American society.[89]

The proposal ultimately did not make it through Congress, but its failure was nonetheless productive. It accomplished its purpose simply by being raised. The court buckled under political pressure and acceded to the constitutionality of the New Deal. In 1937, in the case of *West Coast Hotel v. Parrish*, the court split 5–4 while signaling that it was willing to accept a broad definition of interstate commerce in assessing economic legislation, a stance that the New Deal relied upon. Two weeks later the same 5–4 grouping ruled that the Wagner Act, a signature piece of New Deal legislation that allowed collective bargaining by unions, was constitutional. Via these two rulings the majority of the court heralded that it would take a hands-off approach to legislation that sought to rework American political economy.[90]

To that proposition the majority added a second one that would change the entire constitutional landscape and make way for a secular political order. When the court allowed the New Deal to proceed, it repudiated the contract- and property-based conception of rights it had used up to that point. It immediately faced the question of how to conceptualize rights, of how to understand the relationship of the individual to the social whole. This was exactly the question Brandeis and other liberals had been pursuing for the past forty years or more. Now their thinking could finally enter American law.

A year after the court upheld the constitutionality of the New Deal, it began to work through these questions in a footnote to another commerce clause case, *United States v. Carolene Products Co.* The fact that it was a footnote was consequential. The majority indicated that it was not merely interested in disposing of the issues at hand, because the contents of the footnote had nothing to do with the case. But the court recognized that the New Deal transformation meant that a lot of the legal past needed to be rethought and reinterpreted. The majority used the footnote to sketch the directions that the reinterpretation could go, many of which were far-reaching. Harlan Stone wrote the opinion. He said that even as the court showed deference to Congress in economic legislation, it could and would, in Stone's words, conduct a "more searching judicial inquiry" into laws that negatively affected religious, national, and racial minorities. He did not find it necessary to elaborate on what he meant. It was simply a marker for the future.[91]

With this opinion the court entered fully into a new constitutional world. It broadcast a broad deference to the legislature in matters of political economy but a simultaneous commitment to minority rights that refused to defer to prevailing sentiment. The latter was an accession to civil liberties thinking that had been developed by the ACLU and other dissenters and that was articulated through Brandeis's right to privacy thought and the free-speech cases of the 1920s and early 1930s. The court had embraced a new set of substantive ideals and liberal keywords—diversity, equality, rights—that would control its thinking in the coming years. Its public affirmation of new ideas invited people to use the court's institutional power to achieve a renewed constitutional and political order. As a result, the court soon became the central venue for the elaboration of secularism in public life, more so than any other institution.

Yet the justices did not understand all of what they were doing since they did not have complete control over the agenda. The court's opinions had grown over time in a half-conscious and some-times meandering way as groups appeared before it. When the postwar free-speech cases began to work through the system, even Brandeis was caught off guard. The justices responded to the challenges with fresh thought and so built a new body of doctrine and a new language that others could pick up.

In protecting racial, ethnic, and religious minorities, the court would have to ask about their rights and how their rights squared with those of others in a political system. It could happen only by considering a range of desirable political ends—as the minority had shown in the free-speech cases—which turned legal reasoning into a quasi-policy endeavor. That made the court into a venue that could be used by minorities who could not hope for success through normal political channels.

Given the place of Christianity in the United States, it was in-evitable that litigants would use the court's jurisprudence to ques-tion Christian power and to demand a secular reformulation of the nation's laws in order to protect minorities. The Bible Students, the ACLU, the Catholic church, atheist groups—the entire array of the American religious scene soon began urging the court to elaborate on its promises. The push and pull of these new voices led to secular constitutional structures that were not always coher-ent and that people would view through their own lenses. The varying viewpoints would lead to more conflict in the future, which would push the court further still and build out the constitutional framework in surprising ways.

But all that was to come. The point is that by 1937 the founda-tions were in place. The creation of a secular political order could finally begin.

PART TWO

Structures

CHAPTER FOUR

The Difficulties of Diversity

The American secular order did not emerge overnight, and to some extent, even though the foundations were laid, it would come as a surprise to the Supreme Court itself. The problem for the members of the court was that as their jurisprudence was transforming in the 1930s other developments were occurring beneath their gaze. Groups that might not have been on the radar were becoming organized, ready to challenge the court once they saw an opening. At the forefront of the challengers was the ACLU, which had appeared before the court often, and its odd clients Joseph Rutherford and the Bible Students, who had appeared far less.

While the court refigured its constitutional concepts, the Bible Students were growing more militant, increasingly disruptive, and, as a result, still more persecuted. The reason had everything to do with their message, which had become, if possible, even more caustic during the 1930s. The Bible Students saw the Great Depression as an indication of the rightness, even righteousness, of their theological stance. They started to rail against what they called Christendom, the alliance between corporate giants, professional politicians, and clergymen who they thought worked in combination to control American society. The Depression was, in the Bible Students' interpretation, a result of that unholy alliance, and American leaders' professed anxiety about communism simply sought to disguise Christendom's power. But it also offered a sign that the system was breaking down. "The day of God's vengeance is at hand," the Students declared to whomever would listen.[1]

The Bible Students' straightforward message of divine judgment and theological renewal found fertile soil in the despair caused by economic suffering. But as they expanded their evangelistic activities, they were continually harassed by authorities who believed that their efforts violated the Christian Sabbath, disrupted good order, and incited others to violence through the obnoxiousness of their message. When communities demanded that something be done, the police stepped up their arrests.

In response to the crackdown Joseph Rutherford began to articulate his own legal strategy rather than simply relying on the ACLU. By 1929 he had already published what amounted to a legal brief in the Watchtower Society's journal, *The Golden Age*. The brief mixed scriptural and constitutional justifications to defend the Students' preaching activities, and it explained the general approach of the Watchtower Society on Sundays. Rutherford maintained that when the Bible Students went into a neighborhood to preach the word of God they were exercising their religion according to their conscience. Because their activities were rooted in a fundamentally religious set of commitments, Rutherford said, they had constitutional protection within a neutral state.[2]

The result was a standoff. State and municipal authorities asserted that they were simply upholding order when they shut down the Bible Students. They drew upon a full panoply of laws to support their efforts: those that prohibited preaching door-to-door on Sunday, those that required a permit to go door-to-door, and even those that compelled Sunday observance within a state or locality. But Rutherford thought that freedom of religion had been offered to every American as an absolute guarantee. The existing laws being used to persecute the Bible Students were therefore both illegitimate and unconstitutional. Rutherford wanted every Bible Student to know that he or she was obliged not just to spread the good news of Jehovah's coming kingdom but also to defend their legal right to conduct evangelism without the constraint of law.

To that end, Rutherford gave precise instructions in written form. He told his followers that if troubled by police they should inform the officers that the Bible Students were within their rights. If they were arrested, they ought to get a lawyer, show him the memorandum of authorities that Rutherford had prepared, take the case to trial, and be sure to preserve all records to mount a success- ful appeal. If convicted, they were instructed to appeal to ever- higher courts in order to make their case. "In doing so," Rutherford wrote, "you will be acting strictly according to the law of the land and in harmony with the Word of God."[3]

In 1931, in keeping with this new legal orientation, the Bible Students changed their name to the Jehovah's Witnesses.[4]

The Witnesses had an obviously thorny intellectual stance. In religious terms, they were narrow exclusivists. They believed that they alone spoke the truth of God's Word and that all other orga- nized religions were corrupt rackets functioning as vehicles of Satan. They used the Bible, in the words of one early Witness, "as an offen- sive weapon" to tear down other religious groups and to promote their own vision.[5]

But they paired their exclusivism with a political pluralism and a view of the Constitution as a living document. The American consti- tutional order, according to the Witnesses, was capacious and al- lowed for many political, religious, and economic beliefs. The right to advocate for your belief, whatever it was, was protected through the Constitution. And as the times changed, as technologies changed, and as society itself changed, the Witnesses thought, the Constitu- tion grew in response to those changes. So if, for example, the Wit- nesses were arrested for using sound trucks to amplify their message in a public place, even though recording or amplification technology had not been invented at the republic's founding, the Constitution could develop to encompass the new factors within the old terms, whether those terms were freedom of speech or freedom of religion.[6]

In the 1920s the Witnesses' legal stance was ahead of constitu- tional law. They had a hard time making their case. But once the court announced its new orientation in the *Carolene* opinion, they saw a new angle into the law to accomplish their ends. Rutherford set up a legal department in Brooklyn headed by Olin Moyle, an attorney and dedicated Witness. The goal was to use the court's new orientation to undo the remaining structures of Christendom and thereby make way for the Witnesses' message.[7]

Moyle was a strategic operator. Looking for allies, he reached out to the ACLU to propose a formalized collaboration. The ACLU was open to the partnership. Although none of the ACLU leadership was on board with the Witnesses' theological program—since the organization was composed mainly of post-Protestants and free-thinking or agnostic Jews—it did support the Witnesses' absolutism on civil liberties.

The two organizations immediately found a vehicle to test their alliance in fall 1935, when an eight-year-old Massachusetts boy named Carleton Nichols Jr. refused to salute the flag in his school. Flag salutes were an increasingly ubiquitous requirement across the nation. They went along with the pledge of allegiance and looked like a Nazi salute. The students raised an arm, palm downward, toward the U.S. flag that was often hung in the corner of a classroom. For young Nichols the flag was, in his words, "the devil's emblem" and the salute was a form of deferential worship. School administrators expelled the boy for his refusal.[8]

Baldwin immediately wrote to Carlton Nichols Sr. "The American Civil Liberties Union is following with interest your son's courageous stand against a law contrary to your religious convictions," he said. "We offer you our support since we believe that the American right of freedom of conscience and religious belief is at stake."[9]

It is a remarkable fact that Rutherford had not, at that point, officially forbade saluting the flag. But the entire direction of the Witnesses' message intimated that it was problematic. Nichols Jr. was only applying to his own experience what he had learned about worldly governments and their satanic underpinnings. Pushed by the boy's action, Rutherford soon outlawed flag saluting among all the Witnesses. When other children followed suit, scores in other states were disciplined and expelled from their schools.[10]

Moyle wrote to the ACLU, unaware that it was already in contact with the Nichols family: "I am wondering if your organization would be interested in cooperating in another test case on the subject?"[11]

The ACLU immediately began developing legal arguments to resist compulsory flag saluting in coordination with the Witnesses. But its lead attorney, Abraham Isserman, decided to make the case using the concept of free speech, not religion. His decision was practical. Grounding the case in religious freedom would have created problems since the concept was difficult both to define and to limit. Any coherent legal system would be unable to allow people willy-nilly to decide that a law did not comport with their religious sympathies. As Baldwin later said, "We had our troubles in defining the limits of religious freedom." To avoid the issue Isserman portrayed the flag salute as a case of coerced speech.[12]

There were advantages to the posture other than simple clarity. Unlike a religious freedom claim, free speech had an established place in American jurisprudence. Isserman could use the court's own rulings to make his case. "Compelling words or a gesture equivalent to words," he wrote in his model brief for the cases, "is quite clear as an invasion of the right of free speech as is a prohibition against words or symbols."[13]

The ACLU insisted that it was being careful, not that it was disavowing religious freedom. The organization wanted to raise religion without really debating it. Isserman sought other religious groups to participate in the test cases, and Baldwin urged that they get a Catholic lawyer to argue the cases. "The issue is of importance to Catholics as a matter of principle," he explained. The idea was to ground their reasoning in the issue of speech but to gesture toward religious diversity through the litigants and their legal representatives.[14]

The ACLU worked the press in similar fashion. It issued a memo asking why it was necessary to compel little children to salute the flag. What public reason did it serve? Framing the issue in this way emphasized the public advantage of free debate on all issues of political import, which was the central issue in the court's free-speech jurisprudence. The flag salute seemed to narrow public debate through an enforced conformity and violated freedom of thought and speech.[15]

But the religion issue kept coming up, and the ACLU soon broadened its approach. In a Long Island case involving a thirteen-year-old Witness who was expelled by the school, an ACLU lawyer named Arthur G. Hays questioned the hostile superintendent.

Hays asked him, "You believe in religious freedom?"

"I do when it does not conflict with the rights of the Government," the man responded.

"The guarantee of religious freedom is the first amendment to the Constitution?" he asked.

"Correct," the superintendent replied.

"Don't you know that the first ten amendments to the Federal Constitution are limitations upon the power of the federal Government? Don't you know that?"

"No."

"Don't you know the first amendment of the Constitution is that Congress shall have no power to pass laws that will abridge religious views?"

"When those laws were passed there weren't all these different religions."

"Isn't that the way it is worded?" Hays asked.

"I refuse to answer," the superintendent responded.

As a point of fact, the First Amendment was not worded as Hays claimed, and his interpretation, though certainly feasible, was only one possible interpretation.

Hays eventually got the superintendent to say that he did not know where such expansive declarations about religious freedom would stop. "There is nothing to prevent people from starting a religion to keep them from paying taxes," the superintendent said. "We would have anarchy."[16]

The Witnesses were delighted that the ACLU seemed finally to be coming around to a religious defense. "It is a nice, skillful piece of trial work," Moyle wrote to Hays, "done in the interest of liberty, which you love so well."[17]

But in another sense it raised the problem directly. Speech and religion were different. Speech was free to allow full public debate. Religion, as it had been conceptualized in the past, was a private right that allowed for a person to make sense of the world free of governmental interference. To graft a new jurisprudence of religious freedom onto the free-speech jurisprudence would require either a change in conceptualization or some attention to the limits of religious freedom in the American political order. The tensions went to the heart of American secularism. If religious freedom sim-

ply became a constitutionally protected mechanism of bringing religion into public life and of exempting people from otherwise
applicable law, would that be a secular order? For the Witnesses
the question was irrelevant. Their goal was not a secular order; it
was to make way for the Kingdom of Jehovah. They did not much
care for the larger questions in place, except as those questions
prevented them from their work. But for the ACLU the question
was unavoidable. That was why the organization had so gingerly
raised the question of religious freedom in the first place.

That left the Witnesses to make their cases themselves, not entirely trusting others to articulate their view. They were finally able
to explain their position in early 1938, when the Supreme Court
agreed to hear a solicitation case involving a Witness, Alma Lovell,
who had been arrested in Griffin, Georgia. According to the local
ordinance, all distribution of printed matter required prior approval
from the city manager. Lovell was distributing literature without
permit. She thought that the act of obtaining permission would
submit the truth of her religion for determination to a secular authority, which would have violated her freedom of the press and her
freedom of religion.

As the case made its way through the courts, judges consistently
rejected her position. Their main reason for doing so was a set of
cases from the nineteenth century that had to do with Mormons.
After the Civil War the federal government had banned polygamy,
which the Mormons then practiced, in an attempt to eliminate what
they considered an institutionalized immorality from the federal
territory of Utah. In *Reynolds v. United States* (1878), the Church of
Latter-day Saints challenged the polygamy ban by insisting that it
violated the church members' religious freedom. The court rejected
their stance. Freedom of belief, the court said, was absolute. Freedom of action was not. Religious freedom could not be used to
justify behavior that violated otherwise applicable laws, such as a
prohibition of polygamy.[18]

The decision was the start of a long battle between Congress
and the Mormons. Twelve years later, after Congress disenfran-
chised polygamists in Idaho territory, the Mormons asked the court
to grant them back the franchise. The court refused, again citing
the distinction between belief and action to strike down Mormon

challenges to the law. Polygamists could believe what they wished, but they must bear the consequences of acting on it.[19]

The same year, after Congress stripped the Church of Latter-day Saints of its charter of incorporation and seized all of its property until it modified its church teachings about polygamy, the court again ruled against the church. This time it implicitly acknowledged that the regulation of actions could shade into the regulation of belief. Congress's seizure of church property was a straightforward attempt to reconstruct Mormon doctrine. The court found the reconstruction to be legitimate. Because incorporation was given under the law of charities, which was an expression of "the spirit of Christianity," Congress was within its rights to make sure that expressions of barbarism, such as polygamy, were rejected in law.[20]

For a long time, those three rulings were pretty much the sum total of jurisprudence on the religion clauses of the U.S. Constitution. They did not help the Witnesses.

In oral argument Olin Moyle sought to convince the court to move beyond its own decisions. The issue was broader than the Witnesses, he said, and had to do with the place of religion in society. The court's prior rulings posed a dilemma for minority religions whose practices did not comport with the majority sentiment.

Moyle later wrote Rutherford explaining that he sought to convince the court's sole Catholic justice, Pierce Butler, a seemingly difficult task given the Witnesses' virulent anti-Catholicism. Butler asked no questions, Moyle told Rutherford, "but sat there with a sardonic grin on his face until near the close when I pointed out under the construction as made by the Georgia court that we could very easily be put in the same situation as Russia or Germany where the children were not permitted to be taught anything concerning the Bible or religion." From that point on, Butler's face changed, and he listened soberly. "I guess it dawned upon him," Moyle continued, "that if the court followed the Georgia construction, things might happen in some places to the parochial schools of the holy church."[21]

Moyle's approach turned out to be successful. In the unanimous opinion written by Chief Justice Charles Evans Hughes, the court sided with the Witnesses. Freedom of speech and of the press are among the most fundamental of political rights, Hughes wrote.

The city's prohibition against the distribution of literature was sweeping and not carefully tailored so as to preserve these rights. Since the ordinance banned all literature at all times and places unless approved by the city manager, it tended toward officially approved speech and operated as a de facto method of censorship.[22]

The decision was a huge victory for the Witnesses, though it did not go as far as they had wanted. The court had no interest whatsoever in the religious freedom component. It decided the case entirely on the grounds of free speech, sidestepping the religious claims entirely. Those issues, though the opinion did not quite say so, were difficult to untangle and unnecessary to resolve the case.

But the ruling could still be used in defense of religious freedom as the Witnesses understood it. Moyle wrote to Rutherford, "The decision is so clear and far reaching that we should be able to wallop them all along that line."[23]

The next month Moyle wrote to Rutherford to explain the approach. "The battle line," he said, "has shifted both as to territory and nature. Connecticut is now the place." Like Georgia, Connecticut had a law that required persons who were soliciting to get a license from the secretary of the county public welfare council. But the Witnesses' activities were more widespread than in Georgia, and the authorities' response was more severe. In Connecticut there had been over two hundred arrests of Witnesses in two months.[24]

The first step was to appeal all convictions in Connecticut. There were already 135 appeals pending in the state superior courts. The next step was to seek an injunction from a federal appellate court. Assuming they were turned down, the appeal could go up the line to the Supreme Court. He proposed to continue the collaboration with the ACLU to ensure that everyone had legal representation.[25]

The strategy worked well. Within the year an attractive appellate case emerged. Newton Cantwell and his two sons were arrested for soliciting without a permit. What made their case useful was that they were also charged with violating a statute that broadly defined breach of the peace to include the distribution of "inflammatory literature." The Cantwells had been proselytizing in a neighborhood that was 90 percent Catholic. They approached two Catholic men and asked if they could play a record. When the men said they would listen, the Cantwells played "Enemies," an excoriating denunciation of the Catholic church as a racket and an enemy of God. The men had at first wanted to beat up the Cantwells, but they collected themselves and instead had the Witnesses arrested. At trial one of the chief pieces of evidence against the Cantwells was the publications that they distributed. Many of the Witnesses' aggressive statements were read into the record as evidence that the father and his sons were peddling inflammatory literature.[26]

The case offered a meaty and fully documented test that was perfect for the Supreme Court. By the time the case got to the court, the Witnesses were represented by their new counsel, Hayden C. Covington, who stood before the panel assuring the justices that they could no longer avoid the issue of religious freedom. Covington pressed the court on the way the Connecticut law infringed upon the Witnesses' religious proclamations. Hughes cut him off.

"I suppose these Catholics had some right of religious freedom themselves, did they not? I suppose they have the right to be left alone and not to be attacked with these scurrilous denunciations of their most cherished faith. What do you say to that?"

"I say that we are right," Covington responded.

"Is there no limit at all to what you can do when you think you are worshipping your God?" Hughes asked.

"There is no limit so far as this record is concerned."[27]

After oral argument Hughes was inclined to vote against the Witnesses. The law applied equally to all charitable and philanthropic groups, he pointed out. He could not see how it discriminated against the Witnesses or violated their faith because it also applied to other religious groups. More broadly, the absolute nature of their position alarmed him. The principle seemed ripe for mischief. Although the Witnesses seemed sincere, Hughes noted in conference, "There are fake religious groups." How would the state deal with that? How would it find a way to cabin religious exemptions once the principle was granted?[28]

No one really had an answer. But the other justices were inclined to side with the Witnesses anyhow. The reason went back to the *Carolene* decision, in which the court announced a "more searching judicial inquiry" into laws that discriminated against religious, national, and racial minorities. At the time, the court's stated goal was simply the elimination of prejudice. But several members of the court began to move further toward an embrace of cultural pluralism as a guiding principle in American law.[29]

The majority of the court had been pulled in that direction by its prior reasoning about the purposes of free speech. Given the limitations of an individual's perspective, the court had ruled, ensuring free speech enabled a full airing of political issues from many perspectives so that public policy would more likely be both wise and democratic. Because many members of the court came to the issue of religion through the issue of speech, they adopted a similar stance toward religion without recognizing the difficulties they were about to encounter.

In the case against the Cantwells the court was unanimous. The ruling was the first to apply the free-exercise clause of the First Amendment to the states. It struck down the Connecticut law in order to protect freedom of religion to the fullest possible extent. As Owen Roberts put it for the court, the deciding issue was the cultivation of pluralism as a normative ideal. "In the realm of religious faith," he wrote, "and in that of political belief, sharp differences arise. In both fields the tenets of one may seem rankest error to his neighbor. To persuade others to his own point of view, the pleader, as we know, at times resorts to exaggeration, to vilification of men who have been, or are, prominent in church or state, and even to false statement. But the people of this nation have ordained, in the light of history, that, in spite of the probability of excesses and abuses, these liberties are, in the long view, essential to enlightened opinion and right conduct on the part of citizens of a democracy." The point was to create a political system in which "many types of life, character, opinion and belief can develop unmolested and unobstructed."[30]

The decision's solicitousness toward religious freedom was an outgrowth of the court's constitutional liberalism. It brought the cosmopolitan ideal into the legal realm. But it also raised the question of where these rights ended. The Witnesses cited an absolute right capable of no limitation. In *Cantwell* the court disagreed though it only minimally clarified how it contained the rights. The court did say that free exercise could be limited if it incited violence or breached the peace in a way that deprived others of their liberties. It was, again, thinking of religion as an extension of speech in ways that it had not fully understood.[31]

But the court soon confronted the dilemmas that its jurisprudence created, and the fissures buried beneath the *Cantwell* opinion began to open up. Part of the problem was that cultural pluralism had historically offered a strategy to displace or at least decenter Protestant Christian power. To embrace pluralism was to accept that a singular religious authority needed to recede in the face of multiple and often competing claims.

But when the Witnesses invoked religious freedom their argument functioned in another way. They rejected the authority of others and urged the court to do so as well, while also assuming a nearly unqualified religious authority for themselves. They expected the court both to respect their views and to clear any and all impediments to their attestations of conscience, however they understood them. Their position in effect made secular authority always open to negation by a religious appeal, and it used secular authority as a mechanism for religious advancement.

Some on the court were troubled by the implications of the Witnesses' position. After *Cantwell* they sought to reaffirm the power and appropriateness of secular authority. The court was able to address the issue a few months after it decided *Cantwell* when it accepted a flag salute case that involved Lillian and William Gobitas, aged twelve and ten. Like other Witness children, they had refused to salute the flag after Rutherford had banned it. And like other Witness children they were expelled from school. Following the Witnesses' strategy, they appealed to the district court, which ruled in their favor. The school board appealed to the 3rd Circuit Court of Appeals, which also ruled in the Witnesses' favor. The school board appealed to the U.S. Supreme Court, where it had every expectation that it would lose given the ruling in *Cantwell*.

The Witnesses were confident. The Gobitas children were represented by Witness lawyers as well as by the ACLU. The two groups agreed to split the time in oral argument, the Witnesses emphasizing the religious freedom aspects of the case and the ACLU focusing on the free-speech aspects. It seemed like a solid strategy, as it had worked in the past.[32]

But the Witnesses' case was in trouble from the beginning. Their brief, written by Rutherford, was nearly calculated to put off the justices. It was intemperate. It featured ubiquitous biblical references in the free-associative hermeneutics typical of apocalyptic sects. References to law were thin and often irrelevant. Rutherford continued that posture in oral argument. If the judges were to rule in the Witnesses' favor, they had to look beyond Rutherford when evaluating the issues.[33]

In conference Hughes expressed his bewilderment. "I come up to this case like a skittish horse to a brass band," he told the other justices. "I don't want to be dogmatic about this, but I simply cannot believe that the state has not the power to inculcate this social objective."[34]

Nearly all of the justices agreed. It seemed to be a relatively straightforward decision. So Hughes assigned the opinion to Felix Frankfurter, a junior member of the court whom Roosevelt had appointed to replace Benjamin Cardozo the year before. In many ways Frankfurter had seemed to be an ideal choice for the Witnesses. When Roosevelt's nomination was announced, Moyle had written to Rutherford praising the decision. "With Frankfurter, an avowed advocate of civil liberties, now on the Supreme bench," Moyle said, "we may get a chance for a hearing."[35]

But as much as Frankfurter was in favor of civil liberties, he was also a secularist who distrusted the role of religion in public life. As a Jew, he tended to associate the projection of religion outside of private spaces with the marginalization, even suppression, of minorities. He was a thoroughgoing civic nationalist who extolled national identity over all ethnic and religious collectivities. These other collectivities, religious or otherwise, were, in his thinking, relegated to civil society or to private affairs. So although he had much in common with the Witnesses, their position on religious freedom ran against his sense that secular civic authority needed to retain primacy in the governance of national life.

As he put it in his 8–1 opinion for the court, the American experiment was designed against the backdrop of centuries-long religious strife. The guarantee of religious freedom in the U.S. Constitution sought to mitigate animosity. The court had acknowledged the importance of religious freedom in its *Cantwell* decision, which he had joined and which articulated the importance and expansiveness of existing protections for religious belief and expression. "But the manifold character of man's relations may bring his conception of religious duty into conflict with the secular interests of his fellow men," Frankfurter wrote. In the case of conflict between religious and secular authorities, certain exemptions could be granted, Frankfurter acknowledged. The right of dissident or even obnoxious religious belief was always guaranteed. "But to affirm that the freedom to follow conscience has itself no limits in the life of a society," he continued, "would deny the very plurality of principles which, as a matter of history, underlies protection of religious toleration."[36]

That, according to Frankfurter, was the mistake of the Witnesses. They were deeply committed to the separation of church and state but also recognized no limit to their right of conscience. An avowal of conscience trumped any and all rules of the state. The position made perfect sense to the Witnesses because they saw the state as evil, and they were waiting for the end of the world. They did not require any coherent theory of state power because they looked only to the coming Kingdom of Jehovah. But that was not a position available to the court. To Frankfurter, the right of conscience in a pluralized society was always relative and must be balanced against other factors in a way that preserved the secular authority of the state.

Still, that did not resolve the case. Having dispensed with the absolute claims of the Witnesses, Frankfurter was forced to ask whether they had a grievance in this instance. Their proposition that the flag salute was a gesture in support of the devil implied that all the children, not just the Witnesses, were being coerced. Frankfurter rejected the inference. He explained that American society had agencies tasked to support a common national sentiment. The school was at the forefront of those agencies. The flag was a symbol of collective national aspirations. The desire of school boards to inculcate national fellowship was surely legitimate, Frankfurter thought, even if their means were harsh or foolish.

That left him the option that the Witnesses could be excused from the exercise, but he refused to do that as well. His own positive vision of secularism was surely in play, but he grounded his opinion in judicial deference to legislative authority. There was a range of policy choices available to governments. There was a range of school options, from public to private, that were available to the Witnesses. No student was required to attend public schools. If the Witnesses absolutely could not salute the flag, they were free to educate their children in some other venue. Or school boards were able to change their minds. Or legislatures could modify their laws. All were options that went beyond the capacity of the court, Frankfurter held. Such variety was allowed in keeping with the plural nature of American society. If the Witnesses wanted to attend public school and school officials said they had to salute the flag, the court was not going to say otherwise.

Frankfurter's opinion was long and comprehensive. The majority was overwhelming. It seemed a decisive ruling.

Harlan Stone, who wrote the *Carolene* opinion, expressed the only dissent, though even he disagreed with the Witnesses in their absolutist position on conscience. In explaining his departure from the majority of his brethren, he went out of his way to say that protections of personal liberty were not as absolute as the Witnesses thought. But, leaving that question aside, Stone held, the Witnesses had a legitimate constitutional grievance. The flag salute was a compulsion that unnecessarily denied the Witnesses their liberties and that undermined debate in a free society. "The state seeks to coerce these children to express a sentiment which, as they interpret it, they do not entertain," he wrote.[37]

The speech issue was the problem. The flag salute violated free expression and undermined the social and political function of free exchange. "The guaranties of civil liberty are but guaranties of freedom of the human mind and spirit and of reasonable freedom and opportunity to express them," Stone explained. "They presuppose the right of the individual to hold such opinions as he will and . . . to teach and persuade others by the communication of ideas." But the flag salute violated the purpose of free speech and so could not be constitutionally legitimate.[38]

Stone's dissent went a long way to reframing the debate entirely. He did not deny that legislatures could attempt to inculcate national cohesion, but he thought that they could do so only while upholding a system of protections that allowed for the freest circulations of ideas. In that way his dissenting opinion emphasized the doctrinal continuity of the case with the court's earlier decisions about free speech.

Critics followed Stone's lead. *Christian Century* the house magazine of Protestant liberalism, lamented the decision as "not a wise one," but it speculated that the court had been driven to the position by the Witnesses' absolutist statements. That was the court's mistake. "[The Witnesses'] refusal to go through the ritual of the salute," the magazine continued, "is not half so dangerous to this country as the equally conscientious and equally misguided zeal of the patriots who, mistaking one formula of loyalty for the thing itself, are more anxious to have a symbol of liberty saluted than to have liberty maintained."[39]

Even some Supreme Court justices were persuaded after the fact. Stone had worked on his dissent to the last minute. None of the other judges had time to read it until after the decision was announced. Frank Murphy, who had replaced Pierce Butler earlier that year; William O. Douglas, who had replaced Louis Brandeis in 1939; and Hugo Black, who had replaced Willis Van Devanter in 1937, all immediately felt, upon reading Stone's dissent, that they had decided the case wrongly. They soon met around the swimming pool in Murphy's hotel and agreed that Frankfurter's opinion needed to be overturned as soon as possible.[40]

Contemporary events fed into their reappraisal. The *Gobitis* decision coincided with a wave of violence against the Witnesses. In 1940 alone 335 groups were attacked in 44 states. After a summer of sometimes-bloody conflict, Douglas told Frankfurter that Hugo Black was reconsidering his position on the flag salute case.[41]

"Why, has he reread the Constitution during the summer?" Frankfurter responded, sarcastically.

"No," Douglas replied, "but he has read the papers."[42]

By January the Witnesses' cause was strengthened when Roosevelt delivered his State of the Union. Toward the end of his speech he famously articulated the four freedoms that needed to be secured in both the United States and the world—freedom of speech, freedom of religion, freedom from want, and freedom from fear. Roosevelt promoted the four freedoms as compatible with American institutions and as in keeping with the constitutional modernism embraced by the court. "Since the beginning of our history," he said, "we have been engaged in change—in a perpetual peaceful revolution—a revolution which goes on steadily, quietly adjusting itself to changing conditions—without the concentration camp or the quick-lime in the ditch." His proposal was simply in keeping with the long-held practice of national self-regeneration and constitutional transformation.[43]

Soon the Witnesses were back in court, this time protesting a city ordinance in Opelika, Alabama, that required a tax be paid and a license procured in order to conduct a business, including selling books and pamphlets. The court ruled 5–4 that the tax was legitimate because it applied to all businesses in a nondiscriminatory fashion. Writing for the court, Associate Justice Stanley Reed went out of his way to support the free dissemination of ideas and to acknowledge that one must always be wary of attempts to suppress dissident opinions. But that was not what was occurring in Opelika, he held. "When proponents of religious or social theories use the ordinary commercial methods of sale of articles to raise propaganda funds," he wrote, "it is a natural and proper exercise of the power of the state to charge reasonable fees for the privilege of canvassing."[44]

Stone, in a dissent joined by Black, Douglas, and Murphy, excoriated the reasoning of the majority. The only purpose of the licenses was to suppress the distribution of literature that occurred outside the watchful gaze of city authorities, Stone alleged. Taxation for the dissemination of ideas could easily be made to suppress those ideas. Although it had not happened in the existing case, the city official could revoke the license at any point. Even if the city official did not revoke the license, the system of taxation itself, reproduced in town after town, had the potential to destroy freedom of the press for everyone but the independently wealthy. "It seems fairly obvious that, if the present taxes, laid in small communities upon peripatetic religious propagandists, are to be sustained," Stone wrote, "a way has been found for the effective suppression of speech and press and religion despite constitutional guarantees."[45]

Writing separately, Black, Murphy, and Douglas acknowledged their change of mind since they joined Frankfurter's *Gobitis* opinion. They now detected the operations of older, more mainstream religious groups in these laws. Established groups were using the powers of the state to suppress a religious minority. Black, Murphy, and Douglas thought that court protection was necessary, especially for small, unorthodox, and unpopular groups like the Witnesses, which they had failed to appreciate when they joined the majority in *Gobitis*. Rather than protecting unorthodox expression, they now said, the majority of the court had in effect sustained the suppression of religious opinion behind a veneer of nondiscrimination and an attentiveness toward secular authority.[46]

The fissures were real and deep, though the justices did not fully understand them. Their disagreement turned on their divergent understandings of secular authority and its relationship to religious pluralism. For the majority, led by Frankfurter, secular authority existed independently of the religious position of individuals. But the minority had other priorities. It was not that they wanted to give religious groups veto power over otherwise applicable law, but they thought that religious ideas and expression needed special protection. The defense was not just for the group's own sake but also in order to preserve the effective exchange of ideas necessary to a free society. They did not think that shielding small religious groups would endanger the secular rule of the state.

The disagreement would only grow more fraught. The next year the Witnesses were back in court again, protesting a similar fee for solicitation in Pennsylvania. But in the interim Roosevelt had appointed a new justice, Wiley Rutledge, to replace James Byrnes, who had previously voted against the Witnesses. The additional appointment created a new five-person majority. Writing for the court, William Douglas vacated the holding in the earlier Opelika case and allowed the Witnesses to solicit without fee.

Douglas's reasoning was novel. He proposed that the fee was essentially a tax on the exercise of First Amendment rights. "The mere fact that the religious literature is 'sold' by itinerant preachers, rather than 'donated' does not transform evangelism into a commercial enterprise," he wrote. "If it did, then the passing of the collection plate in church would make the church service a commercial project." The Witnesses' activities were religious, he ruled, regardless of the means of conducting their religion, and so they received strict constitutional protection.[47]

Reed, in a dissent joined by Frankfurter, Robert H. Jackson, and Owen Roberts, was scathing in his criticism. "It has never been thought before that freedom from taxation was a perquisite attaching to the privileges of the First Amendment," he wrote. Newspapers could be taxed, which would seem to make the majority's contention illogical on its face. And the tax itself was nondiscriminatory and nonexcessive. What the majority had ruled was that the religious ideas of the Witnesses had such a high position that governments were powerless to touch them or to raise funds from their activities. This was hardly secular.[48]

Frankfurter also wrote a dissent, joined by Jackson, elaborating on what he saw as the folly of the majority. The logic of the court's opinion actually committed the state to support religion, Frankfurter thought. The Witnesses' activities cost money by requiring cities to provide police, trash pickup, and more. The majority, in declaring that any supposedly religious activity was exempt from taxation, required that the state offer a subsidy for the dissemination of religious ideas. "Such a claim offends the most important of all aspects of religious freedom in this country," Frankfurter concluded, "namely, that of the separation of church and state."[49]

Jackson also wrote a dissent, joined by Frankfurter, that went still further in questioning the majority's reasoning. In his view the First Amendment protected the broadest possible exercise of free speech, free assembly, and freedom of the press, not just for religious purposes but also to spread political, economic, or scientific views. But the majority had, in effect, narrowed the protection of nonreligious communication while gifting a sweeping and absolute protection for avowed religious groups. Jackson thought the holding would involve the court in impossible issues in the future, as it attempted to sort out what received protection and what did not. "This Court is forever adding new stories to the temples of constitutional law," Jackson wrote, "and the temples have a way of collapsing when one story too many is added."[50]

A month later the court handed down another opinion that again favored the Witnesses. This time it reversed the court's flag salute decision from three years earlier. Jackson, writing for the 6–3 majority, ruled that the flag salute was a form of compelled speech that violated the First Amendment's free-speech protection. He specifically did not find that the Witnesses' freedom of religion was being violated. He noted that a decision by the court to exempt the

Witnesses would not interfere with anyone else's right and would not offer an official endorsement of religion in any way. That made the case easy, according to Jackson. "To sustain the compulsory flag salute," Jackson said, "we are required to say that a Bill of Rights which guards the individual's right to speak his own mind left it open to public authorities to compel him to utter what is not in his mind." Since that was obviously nonsensical, the flag salute could not be compelled.[51]

But Jackson was not content to leave it there. Although he wanted to preserve secular authority and although he was wary of absolutist statements of religious freedom, he distrusted the equally unbending secularity of Frankfurter. Jackson offered instead a negative secularism. By grounding the opinion in freedom of speech, he had effectively neutralized the problem of religious freedom. So for the rest of his opinion he turned his attention to a demonstration of how Frankfurter's position, far from preserving public secularity, would actually endanger it.

As Jackson saw it, if public education was faithful to the idea of secular instruction it could not be an enemy of any class or creed or faction. To declare an orthodoxy and to require submission to it, as the flag salute seemed to do, would start a scramble between groups to control the system of education in order to preserve that faction's own interest. Failing that, groups would seek to weaken the system of education so that it was ineffective in achieving public goals. Preserving secular education, by contrast, required a return to the balancing tests supported by an earlier generation of sociological jurisprudence. When approached in that way, it became clear that accommodating the Witnesses would strengthen the system of secular instruction by adopting a posture of political and religious neutrality. "We apply the limitations of the Constitution with no fear that freedom to be intellectually and spiritually diverse or even contrary will disintegrate the social system," Jackson wrote. The only unity required was a shared commitment to protect the individuality of all.[52]

Frankfurter's dissent was bitter and personal. He began the opinion with reference to his Jewishness. As he put it, he was "one who belongs to the most vilified and persecuted minority in history." If anyone on the court was sensitive to the oppression of mi-

norities, he declared, it was, given his experience as a Jew, him. And
if it were up to him he might accommodate the Witnesses. But his
personal perspective was not at issue. The real concern was who
was supposed to make the accommodation. That power rested with
the legislature, not with the courts.[53]

He could have ended his opinion there, justifying it entirely on
the basis of deference to legislative prerogative. But his position was
more expansive and was intimately tied to a wider political philosophy of secularism, not simply judicial deference. The problem was
that the majority had misconceived the rights granted by the Constitution and in so doing had threatened the American political arrangement. The American Founders, in Frankfurter's understanding,
created a system in which there was neither orthodoxy nor heterodoxy before the state. Religious minorities and religious majorities
were equal insofar as their religious belief was irrelevant to the state.
Their belief was private. The majority misunderstood just this point.
"The constitutional protection of religious freedom terminated disabilities, it did not create new privileges," Frankfurter wrote. "It gave
religious equality, not civil immunity. Its essence is freedom from
conformity to religious dogma, not freedom from conformity to law
because of religious dogma."[54]

Frankfurter's understanding, though he did not say so, was shaped
by the French model of secularism known as *laïcité*, a system that
emerged during the 1880s as part of the Third Republic. The goal, as
the historian Joan Wallach Scott has explained, was "the separation of
church and state through the state's protection of individuals from the
claims of religion." What that meant in the French case was that the
state took no cognizance of religious belief in the sense that a person's
religion was relegated to the private sphere, the area of family. The
state demanded undivided loyalty of citizens to the French nation as
a whole. The secular school mediated between these two realms. It
served as a transition between private and public, from the world of
the family to that of the nation. A child entered school loyal to the
household. But it left school committed to the French state. Insofar as
freedom of religion required the performance of one's belief, that kind
of freedom, which threatened the undivided loyalty to the republic if
left unchecked, was only for the private realm.[55]

Frankfurter articulated a similar idea but transposed into American history. It was this commitment, more than his deference to legislative authority, that made him reject the position of the Witnesses. As he put it in his dissent, "The validity of secular laws cannot be measured by their conformity to religious doctrines. It is only in a theocratic state that ecclesiastical doctrines measure legal right or wrong." Frankfurter fretted that if religious freedom meant an automatic or nearly automatic exemption from applicable law, then the separation of church and state would be a farce, and instead all religious groups would receive power over and above the state.[56]

Frankfurter had already said a lot and, again, he might have left it there. But he offered one final word of warning. A person might want to support religion, he acknowledged, and a person might worry that failing to accommodate religious claims would jeopardize deep human commitments. But as Frankfurter saw it, the state really had no choice. It had to disregard some people's religious ideas. "When dealing with religious scruples," he wrote, "we are dealing with an almost numberless variety of doctrines and beliefs entertained with equal sincerity by the particular groups for which they satisfy man's needs in his relation to the mysteries of the universe." The sheer number and variety of claimants meant that the state could not recognize all of them and still have a functioning government. Someone would have to determine who was sincere and who was not, which groups received accommodation and which did not, and what was to be considered religion and what was not. That should be the legislature, not the courts, Frankfurter said, otherwise such determinations were all the courts would do given the number of issues and potential appellants involved.[57]

If Frankfurter had a crystal ball he could not have been more accurate. He ultimately grounded his stance in a practicality that the majority had not entertained. The right of religion was a morass that the court would soon find continually problematic.

CHAPTER FIVE

Stumbling toward Secularism

The Supreme Court's decisions, in the short term, left many people uncertain. Protestants were especially torn, not because they did not understand the cases but because they could not quite figure out their proper political response. The United States had historically had a Protestant cast to public life. Protestant cultural influence was so great that, as late as 1942, Franklin Roosevelt could say to two advisors, without any sense of shame, that Catholics and Jews lived in the United States only "under sufferance." The fact that one of the advisors was Catholic and the other was Jewish suggested that Roosevelt thought he was simply articulating an obvious truth.[1]

If Protestant religious leaders did not go quite that far, at least not publicly, that was because they had begun to sense their own weakness. Starting in the late-nineteenth century some Protestant modernizers had begun to undertake a series of strategic shifts. The first was a modification of their belief, adapting Christian dogma to the discoveries of science and the historical study of the Bible. These discoveries challenged past beliefs, rendering many specific dogmas untenable and systematically undermining components of Christian doctrine. But because theologians had long acknowledged that an infinite God used metaphor to appear before finite human beings, the challenge left Protestant modernizers only momentarily troubled. God spoke in the Bible in a way that was inexact but keyed to the understanding of the people of the time, they believed. Now that human understanding had changed, the task of theology was to extract the timeless universals from the historical particulars. The obsolete specifics were the accidents of history that did not affect the timeless core of revelation that remained.[2]

The reconsideration of their doctrine allowed for other shifts, especially a new attempt to make peace with religious diversity. To some extent that meant making their peace with the American religious scene. There had long been a centrifugal force within American spirituality that produced a bewildering congeries of new religious forms. Universalists, Ethical Culturists, Theosophists, Spiritualists, New Thought proponents, Vedantists and other converted Hindus, Buddhists, Quakers of both traditional and Hicksite persuasions, apocalyptic sects such as the Jehovah's Witnesses—all proliferated in a wildly chaotic religious arena. By the end of the nineteenth century Protestant missionaries had begun to bring back a changed outlook on foreign peoples, offering a perspective at once deeply sympathetic to other cultures and deeply conflicted about the program of Christian civilization at the heart of the missionary enterprise. Other Protestant leaders began to wrestle with an awareness of the world's religions generated by comparative religion scholars and by events like the World's Parliament of Religions at the Columbia Exposition in 1893.[3]

The challenges grew more acute with a demographic transformation of American society that began after the Civil War. The nation had begun to diversify to the point that Protestant Christianity could not simply presume a custodial relationship over American culture and values, Roosevelt's comments to the contrary. Both Catholics and Jews, who had been in the country from the beginning, began to increase their presence through immigration. Catholics began their first mass migration in the 1840s, fleeing first poverty and then starvation as a result of the Irish potato famine. After the Civil War the migration continued in even larger numbers, with Jews joining Catholics in what historians now call the New Immigration. By the 1890s Jews would constitute a sizable force in American cities, and Catholicism would become the largest single denomination in the United States.[4]

In response, some Protestant modernizers turned to social science in order to reconstruct their own faith. They drew on the emergent field of psychology to reimagine the urgent existential and emotional function that religion served. Because religion was supposed to meet a stable set of human needs, psychologists like the early William James, Edward Diller Starbuck, and George Albert Coe thought that religion emerged in a predictable way across societies. That predictability affirmed the necessity of religion to all civilizations across time and space, even if the specific tenets of religion needed to be reconstructed in the modern era.[5]

Protestant ecumenicals soon began to reach out to modernizers within both Catholicism and Judaism, recognizing people they considered allies in the ongoing effort to reconstruct religion. The resulting liberal alliance affirmed the universal brotherhood of man under the fatherhood of God as the essential religious creed. It worked outside the specific confines of one denomination or religious tradition to find a universal religious sensibility that could serve as a more authoritative basis for their influence on American society. The efforts diluted a specifically Protestant message while attempting to preserve a religious one.[6]

Not everyone made the ecumenical turn. Protestant denominations began to fracture. Fundamentalists, as they called themselves, objected to the liberalizing movement within Protestantism and wanted to hold onto their preeminent place in American life. When they failed to move their colleagues they began to leave the major denominations in the 1920s to start their own organizations, schools, and civil society groups. They would reemerge in the 1940s calling themselves evangelicals.[7]

The split left liberal Protestants even more organizationally compromised, though it also reinforced the tendency to ecumenicism. Having purged the fundamentalists from mainstream Protestant leadership, the big Protestant denominations soon pursued even wider alliances. By the 1930s they brought Catholics and Jews into national power through Roosevelt's New Deal coalition. They welcomed them to cultural influence under the banner of Judeo-Christianity, a relatively new term that had gained salience in the ecumenical movement. After the Second World War and the traumas of fascism the Protestant ecumenical leadership went still further, seeing in the horrors of the war the necessity of forging pan-religious alliances to create a better world. Their impulse, as the intellectual historian David A. Hollinger has put it, was "to include everyone—all human souls—into a single community of love."[8]

Yet there were limits to their embrace of diversity. Liberal Protestants worried about the status of religion in American society. The secularization of American life—or the advancement of what Lyman Beecher had called "political atheism"—was not the goal of many Protestant leaders. According to Beecher, if a person assumed that God existed, that God established norms, and that human law was built to enforce those norms certain things followed. The crucial thing was that American politics, culture, and society needed to recognize God's law and needed to enforce that law. If someone did not recognize the dominion of God in political affairs, Beecher had said, they were guilty of political atheism.[9]

By the 1940s Protestant liberals disagreed with the specifics of Beecher's theology—strongly so. But they agreed with him that God and religion were the ultimate ground for human society and that religious authority was a necessary component of social cohesion. That made them resist the actions of the court. They sensed that secularization did not require the absolute abandonment of religious belief or adherence, something that contemporary sociologists have more recently pointed out. It involved, more fundamentally, an abandonment of the public authority and social significance of religion. Many people might still believe, but if that belief was not relevant to culture and politics then a secular society could be the only result. As the court encountered the variety and incompatibility of religious authorities within the United States, Protestant leaders began to fret that the justices would seek to constrict the public relevance of religious ideas and thereby render their authority irrelevant to the wider culture.[10]

As Charles Clayton Morrison, the editor of *Christian Century*, put it, the court had adopted a theory of neutrality toward religion that threatened, in effect, to neutralize the cultural power of religious ideals. In that way the court's supposed evenhandedness toward religion was not what it professed to be. "It is positive," Morrison explained. "It takes the form of secularism which, when not overtly hostile to religion, is ignorant of it and indifferent to it."[11]

In fact, Morrison was wrong. Felix Frankfurter and others in the minority had articulated a positive secularism, but they had not prevailed. The majority of the court articulated, through Robert H. Jackson, a negative secularism or, through Harlan Stone and William O. Douglas, a solicitousness toward public religion in a variety of forms. Yet it was an indication of the softness of Protestant power that someone like Morrison would see the erosion of Protestant cultural authority, articulated by the court, as a creeping toward established unbelief.

Other groups saw the dynamic more clearly. The court's recognition of the diversity of American religion opened up space for religious groups that had been subsumed under Protestant dominance of public life. The obvious potential benefactor was the Roman Catholic Church.

Catholics had long objected to the Protestant cast of public life and had held themselves aloof from what they considered Protestant political institutions. Their suspicion started with the public school. Dating back to the beginning of the public-school system in the 1830s, religious exercises had been an essential component of the day-to-day life of the curriculum. Because the development of the American school system had overlapped with the evangelical awakening, state curricula tended to infuse a basically Protestant ethos into the students as part of their educational goals. Daily religious exercises included Bible reading, recitation of the Ten Commandments, teacher-led prayers, and recitation of the Lord's Prayer. These religious practices were ostensibly nonsectarian, but in reality they were thoroughly Protestant.[12]

Catholics accordingly had a long list of grievances with the schools. A Catholic did not often read the Bible individually and did not partake in many religious practices outside the priestly mediation of the church. But the schools circumvented Catholic religious authority and assumed the priesthood of all believers, a Protestant concept. The schools also used the Protestant King James Bible rather than the Catholic Douay Bible. They recited the Protestant version of the Ten Commandments, which had a prohibition against graven images that tended to challenge Catholic devotional practices and the cult of the saints. Schools also used the Protestant form of the Lord's Prayer, which included a final line not usually included in the Catholic one that ascribed kingship and rule to God alone, implicitly undermining the papacy.[13]

The Catholic hierarchy sought various solutions to the problem of Protestant practices. At a minimum it wanted separate devotional services, led by a Catholic priest. Better yet, it wanted the public-school fund divided in order to use a portion to support separate Catholic schools. In 1866 Catholic bishops gathered at the Second Plenary Council of Baltimore, one of the three national meetings of American bishops in the nineteenth century. The Catholic leadership was growing irate and issued a decree condemning public schools. A Catholic child attending such a school risked, they said, "great danger to faith and morals." The schools promoted, they said, "either a false religion or none at all."[14]

But Catholic leaders were stymied in their efforts. Bitter disagreement and antagonism soon followed. Philadelphia, Boston, and Cincinnati became sites of social conflict. Some of the disputes involved rioting and violence. Catholics were often left unsatisfied or in a worse situation than before. The Catholic hierarchy became convinced that their only option was to withdraw from the public schools. So in 1884, at the Third Plenary Council of Baltimore, the American bishops decided to build a separate Catholic parochial school system. Every parish was required to have a school within two years. All Catholic parents were instructed to send their child to a Catholic school.[15]

The commitment to Catholic separatism and conservatism only grew from there. In 1895 Pope Leo XIII released an encyclical on Catholicism in the United States that summarized the main components of the hierarchy's position. The encyclical rejected church–state separation and noted that any government that endorsed separation was an inferior form of government, even if Catholicism flourished under such a system. Leo warned American Catholics against associating with non-Catholics. And he urged American Catholics to aid the United States by bringing the nation into submission to the church.[16]

Leo's papacy inaugurated a conservative entrenchment in Catholic doctrinal development that rejected any concession to the modern world. In 1907, Pope Pius X extended the barricades. He issued an encyclical denouncing those within the church who sought to update doctrine. These "partisans of error," who often took their cues from Protestants, were abandoning church teaching under the banner of modernism. To Pius, modernism was flawed in so many ways that it contained a "synthesis of all heresies." The best that could be done was to resist the modernist trend in contemporary life while upholding spiritual purity and separation. In 1928 Pope Pius XI issued another pronouncement that again denounced religious interaction between Catholics and Protestants as contrary to the supremacy of the church. American bishops applied these rules by prohibiting Catholic parishioners or priests from engaging in goodwill efforts or ecumenical initiatives.[17]

By the 1930s, after a round of canon law codification, the impulse toward purity and authority had absolutely triumphed within the church. In the hierarchy's conception all teaching authority flowed from the Roman pontiff. The hierarchy claimed a sweeping control over the lives of its parishioners and, in principle, over every living person on earth. Catholic law commanded that the faithful not enter into dispute or conference with non-Catholics without permission from the Holy See. It required that children attend schools where nothing contrary to Catholic doctrine was taught. It assumed the right to remove teachers and books from those schools and the right to forbid the faithful to read books. It commanded Catholics to avoid publishing in papers and magazines that were contrary to the Catholic faith. And it set up the church as the sole arbiter of truth in public life, whether a person was Catholic or non-Catholic. To that end, the hierarchy declared it had the power to censor or to prohibit the publication of books, movies, or other media that defended heresy or schism, that undermined morals, that ridiculed the Church, that weakened Catholic discipline, or that defended other sects.[18]

In that way the Catholic church worked in two ways at once. It required Catholics to hold themselves apart while at the same time it announced a public authority over everyone.

This conception of Catholic public authority led to far-reaching changes in American life. The most successful was the Motion Picture Production Code in 1930, which applied a rigid standard of public morality to the movies. The League of Decency, which used Catholic parishes as an organizing platform to pressure studios into adopting the code, produced a template for other forms of political action. Soon another Catholic group, the National Organization for Decent Literature, sought to censor print material that Catholics found problematic. Catholic groups were also successful in outlawing birth control in Connecticut and elsewhere during the same period.[19]

If anyone wondered where all of this was going, the hierarchy was clear. The goal was to bring about the cooperation between church and state in all the nations of the world. To that end the church signed concordats, or treaties of mutual recognition, with Mussolini's Italy, Franco's Spain, and Hitler's Germany. In the United States, American bishops professed open regard for fascist regimes because they offered special privileges to the Catholic church. Although many of these voices would, after the war, express regret for their support of fascism, they did not recant their political rationale or their overall theological commitments. Italy, Spain, and Germany offered a step toward the final goal, or what Father John A. Ryan called the normal relation between church and state. This normal relation was, he explained, "the union of Church and State," with the Catholic church overseeing many aspects of public life. Catholics needed to hold themselves separate and apart and therefore pure, awaiting the normal relation to come into effect.[20]

Unlike Protestants, in other words, Catholics by the 1940s were feeling emboldened and optimistic about their political power. They began to press legislatures to pass laws aiding Catholic education. Partly these laws were a recognition of how large the Catholic school system had become and how difficult it was for the church to support all its children. For much of its existence the system had been possible because priests and nuns administered the instruction. But by the 1940s they faced a squeeze. There were not enough priests or nuns available, which meant that the schools had to hire lay teachers, who were far more expensive. At the same time, the schools were growing rapidly as more children were born and enrolled. In a number of states the Catholic church lobbied legislators to subsidize aspects of the Catholic school system in order to mitigate the financial burden.[21]

It did so on the basis of what became known as the child-benefit theory. The general idea was that these children were as much a part of society as those who attended public school. If the state paid for, say, textbooks or transportation or even salaries for teachers who covered non-religious subjects, then that public support could be said to benefit the child rather than the school. The purposes of education could be preserved without violating the conscience or the free exercise of Catholic citizens.[22]

Their argument was persuasive to many in those states with large numbers of Catholics. By 1946 seventeen states and the District of Columbia had passed bills to subsidize public transportation to private schools. The laws overwhelmingly aided Catholic schools.[23]

Protestants were alarmed with the development. When combined with the decisions of the court, they began to feel pinched between an encroaching secularism on the one side and an emboldened Catholicism on the other. The pages of Protestant journals became filled with hand-wringing about the appropriate response.[24]

But Protestants were not alone in their suspicion of Catholic activism. Many intellectuals, of both post-Protestant and post-Judaic varieties, saw Catholicism's increased public presence as a threat to American freedom. The educational theorist and liberal pragmatist John Dewey thought the public subsidy of Catholic schools risked the public-school system and might lead the United States back, in his words, through "centuries of systematic stultification of the human mind and human personality." Horace Kallen, the Jewish theorist of cultural pluralism, pled with Catholics to reject, as he put it, the "separatist pull" that led them apart from their "non-Catholic neighbor." The Catholic separatist impulse, he said, aroused doubts in many people about Catholic loyalty to a pluralist democracy. Their shared suspicions about Catholics led Protestants, post-Protestants, and post-Judaic Jews into a loose, sometimes uncomfortable, alliance.[25]

All of these developments fed into the court, just as Frankfurter had predicted. Because of the court's earlier decisions it found itself embroiled in a bitter policy dispute that took on increasingly overt constitutional overtones. It also pulled other groups into the conflict through a transformation of court practice.

The change had to do with amicus curiae, or friend of the court, briefs. Before the 1940s the parties in a legal dispute filed briefs before the court prior to oral argument. The idea was to lay out the issues in a written form that the court could later tease out in person. Occasionally other parties also filed briefs that, in a friendly help to the court, sought to offer a more comprehensive view of the issues. Advocacy was generally frowned upon unless someone was a party to the dispute. But faced with cases that involved large policy questions, groups by the 1940s began to take amicus briefs and turn them into a mechanism of political and legal activism. That made the amicus brief into an instrument of access in a quasi-political process and left the court sorting through serious group conflicts that were normally handled in the political arena.[26]

The first of many disputes began in New Jersey after that state passed a law allowing parents to be reimbursed for public transportation to private schools. As in other states, 96 percent of schools that benefited from the law were Catholic. A suit by Arch R. Everson, a taxpayer in Ewing, New Jersey, alleged that the law violated the First Amendment's provision that Congress could establish no religion.

The Catholic hierarchy responded immediately to the challenge. As the case made its way through the court system, Francis Cardinal Spellman of New York and Samuel Cardinal Stritch of Chicago committed church resources to help the Ewing School Board defend its position. By the time the case made it to the Supreme Court, the National Catholic Welfare Council had submitted an amicus brief written primarily by the Jesuit priest John Courtney Murray. The brief emphasized the public rather than the sectarian purpose of what Murray called nonprofit, private schools. It also reminded the justices that the First Amendment protected religion, which was what the New Jersey bill did, rather than public secularism. On those grounds, the arrangement ought to be upheld.[27]

In an opinion that satisfied no one, the court ruled in a five-person majority that the New Jersey law could stand. The opinion, written by Hugo Black, loudly proclaimed a theory of church–state separation that, critics thought, it violated in upholding the law. Black's ruling read like a history lesson. It offered a tale of persecution that began in Europe, continued in the colonial era of the United States, moved through Madison's Memorial and Remonstrance, and culminated in the First Amendment as the American solution to the religious conflict that had long plagued Europe. Along the way Black explicitly incorporated the establishment clause of the First Amendment into the Fourteenth, which the court had implicitly done in *Cantwell*. He acknowledged that the Constitution prohibited all aid to religion, even on a nonpreferential basis. "The First Amendment has erected a wall between church and state," he wrote. "That wall must be kept high and impregnable. We could not approve the slightest breach." But in spite of the strident rhetoric, Black swerved in the end to rule that the New Jersey scheme was perfectly permissible. It aided the family rather than the church, and even if it indirectly aided the church it did so only in an attempt to benefit the child in his secular education.[28]

Writing in a dissent joined by Frankfurter, Jackson, and Burton, Wiley Rutledge noted that the majority's position made no sense. He agreed with the majority's declaration of church–state separation and its application of the establishment clause to the states. He concurred that a state could not support religion. But he thought those two principles required striking down the law. The reason was simple logic. According to Rutledge, the child-benefit theory was self-contradictory when paired with Catholic doctrine. Catholics thought, in Rutledge's explanation, "that the basic purpose of all education is or should be religious, that the secular cannot be and should not be separated from the religious phase and emphasis. Hence the inadequacy of public or secular education and the necessity for sending the child to a school where religion is taught." Yet in order to uphold the law, the majority had to look past the official justification for Catholic schools while allowing taxpayer support for a basic educational expense that these schools incurred. The series of evasions required to pull that off were, to the minority, unpersuasive.[29]

Robert H. Jackson, in an opinion joined by Felix Frankfurter, piled on. In the process, he betrayed his own anti-Catholicism. The issue in the case, according to Jackson, was the alien nature of Catholic doctrine to American democracy, which the public-school system sought to support. "Our public school, if not a product of Protestantism, at least is more consistent with it than with the Catholic culture and scheme of values," Jackson wrote. "It is organized on the premise that secular education can be isolated from all religious teaching, so that the school can inculcate all needed temporal knowledge and also maintain a strict and lofty neutrality as to religion."[30]

The public's response to the court's decision demonstrated the bitterness to come. Protestants immediately decried the ruling. It seemed part of a wider wedge strategy pursued by the hierarchy. The Catholic church started small by asking the state to subsidize books or transportation. Once the public became used to that idea, Protestants alleged, larger things would follow. Soon the public would be subsidizing the entirety of the parochial school system.

The Council of Bishops of the Methodist Church, the largest Protestant body in the United States, issued a statement expressing support for church–state separation and denouncing the Catholic position. The bishops referenced the church's political activities around the world, especially in Argentina, Italy, and Spain. They observed that in countries where Catholicism became dominant religious freedom was inevitably curtailed because the Catholic church had specifically rejected it in numerous papal pronouncements. But instead of recognizing the threat, the bishops said, the court's decision reinforced the power of the Catholic church and so undermined American freedom.[31]

The Southern Baptist Convention echoed the Methodists. It warned that the decision weakened, in its words, "religious liberty and its inevitable corollary, the complete separation of church and state."[32]

"Now Will Protestants Awake?" the *Christian Century* asked. The decision, the magazine said, "should open the eyes of all American-minded citizens, and especially of Protestant citizens, to the strategy of the Roman Catholic Church in its determination to secure a privileged position in the common life of this country."[33]

Catholics were, ironically, also unhappy with the decision. Although the outcome was good for the church, the court's rhetoric was troubling. The Jesuit magazine *America*, the leading Catholic magazine in the United States, rejected talk of a wall of separation between church and state. It led to bad thinking, the magazine said, which was evident in the dissenting opinions. Jackson's opinion was revealing of the point. It displayed the bias inherent in talk of a wall of separation, *America* thought, which verbally promoted neutrality while actually supporting Protantism.[34]

But Catholics were in a difficult position. Protestants had accurately summarized the doctrinal commitments of the Catholic church. The Catholic hierarchy could not and did not deny those doctrinal commitments. What it could do was to explore Protestant assumptions. Shortly after the decision, Francis Cardinal Spellman, in a commencement speech at Fordham University, complained that the criticism of the church was really a form of anti-Catholic bigotry. "It is assumed that all American people must agree to the dogma that in the sight of God all churches are of equal value," he said. "From this assumption it is concluded that any American who does not accept this brand of toleration is a heretic from the democratic faith."[35]

Catholic leaders said in response that a truly democratic faith and a real commitment to pluralism would allow for multiple kinds of educational systems rather than a suffocating secularism. At a meeting of the National Catholic Education Association in Boston, Archbishop Richard J. Cushing told the crowd, "We must never allow legislators or courts or anti-Catholic spellbinders of the moment to distract attention from the central place of the parent and the home in all democratic and Christian educational theory." Cushing did not deny that the church wanted more subsidies. But he did not view those subsidies as aids to the church. They helped parents in their democratic and Christian ability to choose.[36]

Others pressed the issue still further, contending that Protestant rhetoric about church and state obscured the questions at stake. As the Catholic scholar James M. O'Neill put it, the secularist movement worked by appealing to "categorical slogans and unhistorical myths." Like the advertising industry, Robert C. Hartnett wrote in an essay in *America*, these slogans operated through the power of suggestion. "You merely keep repeating a few well-chosen words until the public, without any rational grounds or mental operation at all, finds the simple idea implanted in its consciousness," he said. Meanwhile, an "ominous intolerance" marched behind the rhetorical screen that concealed Protestant self-righteousness.[37]

Protestants, for their part, decided to mobilize. After several months of trading barbs with Catholic leaders, a group of prominent Protestants formed a new advocacy organization that they called Protestants and Other Americans United for Separation of

Church and State (POAU). At their first meeting they issued a manifesto that sought to respond to what they called the specious propaganda put out by Catholic leaders. They agreed with Catholics that, as the manifesto put it, "This is a cultural and spiritual democracy."[38]

But democracy, they said, required open debate, which in turn relied upon governmental neutrality in religious matters. The Catholic church, by contrast, wanted more. "This church holds and maintains a theory of the relation of church and state which is incompatible with the American ideal," the manifesto said. "It makes no secret of its intention to secure for itself, if possible, a privileged position in the body politic. In pursuit of this policy, it has already made such gains that the principle of separation of church and state is in peril of nullification by legislatures and courts, and by federal, state, and local administrations."[39]

POAU leaders rejected the accusation, which had yet to be made but that they were confident would come, that their organization was sectarian. It was led by Protestants, who had a preponderance in American society, but it had also reached out to and encompassed Jews, fraternal orders, and those who belonged to no church. It even claimed to welcome Catholics who, rejecting the teaching of their clerical leadership, recognized the freedom of separating church and state.[40]

Catholics responded immediately. The day after the POAU issued its manifesto, John E. Swift, the head of the Catholic fraternal organization the Knights of Columbus, issued a statement through the Catholic Archdiocese of New York. The POAU, Swift announced, promoted organized bigotry. It also lost sight of the real challenge facing all religious groups, Catholic and Protestant alike. "What the nation urgently needs is a united effort by all groups to check the godlessness which is tearing away the very roots of our American political and social institutions," Swift announced.[41]

The National Catholic Welfare council issued a statement trying to clarify the Catholic position. "We deny absolutely and without qualification that the Catholic Bishops of the United States are seeking a union of church and state by any endeavors whatsoever," the bishops declared. But the Catholic position was so bound up in its own terms that they strained to articulate the hierarchy's commitments in a way that could be understood by a non-Catholic. The bishops denied *both* a union of church and state and a separation of church and state. A variety of Catholic leaders and several encyclicals had stated clearly that the Catholic church sought an orderly cooperation between church and state. The state would remain separate but it must acknowledge the Catholic church as the one true church and defer to its authority. The orderly cooperation between church and state would promote God's truth in all aspects of life, even as church and state remained distinct. To a non-Catholic this looked a lot like a union of church and state regardless of Catholic protestations.[42]

Catholic leaders also began to smear the leaders of POAU. Archbishop Richard J. Cushing thought that it was obvious that the POAU, with its talk of separation, was responsible for "a tempest of talk in behalf of communism." Others alleged that the POAU leaders were "breeders of religious hatred," "a society of organized bigotry," and "a reorganized Klan with the 'new look.' " In all cases Catholic leaders complained that Protestants disguised their anti-Catholic bigotry behind high-minded rhetoric in order to conceal their own power.[43]

Unfortunately for Catholic leaders, the POAU was only one of several groups that began to mobilize against them, and the other groups were harder to critique. The POAU was joined by Jewish groups, including the Anti-Defamation League (ADL), the American Jewish Committee (AJ Committee), and especially the American Jewish Congress (AJC), which had been formed by liberal Jews including Louis Brandeis in 1918. In addition, the ACLU continued its work in defending church–state separatism and in resisting the Catholic attempt to divide the public-school fund.[44]

The Jewish groups' entry in the dispute offered particular challenge, though it was not without internal division. In *Everson* Jewish groups declined to join the case, even though they opposed state payment for religious schools, for fear that the controversy surrounding the case would spur anti-Semitism. Instead, the groups focused on interfaith and goodwill efforts. But with the mobilization of the Catholic church, Jewish groups reluctantly came to recognize that their interfaith efforts would not gain equality in American public life. They began to move from a focus on public relations to legislative lobbying and litigation in an attempt to secure equal treatment.[45]

The central figure in the shift was a youngish lawyer named Leo Pfeffer. He had been born to a rabbi in Austro-Hungary in 1910, but the family emigrated when he was two years old to the Lower East Side of New York City. He went to public schools where religious exercises were a daily occurrence. The ritual was pretty much the same each time. A teacher, usually a Protestant, read from the Psalms because the entire population of the school was Jewish. That was fine with his parents—or at least tolerable. But when he was in fourth grade the state of New York proposed releasing children for part of the school day to attend religious instruction through a denomination of the parents' choice. His father, still a rabbi, immediately objected to the infusion of sectarian religion into the schools. He pulled Pfeffer from the school and enrolled him in a Yeshiva.[46]

In time Pfeffer rejected the Judaism of his parents and became an avowed humanist. After college and law school he became the legal advisor to the AJC. By the 1940s Pfeffer had begun to build a network of legal communication connecting the three big Jewish organizations to the ACLU and, to a lesser extent, to the POAU.[47]

Those connections soon became quite useful when a case began to make its way to the Supreme Court. It started a few years earlier when a woman named Vashti McCollum found that her son was to receive religious instruction as part of a release-time program in his Illinois school. The program was built on the kind of instruction that Pfeffer's father had objected to. Unlike the New York model, it modified the procedure by releasing students for religious instruction that was held on school grounds. The children were divided by Protestant, Catholic, and Jewish faiths and sent to parts of the school to be instructed by religious leaders. Those who declined to participate were sent to study hall.[48]

McCollum reluctantly allowed her son to take part in the Protestant instruction, even though she was a secular humanist. She thought he would receive ethical and moral teaching. But when she saw the materials she realized it promoted a fairly exclusivist form of Protestant Christianity. The next year, when her son moved schools, she decided that he would not participate. Her son's teacher pressured McCollum to let him take the religious course, telling her that it would help her son fit in.

"You know that I'd do anything to help my boy get along," she replied, "but I will not let him take something we feel is unconstitutional and undemocratic." In response, the teacher made her son sit alone in the hall, like punishment, while others were released.[49]

When McCollum found out, she was enraged. After meeting with the school administrators, she realized that they were entirely unsympathetic to her complaints and that she was unlikely to change any of the arrangements. She decided to bring suit, first in state court, where she lost, and then in federal court, where she also lost.[50]

As the case made its way through the courts she started to receive increasing amounts of hate mail. People started calling her house with threats. Halloween pranks turned ominous and somewhat sinister. Her son Jim regularly arrived home with a bloodied nose and torn clothes. By the time the case was appealed to the Supreme Court the abuse had become so regular that the McCollums sent their son to New York to live with his grandparents.[51]

The national civil liberties organizations soon became aware of the case. The school board's position troubled Pfeffer. The board's attorneys made two assertions. They argued, first, that the First Amendment's establishment clause applied only to Congress, not to the states. The Supreme Court had already rejected that view in *Everson*, but given the confused holding of the majority opinion, which proclaimed separation of church and state while signing off on state aid to religious schools, it seemed like a proposition worth testing. Failing that, second, they proposed that the First Amendment did not forbid governmental aid to religion on a nonpreferential basis. It forbade only discriminatory aid to religion.[52]

To Pfeffer that was a dangerously misguided point of view. So when the court decided to hear McCollum's appeal shortly after *Everson* Pfeffer and other civil liberties attorneys leaped into action. Among the Jewish organizations there were serious reservations about joining the case. McCollum's atheism bothered the ADL and the AJ Committee, who were disquieted by the thought of backing someone who was so obviously irreligious. But Pfeffer convinced them that, given the gravity of the issues involved, they could not remain out of the case.[53]

When leaders of the other organizations conceded the point, Pfeffer wrote an amicus brief for the National Community Relations Advisory Council (NCRAC), a joint policy-making body created by the major Jewish organizations. So as not to be misunderstood, he began the brief with what amounted to a disclaimer. "We wish to make clear our regret," he wrote, "that the appellant chose to use the case as a medium for the dissemination of her atheistic beliefs and injected into the record the irreligious statements it contains." The NCRAC's support for McCollum, Pfeffer suggested, ought not to be understood as support for her irreligion. But, having renounced irreligiousness, Pfeffer expressed an absolutist commitment to the separation of church and state. The First Amendment, which required separation, ought to have prevented the intrusion of religion into the secular public schools, he alleged.[54]

In this, Pfeffer was following the lead of David Petegorsky, the executive director of the AJC. In a memo to other Jewish organizations before joining the *McCollum* case he noted that confronting any one of the myriad forms of public Christian observance in the United States held risks. The obvious risk was the possibility that a challenge might make some believe that Jewish groups were indifferent or hostile to religious teaching. But, while taking all-due-care to avoid such a misunderstanding, the fear of being portrayed as irreligious was somewhat overblown. Petegorsky explained, "The attitude of the non-Jewish community towards Jews is only one of the many factors determining the status and security of the Jewish community. A far more important factor affecting that status is the strength and health of the democratic system under which we live. In opposing any impairment of the separation of church and state, we stand firmly on sound and tested democratic principle."[55]

The decision of Jewish organizations to enter the fray would have a profound effect in the future.

In the short term, the court was almost entirely persuaded by McCollum's argument. The 8–1 majority opinion, written by Black, dispensed with the case in a few crisp paragraphs. It referenced the wall of separation language that the court had used in *Everson*. The court said that school officials had not respected the constitutional barrier between church and state. "Here not only are the State's tax-supported public-school buildings used for the dissemination of religious doctrines," Black wrote. "The State also affords sectarian groups an invaluable aid in that it helps to provide pupils for their religious classes through the use of the State's compulsory public-school machinery. This is not separation of Church and State."[56]

In a concurring opinion the four justices who dissented in *Everson* put a finer point on the issue. Written by Frankfurter, it narrated the history of public education in the United States as one of progressive religious confinement. Frankfurter went out of his way to obscure the Protestant history of public schooling and to affirm the public secularity of the school system. That secularity, he thought, allowed it to promote cohesion among a heterogeneous population. "The public school is at once the symbol of our democracy and the most pervasive means for promoting our common destiny," Frankfurter wrote. "In no activity of the State is it more vital to keep out divisive forces than in its schools, to avoid confusing, not to say fusing, what the Constitution sought to keep strictly apart."[57]

Stanley Reed was the only dissent in the case. He believed that the court was applying an overly broad interpretation of the First Amendment that was in tension with established religious practices. There were, as he pointed out, "many instances of close association of church and state in American society." Were they really going to strike down all of those instances?[58]

Reed was not alone in asking the question. Catholics saw their darkest fears realized in the *McCollum* decision. In rejecting the notion that the First Amendment would allow nonpreferential aid to religion, Catholic leaders saw that separationism yielded secularism, as they had long said. The editors of *Commonweal*, a journal of Catholic lay opinion, decried that the court would take such a step simply to appease, in its words, "the mother of a maladjusted boy." "In order to avoid her son's being laughed at," the editorial continued, "Mrs. Vashti McCollum and the groups that supported her are attempting to pull down the whole public-school system, Samson-like."[59]

The court took the step it did, *America* complained, in seeming ignorance of the consequences. The editors noted the pervasiveness of government support for religion, from chaplains and prayers in Congress, to compulsory religious services in the military and in military academies, to the ritualized invocation of God at the

Supreme Court itself. "There must surely be some way in which the citizens of these United States can prevent the Establishment of Atheism in the name of a few dissatisfied persons," the editorial concluded.[60]

The Catholic hierarchy agreed with *America*. After the ruling, Catholic bishops released a statement that construed the controversy as one "between secularism and society." "Human life centers in God," they said. "The failure to center life in God is secularism— which, as we pointed out last year, is the most deadly menace to our Christian and American way of living." The statement cited the Catholic social philosophy first put forward by Leo XIII and elaborated by Pius XI that required religion and citizenship to be connected. Secularism broke the connection, separating human law and natural law, eliminating the cooperation of religion and the government. It would pave the way "for the advent of the omnipotent state." "We, therefore, hope and pray," the bishops concluded, "that the novel interpretation of the First Amendment recently adopted by the Supreme Court will in due process be revised."[61]

The *McCollum* case started a cottage industry of Catholic writers denouncing the court. They pretty much all followed the bishops in decrying the court's desire to quarantine religion from public life. The court based its opinion, the Jesuit Wilfred Parsons announced, on "a constitutional and historical absurdity" that promoted "one particular sectarian ecclesiology"(that is, Protestantism) over others. The deracinated Protestantism of the court eventually cashed out as "an extreme form of secularism in the state." All of it would soon culminate in a judicial dictatorship, he predicted.[62]

Protestants also began to reconsider. The court's decision intimated that many justices were unwilling to permit the cozy connections between Protestantism and the nation's civil institutions just because they were long-standing. It was becoming clear that the social and cultural preeminence of Christianity, even Protestant Christianity, was on a shaky foundation. The editors at the Protestant *Christian Century* saw those implications immediately. Although in the main the magazine welcomed the *McCollum* decision, it noted that "if the total application of this principle is to be made consistent," it would limit the ability of religious forces "to perform their function in erecting a barrier against the advance of secularism."[63]

A few months after the court handed down its decision, a small group of influential Protestant leaders gathered at Union Theological Seminary. They fretted, as they put it, about "the religious foundations of our national life." The court's decision had begun to undercut the support structures in a way that they thought needed to be reconsidered. "We believe that, whatever its intention may be, this hardening of the idea of 'separation' by the Court will greatly accelerate the trend toward the secularization of our culture," the group announced.[64]

One of the most surprising attendees at the Protestant meeting was the Jesuit John Courtney Murray. He even addressed the group, and, it turned out, he had much in common with them. Following the *McCollum* decision he had begun to talk to anyone who would listen about what he saw as the antireligious conspiracy that sought to remove religion from public life. The ruling was, Murray said, "a legal victory for secularism" even if the Supreme Court did not see it that way. In response to the disaster Murray began to call for religious men of all types—Protestant, Catholic, and Jewish—to overcome their divisions in order to unite against the new secular thrust of American law.[65]

But Murray's position required him to defang the traditional Protestant suspicion of Catholicism. During the meeting at Union, the Protestant theologian Reinhold Niebuhr listened with interest to Murray's call for a joint response to the court. Yet he noted that the Catholic position on church and state did not usually invite cooperation. Catholic acceptance of special privileges from foreign governments made Protestants uncomfortable. And the record of Catholic defense of fascism also did not inspire confidence. Catholics refused to defend religious freedom even in principle, Niebuhr noted, since it declared that the Catholic church was the one true church. This was hardly the basis for cooperation. Murray privately admitted, "The theory of church and state expressed in Catholic writings on politics could disturb the Protestant mind."[66]

In spite of these liabilities there was some indication that Murray's strategy might work. Protestant fear of political atheism aligned precisely with Murray's worries about secularism. Liberal Protestants had supported the opening up of categories of faith to generate greater freedom of belief. But because many still regarded religious authority as essential to the perpetuation of any society, the secular-izing and liberalizing move of the court put them off. Protestants saw no difference between a negative secularism that privatized be-lief and a positive secularism that sought to establish unbelief. All eroded religious power and authority.

Protestants accordingly began to respond in what Murray viewed as fruitful ways. Some began publishing books with titles like *Christianity and the Crisis of Secularism* and *The Modern Rival of the Christian Faith: An Analysis of Secularism.* In 1950, at the first meeting of the National Council of Churches, a large ecumenical body composed of Protestant denominations, the new organization made clear its essential agreement with Murray. The leaders hung a giant sign that extended the length of the dais and proclaimed in huge letters, "This Nation Under God." Bishop Henry Knox Sher-rill, the first president of the National Council, told the attendees that their gathering "marks a new and great determination that the American way will be increasingly the Christian way, for such is our heritage."[67]

But other Protestants saw the Catholic position on church and state as a stumbling block too big to surmount. The *Christian Cen-tury,* which regularly featured distressed articles about the triumph of secularism, still denounced Catholic invocations of democratic pluralism as a "national menace." The magazine did not believe that the Catholic appropriation of liberal language could be trusted. It seemed as though the hierarchy was using parts of the political vo-cabulary for spurious ends.[68]

Jews were also suspicious. *Time* magazine, in an article on the religious conflict of the era, quoted Rabbi Philip S. Bernstein to ex-plain the dilemma. "It seems," Rabbi Bernstein said, "that Catholics do not realize the offensiveness to non-Catholics of the Church's claim to exclusive and final truth."[69]

Meanwhile, Leo Pfeffer and the AJC were readying the next chal-lenge. In the aftermath of *McCollum* Pfeffer wanted to move ahead immediately in a steady campaign to remove religion from the pub-lic schools. And he wanted Jewish organizations to take the lead.

The court's turn toward civil liberties, Pfeffer saw, made it nec-essary for advocacy organizations to control all aspects of the case.

Too much was at stake to risk another Vashti McCollum. The right plaintiff needed to be found. The right case with advantageous circumstances needed to be selected. And the case needed to be litigated, from the beginning, with an eye toward appeal. All of it required more active control during the entirety of litigation rather than simply using amicus briefs to direct the legal argument after the case was brought.[70]

To that end Pfeffer consulted with the ACLU, the Public Education Association, and the United Parents Association to find the ideal plaintiff. He also tried to persuade the ADL and the AJ Committee to come aboard, though they were both wary. Eventually he convinced the Jewish organizations, but only with the promise that Pfeffer would find a non-Jewish plaintiff so as to reduce the risk of anti-Semitism.[71]

After much searching Pfeffer found Tessim Zorach, the son of the left-wing sculptor William Zorach. The younger Zorach, unlike his father, was an active Episcopalian who had no political record. The ADL and the AJ Committee approved the choice, as did Pfeffer's other allies. In his own evaluation a lawyer for the ACLU said, "Zorach may not be the ideal plaintiff, but I believe he comes as close to it as we are likely to find."[72]

The ADL and AJ Committee still were uneasy. They did not want Jews being too far in front of the case, and they wanted Pfeffer to get a non-Jewish lawyer to be the public face. Jewish organizations would still build the case, write the briefs, and direct the litigation, but from behind the scenes. Pfeffer obliged by retaining Kent Greenawalt, another Episcopalian.[73]

Having alleviated their unease, Pfeffer went about building the record. Tessim Zorach was a student in New York City who objected to New York's release-time program, a later version of the same scheme that three decades earlier had caused Pfeffer's father to pull him out of the public school. Pfeffer thought that New York's program was similar in every respect to the one the court struck down in *McCollum*. The sole exception was that it was held off-campus for those who decided to participate.

To build the record at trial Pfeffer gathered extensive affidavits from students, parents, and former students in New York City schools. All testified about the pressure on children to participate and the divisiveness that resulted from schools' categorization of children by religious faith. Many students and parents spoke of being ridiculed by classmates and sometimes teachers when they declined to participate. Anti-Semitism was frequent. One former student told Pfeffer that "Jewish students in the class did not participate in release time and the released students assumed that anyone remaining in the school during the released time hours was Jewish, which was not true in my case since I am an Episcopalian." Another student, who was Jewish, told Pfeffer that her classmates called her "Christ killer" and "dirty Jew." Pfeffer also introduced social science data and psychological expertise to explain the social pressures and the implicit coerciveness of the program.[74]

But the New York trial judge ruled against Zorach and excluded all of Pfeffer's affidavits from the appeals proceedings. Lacking the affidavits, Pfeffer had a much harder time showing that the program was coercive in practice. That was not necessarily a problem, given the expansive prior opinion of the court. Still it was not a good sign. Pfeffer pursued the case patiently, moving from the New York courts, to federal circuit courts, to the U.S. Supreme Court.[75]

At oral argument Felix Frankfurter pushed the lawyer for the schools, Charles H. Tuttle, on the administrative mechanics of the program. Tuttle had said that those students who wished to participate left the school for religious instruction. The others were kept at school in a study hall with nothing to do.

Frankfurter asked, "Why aren't you satisfied to have every child dismissed at 2 o'clock each Wednesday and Friday?" That way those who wished could go to religious instruction and those who did not could do something else. This option was known as "dismissed time."

"It isn't a question of my satisfaction," Tuttle responded. "The question is whether the Legislature is bound to say that 'dismissed time' is the only Constitutional alternative."

But Tuttle sensed that Frankfurter was implying more, so he went on. The release-time arrangement was not, he said, an "organized conspiracy of religious sects." It was instead a response to parental fears that, in his words, "the momentum of secularism is pushing religion and the church into the backwaters of life."

He had walked into a trap. Frankfurter pounced.

"So they need public schools to help them accomplish their religious purposes?" Frankfurter asked.

Before Tuttle could answer, Justice Sherman Minton stepped in. "They don't need the school system," he said, "they just need their children for a few minutes."[76]

In conference, the familiar divide emerged.

On one side, Frankfurter reiterated that religious instruction during school time was a sectarian project that violated what he saw as the nation's historical commitment to secularism. On the other side, Stanley Forman Reed, the sole dissenter in *McCollum*, defended his position that there was nothing wrong with the release-time arrangement. The program continued the blending of religion and the state that had long characterized American history. The rest of the justices were somewhere in the middle. But they clearly leaned toward Reed.[77]

The resulting decision was a total departure from the earlier rulings. William O. Douglas, writing for a six-person majority, ruled that the release-time arrangements could stand. But to explain the ruling he had to go through some gymnastics. He denied any tension between his opinion and the court's earlier holdings. "There cannot be the slightest doubt that the First Amendment reflects the philosophy that Church and State should be separated," he began. "The First Amendment, however, does not say that, in every and all respects there shall be a separation of Church and State." To explain this mind-bending contradiction, Douglas announced that the Constitution required that church and state remain separate but friendly. "We are a religious people," he explained, "whose institutions presuppose a Supreme Being." There were many religious aspects to government. The release-time system was simply one of those aspects.[78]

The dissenters were incredulous. It was now clear that the majority of the court had no firm opinions at all on church and state. They had been, in effect, stumbling toward secularism. Jackson lambasted the court's opinion as unwilling to recognize the coercion of the arrangement that it now upheld. The scheme operated in two stages. First, the children must attend school as mandated by the law, a coercive mechanism. Second, they could be released but only if they would go to religious education. During the release time the school functioned "as a temporary jail for a pupil who will not go to Church." Jackson could hardly bear to refute the majority opinion. It had no coherent position to refute, consisting more of emotional sloganeering than legal reasoning. "Today's judgment will be more interesting to students of psychology and of judicial processes than to students of constitutional law," he concluded.[79]

Pfeffer was deeply disturbed, partly because the court did not seem to recognize just how much the release-time program fed anti-Semitism. He had not been expecting that the court would so decisively depart from its earlier rulings. Now that program had received court approval. It also created an organizational problem for him. After the decision the ADL and the AJ Committee decided that they had been right all along. They declined to participate in any more litigation.[80]

The whole debacle left Pfeffer to work in state courts, looking for an adequate vehicle to return to the Supreme Court. But his wait would be a long one. The court did not decide another establishment clause case for the rest of the decade.

The court's ruling and subsequent silence demonstrated the confused, even perilous, state of religion in American public life at midcentury. Religious leaders complained constantly of a creeping secularism in American life. They used that complaint to inject religion more deeply into the schools and other American institutions. The justices on the court, who tried to regulate this dynamic, faced sharp criticism and accusations of antireligious bias that made them pull back when they went too far. But the more prominence that religion gained in public life, the greater the chance of sectarian conflict over morals, mores, and the precise contours of institutional control. That conflict led to calls to privatize religious difference, which had the effect of advancing the secularization that religious leaders had decried.

Part of the dilemma was the state of the Catholic church. It had come into its own over the previous thirty years as a serious force in American life. But the church paired its newfound prominence with a variety of positions that critics found both reactionary and undemocratic. Many of its commitments were both old and had been constantly reaffirmed. And the church showed signs of burrowing more deeply into its position. In 1950, Pope Pius XII released an encyclical, *Humanis generis*, that confirmed the confrontational posture of the Catholic hierarchy that often led to sectarian conflict.[81]

Pius's suspicion toward change was deep and directed as much within the church as outside of it. The encyclical acknowledged that the church was facing unparalleled challenges in the modern world. It recognized that some people within the church responded by attempting to accommodate contemporary realities. Their concessions usually assumed a posture of what Pius called *eirenism*, or an attempt to suppress or massage doctrinal animosity for the sake of Christian fellowship or to jointly address a common enemy. The pope rejected their posture, stating that the Catholic church needed to proclaim the whole truth and to confront all error so that, as the encyclical put it, "the dissident and erring can happily be brought back to the bosom of the Church."[82]

The all-out confrontation with error moved through all levels of Catholic organization in an attempt to quash dissent, but it soon moved outward to address American life as a whole.

The internal process began with John Courtney Murray, who in many ways seemed to be the target of Pius's encyclical. Murray had long believed that church doctrine had not caught up to modern realities or had really accepted, in a full-fledged sense, the aspirations of American political democracy. "Many Americans believe that the Catholic Church is prepared to support democracy only provisionally, and on the grounds of expediency," he pointed out in a 1950 memo, "until what time she acquires sufficient power within society to do away with the forms and institutions of democratic government, and introduce some form of dictatorship subject to authoritarian, ecclesiastical control."[83]

Murray thought that such a view was mistaken but understandably so. The church had a long history of papal pronouncements against religious liberalism, against socialism, and against modernity. Murray fretted that secularists increasingly held sway in American life, that Protestants were estranged from Catholics through the past Catholic pronouncements, and that the hierarchy's rejection of modernism risked, as Murray put it, "a progressive alienation of the American mind from the Catholic Church, with consequent damage to the apostolic activity of the Church."[84]

Other events tended to confirm Murray's apprehension. The same year that Pius released his encyclical and that Murray wrote his memo, Senator Joseph McCarthy gave his "Enemies Within" speech on Lincoln Day. The speech is remembered for McCarthy's accusation that 205 people in the State Department were known members of the Communist Party. But his wider purpose was to reframe the Cold War not as a geopolitical conflict between empires or rival economic systems but as "a final, all-out battle between communistic atheism and Christianity."[85]

McCarthy's speech proved to be the start of an extended campaign against nonconformists in American life. He used the categories of Christianity in the effort. McCarthy brought a variety of actors, writers, and cultural workers into public disrepute by accusing them of having communist sensibilities, hauling them before a special Senate investigative committee, and then denouncing them when they appeared.

Beneath his method was the familiar Protestant–Catholic divide, barely submerged. It is not too much to see in McCarthy's program an application of Pius's call to confront error. McCarthy himself was Catholic. Much of the support for McCarthy came from American Catholics in the Midwest. The hierarchy supported McCarthy almost uniformly. Although *America* and *Commonweal* both immediately spoke out against him, they were largely alone among Catholic journals. And by the time of the *Zorach* decision McCarthy was making the sectarian nature of his program more overt. He began to edge toward public criticism of liberal Protestants as a group of communist fellow travelers.[86]

Soon the criticism became explicit. In July 1953 a McCarthy aide denounced the Protestant clergy to the press as "the largest single group supporting the Communist Party." After fierce blowback, McCarthy tried to modify the criticism by noting that "the vast majority" of Protestant leaders were loyal. But he did not deny that Protestant clergy were the largest single group of Communist supporters.[87]

Protestants condemned McCarthy's campaign, which revealed, in the National Council's words, "a degree of stupidity and misrepresentation which can be reached only in an atmosphere of suspicion, distrust, and fear." The Presbyterian Church of the USA dismissed

McCarthy as nothing more than a sore Catholic. The *Christian Science Monitor* ran a story stating flatly that "the open Roman Catholic attack on communism spearheaded by Senator McCarthy actually is directed as much against Protestantism at home as it is against the Kremlin abroad." Robert J. McCracken of the prominent Riverside Church in New York City noted that McCarthy was "a member of a church that has never disavowed the Inquisition, that makes a policy of censorship, that insists on conformity." Those dynamics, McCracken said, were at the heart of McCarthyism.[88]

The most damning response came from the prominent Methodist bishop G. Bromley Oxnam, who simply observed, "No Protestant nation has been seriously infiltrated by communists." The same could not be said of Catholic nations.[89]

Oxnam's statement enraged McCarthy's supporters, not least because it made the United States into a Protestant rather than a Catholic country. On the floor of the U.S. House, Representative Donald Jackson (R-CA) said in response, "The Bishop serves God on Sunday and the Communist Front the rest of the week."[90]

That accusation led to an eight-hour appearance by Oxnam before the House Un-American Activities Committee. He used the occasion to defend Protestant liberalism and to critique Catholicism by implication. "Free man must discover concrete measures through which the ideals of religion may be translated into the realities of world law and order, economic justice, and racial brotherhood," he told the committee. Those were vital components of Protestant ethical thought, he said, but he denied that such commitments made him a communist.[91]

The testimony turned into a big win for Protestant clergy. At the end of the hearing the committee passed a motion that declared, "This committee has no record of Communist Party affiliation or membership by Bishop Oxnam."[92]

Still, that was not the end of it. A few months later Francis Cardinal Spellman waded into the debate by defending McCarthy's methods in a speech in Europe. "No American uncontaminated by communism has lost his good name because of Congressional hearings on un-American activities," he said. "However, there are individuals who have seriously compromised themselves by a flat refusal to state whether they are now or have been communists. It is impossible for me to understand why any American should refuse to declare himself free of Communist affiliation, unless he has something to hide."[93]

Two days later, at a conference titled "The Church and the World Order," four hundred Protestant leaders expressed their dismay at Spellman's endorsement of McCarthy. The instantaneous Protestant response showed the depth of Protestant alarm and outrage.[94]

Spellman refused to back down. Less than two weeks later, at a surprise appearance before six thousand Catholic policemen and guests, he again stated his endorsement of McCarthyism and implied, again, that critics of McCarthy were communists. At the same meeting, McCarthy himself addressed the crowd. In response to his remarks he received what the *New York Times* described as "repeated and roaring ovations."[95]

Yet some in the hierarchy began to have doubts. McCarthy had long since grown reckless. A few weeks later Bishop Bernard J. Sheil of Chicago denounced McCarthy, the first such statement by any member of the Catholic clerical leadership after nearly four years of McCarthy's campaign. It was the start of a stampede away from McCarthy, as the ship seemed to be sinking. Soon McCarthy would be disgraced and face censure by the Senate. The censure finally calmed tensions on the surface.[96]

But the entire episode validated Murray's point. The way that Catholic leaders lined up behind obviously illiberal political tactics damaged Catholic prospects in the United States. That those same leaders could point to a variety of doctrinal and papal statements as a justification for their position made their actions difficult to critique. To get around the dilemma Murray began to urge church leaders to think about what he called historical factors that had shaped doctrine. Pope Leo XIII's pronouncements against liberalism and church–state separation at the end of the nineteenth century needed to be understood in the temporal context of Jacobin democracy and the subsequent development of nineteenth-century French liberalism. Likewise, Pius XI's pronouncements against modernism in the early twentieth century needed to be understood in light of the theological disputes of the time. Understanding the historical context of papal pronouncements relativized them, Murray implied, so that Catholic leaders could determine, as he put it, what is "principle and what is contingent application of principle, what is permanent demand and what is legitimate temporary expedience." In that way Catholic doctrine could develop.[97]

Murray's strategy essentially followed nineteenth-century Protestant liberalizers. He assumed that there was an eternal truth in all ecclesiastical pronouncements but that those truths had been expressed or encoded in response to local developments that did not necessarily apply across time and space. The trick was to extract the eternal from the particular, which also had the benefit of allowing the interpreter to discard past pronouncements that no longer made sense.

Unfortunately for Murray, many people rejected his views. More problematic still, he could not historicize Pius XII's call to confront all error, since the call had been issued quite recently. As he tried to solve that puzzle, Murray's enemies began to circle. Alfredo Cardinal Ottaviani of the Holy Office, the supreme doctrinal body in the Vatican, condemned Murray's "liberalizing thesis" and his corresponding call to open up and to develop Catholic doctrine. The next year Ottaviani initiated a process to have Murray's views scrutinized by the Holy Office itself.[98]

To do so, Ottaviani had to explain the error of Murray's position. He summarized Murray's thinking in four compact propositions. First, he wrote, Murray held that the Catholic confessional state was not the universal ideal. Second, Murray argued that full religious liberty is a political ideal that the church ought to support. Third, Murray maintained that the democratic state had done its duty when it offered a guarantee of full freedom of religion. It need not grant the truth affirmed by the Catholic church. Fourth, Murray claimed that Leo XIII's renunciation of religious freedom did not apply in a modern democratic state. Though succinct, it was an accurate account of Murray's stance.[99]

Many people within the hierarchy were repulsed. Ottaviani had the Holy Office reject each of the propositions. By 1955, as the condemnation moved forward, Murray's Jesuit superiors ordered him to cease all work on church–state issues in anticipation of an official papal condemnation. After the order of silence came down, a friend remembered Murray combing his bookshelves with an air of dejection to find anything that had to do with church and state. Those books had to go back to the library. Only innocuous ones could remain.[100]

Yet the sectarian strife had surprising effects within public culture. Politicians who had been calling for a renewed role for religion had to find a way around the disagreement. A common response was to affirm the importance of religion in general without offering any specifics. President Dwight Eisenhower took the lead.

Eisenhower was not an obvious spokesperson for the public role of religion. He had been raised as part of the River Brethren until his early teens, when his mother (and possibly his father) turned to the Jehovah's Witnesses. Eisenhower himself moved away from religion until he ran for president in 1952. Then, under the pressures of the campaign, he made nearly constant reference to religious ideas and affirmed at every turn the importance of spiritual strength in the battle against communism.[101]

His gestures toward religion continued even after the election. In a Christmastime address in 1952 Eisenhower explained his point of view. The battle against communism, which he promised to continue, was "a struggle for the hearts and souls of men—not merely for property or even merely for power."[102]

To explain his thinking, Eisenhower recounted a conversation he had had back in the Second World War with the Soviet marshal Georgi Zhukov about the differences between the Soviet and the U.S. political systems. The deeper they went, Eisenhower said, the more at a loss they had been to find common ground or even to communicate. Every subject yielded another disagreement that terminated in the gulf between "the Bolshevik religion" and what Eisenhower considered the American one. American religious fervency really supported all aspects of American life, he thought, just like the Bolshevik rejection of God supported communism. The recognition of the essentially religious nature of the conflict required a commitment on the part of the American people to God as the foundation of the American political system. After all, as Eisenhower said, "Our form of Government has no sense unless it is founded in a deeply felt religious faith, and I don't care what it is. With us of course it is the Judo-Christian [*sic*] concept."[103]

At his inaugural address a month later he continued the theme. He stood on the dais of the Capitol, looked out over the crowd, and said, "I ask that you bow your heads." He then offered a prayer, the first time in American history that a president prayed prior to his inaugural address.[104]

Once in the White House, he worked to install public religious observance throughout his government. He joined a church and was baptized, the first time a president had been baptized while in office. He required all cabinet meetings to begin with prayer, another first. Soon he was the first to preside over a National Prayer Breakfast.[105]

Critics wanted to know what it all meant. G. Bromley Oxnam decried the "danger of developing a holy war against Communism" as a consequence of sanctifying the U.S. government.[106]

But Eisenhower was unmoved. About a year into his first term, facing continuing questions, he further laid out his position. His solicitousness toward religion was really about how to support political equality and how to perpetuate democracy. It was an old issue, as he acknowledged. "The Magna Carta, our Declaration of Independence, and the French Declaration of the Rights of Man were certainly nothing less than the attempt on the part of men to state that in their government there would be recognized principles of the equality of men, the dignity of man," he said. But how could one uphold the equality of men? Men were obviously not equal. The equality of man was, he said, "a completely false premise, unless we recognize the Supreme Being in front of whom we are all equal."[107]

Others took his idea and ran with it. It needed to be institutionalized in some way. There had already been a variety of attempts to recognize the notion that God established the foundation of the U.S. political system. The most prominent was an attempt to modify the pledge of allegiance to include the words "under God." Instead of the usual wording, which went, "one nation, indivisible, with liberty and justice for all," the idea was to say, "one nation, under God, indivisible, with liberty and justice for all."

Eisenhower apparently did not know about the proposal. But a few months after his speech on religion and equality, he was sitting in church when the Reverend George Docherty endorsed the inclusion of "under God" as befitting the religious commitments of the United States. Eisenhower agreed with his call, and a legislative push immediately formed. Four months later Eisenhower signed the bill into law. He thought the additional language was quite significant. As he said in a signing statement, the reference to God rightly affirmed "the transcendence of religious faith in America's heritage and future." "In this way," he continued, "we shall constantly strengthen those spiritual weapons which forever will be our country's most powerful resource, in peace or in war."[108]

Yet critics were not convinced. Looked at in one way, Eisenhower's campaign might suggest an increase of religion in public life, even a kind of religious revival. But looked at another way, it exposed the internal secularization characteristic of Protestant liberalism, a deracinated form of ecumenicism that had no substantive content whatsoever. Eisenhower's high level of generality was necessary to keep religion in public life, given the threat of sectarian conflict that had emerged since the end of the Second World War. The public affirmation of religion worked only if a person brought forth no specifics to cause disagreement.

It made for an odd religious situation, as people at the time recognized. In 1955, for example, the Jewish sociologist Will Herberg published his classic book, *Protestant-Catholic-Jew*, seeking to make sense of the religious position at midcentury. According to Herberg, Protestants, Catholics, and Jews composed the three religious identities that formed the building blocks of American religious life. But the public religion that he observed in American cultural and political institutions did not quite match these identities. The public religious idea seemed to be broadly shared and was acknowledged by many, but it was a pretty mushy concept. When Herberg forced himself to articulate its tenets, all he could muster was that American public religion stood for "spiritual values" at the heart of American democracy, "the fatherhood of God and brotherhood of man, the dignity of the individual human being, etc."[109]

The vagueness left Herberg uncertain about how to characterize the moment. "The religion which actually prevails among Americans today has lost much of its authentic Christian (or Jewish) content," he wrote. "Americans think, feel, and act in terms quite obviously secularist at the very time that they exhibit every sign of a widespread religious revival. It is this secularism of a religious people, this religiousness in a secularist framework, that constitutes the problem posed by the contemporary religious situation in America."[110]

Protestants themselves acknowledged as much. Some, such as the Yale religion scholar William Lee Miller, complained of the emptiness of Eisenhower's religious pronouncements. "President Eisenhower, like many Americans, is a very fervent believer in a very vague religion," he said. Others, often in the pages of the *Christian Century*, began to speak of a post-Protestant era. The Lutheran minister and journalist Martin E. Marty pointed to the "secular national religion that now is flowering" as evidence that Protestantism no longer had a privileged position in the United States.[111]

For Marty, the post-Protestant era was a liberation. "Protestantism, in the interests of truth and strategy, should begin to learn to enjoy the luxury of its minority status in a pluralistic post-Protestant society," he wrote. There was freedom to be found in renouncing a custodial obligation for the nation. If the United States was no longer a Protestant country, Marty noted, then Protestants ought to mount a strategic retreat in order to cultivate a more authentic religious voice that worked beyond the categories of Cold War politics.[112]

Others feared the consequences of such a retreat but could find no obvious way forward. In a 1958 study sponsored by the Fund for the Republic, a group of scholars representing Protestants, Catholics, and Jews announced that Eisenhower's national religion actually posed a significant peril to the nation. William Lee Miller, one of the leaders, told *Time* that people ought to reject "the widely prevalent and intellectually debilitating relativism" and "the belief in believing, the faith in faith." But what did that leave?[113]

The problem, as the Catholic layman William Clancy explained to *Time*, was that the official Washington piety had to draw upon an ever-narrowing national consensus about religious and moral principles. Separationists were working through the courts to suppress real religious ideas by labeling them as sectarian. At the same time, the Catholic leadership, as Clancy put it, "act as though the last few centuries had never happened." In that toxic mix, the public role of what he considered authentic religion could only grow slighter and secularism could only increase.[114]

As it turned out, Clancy's apprehensions were right on the money. The conflict between religious groups left little choice for governing authorities other than mealymouthed platitudes or, better still, the relegation of religion to the private sphere. And once the latter option became politically viable, the secular settlement arrived.

CHAPTER SIX

Religion Is Personal

In early 1958 John Courtney Murray wrote to his Jesuit superiors with news. Senator John F. Kennedy, the Catholic Democrat from Massachusetts, had written him asking for some guidance on what Murray characterized as "the perennially troublesome question." Kennedy wanted to know, "Can a Catholic support, in principle, the religion clauses of the Constitution?"[1]

Kennedy was gearing up for a presidential run. His Catholicism seemed to offer both an opportunity and a problem. Given the increasing numbers and therefore electoral strength of Catholics in American life, Kennedy's own Catholic faith afforded him a ready political base. But the ongoing sectarian division in public affairs and the conservatism of the Catholic hierarchy raised flags among Protestants, which meant that his Catholicism had the potential to turn off many non-Catholic voters.

Fortunately, Murray had been happy to advise. He wrote Kennedy back with assurances that a Catholic could support the religion clauses of the Constitution while remaining solidly within the parameters of Catholic doctrine. A politician could do so, he later wrote, because there was an American consensus that the government was built upon God.[2]

Kennedy only half-listened to Murray. He accepted the assurance that he could support the Constitution. But he was not likely to talk of a government built upon God. Pierre Salinger, Kennedy's press secretary, later recalled that Kennedy was "determined to lean over backward to disprove the suspicion that he would be a *Catholic* president."[3]

It turned out that Kennedy's outreach to Murray was part of a larger effort to get ahead of the issue. His advisors also reached out to journalists. The thought was to get a friendly scribe willing to write an article that would reassure the non-Catholic public. Their efforts culminated in an interview, conducted by Fletcher Knebel and published in *LOOK* magazine. Kennedy came prepared. To Knebel's repeated questions about the relationship of his faith to his public life, he responded with a consistent refrain that did not follow Murray's advice.

"Whatever one's religion in his private life may be," Kennedy said, "for the officeholder, nothing takes precedence over his oath to uphold the Constitution and all its parts—including the First Amendment and the strict separation of church and state." Later, reflecting on Kennedy's answers, Knebel went further. "In a capsule," Knebel wrote, "his theme is that religion is personal, politics are public, and the twain need never meet and conflict."[4]

Kennedy's position was essentially that of Robert H. Jackson: a negative secularism that privatized faith. He emphasized that the church remained subordinate to the state, that the officeholder owed allegiance to the state in standing by his oath, and that whatever private religious sensibilities he held would always remain out of view in the performance of his public duty. In that way he hoped to neutralize Protestant suspicion.

But Kennedy was so focused on pacifying Protestant suspicion that it never occurred to him that he might lose his Catholic base. He should have listened more carefully to Murray because, to many Catholics, Kennedy's endorsement of the privatization of religion made him seem like an out-and-out secularist or like a quasi-Protestant, not like a Catholic communicant. Shortly after the interview, the hierarchy publicly disagreed with Kennedy in its *Catholic Almanac*. To Kennedy's avowal that his faith would remain private, the bishops responded that there was no real way to separate one's religion from public life. "The demands of integrity," wrote the bishops, meant that the officeholder was "answerable to God for actions whether public or private."[5]

Once the bishops spoke, Catholic journals from around the country piled on. They denounced Kennedy's interview as pathetic and as mouthing the formulas of secularism while not really believing them. "We wish he had thought as much of his fellow Catholics as of his potential non-Catholic critics," *America* wrote.[6]

Kennedy was surprised, unreasonably so. His knowledge of Catholic doctrine was limited, but he did not think he had stated anything terribly radical. He also did not think he was selling out to Protestant bigots. "Quite frankly," Kennedy wrote to one critic, "I do not feel that I have made any compromises; and I certainly am not, as you suggest, attempting to placate any particular group, anti-Catholic or otherwise. I am merely trying to state in my own way what I consider to be orthodox principles regarding the relationship between a Christian politician and his beliefs."[7]

His strategy also did not fulfill its original intent. Protestants remained suspicious of him. Once the Catholic bishops stated that his position did not accord with Catholic doctrine, many Protestants wondered if Kennedy would actually repudiate the position of the bishops?

"How do you feel about a Catholic for President?" *LOOK* magazine asked G. Bromley Oxnam after Kennedy's interview. "Uneasy," Oxnam answered.[8]

The unease continued to bedevil Kennedy throughout the campaign, even after he locked up the Democratic nomination. He did not want to invite more Catholic criticism of his position. But he needed to win over Protestants and secularists to secure the presidency. He eventually concluded that he would have to address the issue again.

This time, his advisors went big. They decided against using another friendly journalist. That had not done the trick last time. The public needed to hear his response to Protestants directly, so the campaign decided to have him stand before hostile ministers from the Greater Houston Ministerial Association. He would make a statement. They would ask questions. The exchange would be televised to maximize the effect.

Prior to the event, Kennedy asked Pierre Salinger, his press chief, "What's the mood of the ministers?"

"They're tired of being called bigots," Salinger responded.[9]

In that somewhat tense atmosphere, Kennedy took the podium. He read his prepared five-page statement word for word, only furtively looking up so as not to lose his careful formulations. His message expressed an even starker vision of religious privatization than the one he had offered in his *LOOK* interview. "I believe in an America where the separation of church and state is absolute," he told them, "where no Catholic prelate would tell the president, should he be Catholic, how to act, and no Protestant ministers would tell his parishioners for whom to vote."[10]

The statement was just the beginning. In the question-and-answer that followed, the ministers repeatedly quoted from papal pronouncements that rejected freedom of conscience, church–state separation, and the right of non-Catholic faiths to propagate themselves. Kennedy was, again, in a difficult position. He responded by referencing the 1948 statement American bishops made after *McCollum* that, he incorrectly claimed, endorsed church–state separation. But the ministers kept pushing him with statement after statement from the church that contradicted his views and that corrected his understanding. They seemed to know more about Catholic doctrine than he did. When backed into a corner, he finally admitted that he lacked theological, philosophical, or sociological expertise. But he remained firm in his commitment to the privatization of religious faith and to the supremacy of his oath of office over any other declaration of conscience.[11]

It was, in the end, enough. He adequately satisfied Protestants' questions, and a sufficient number of Catholics stuck with him in spite of his efforts. He won the 1960 presidential election. And when he took office in early 1961 he found himself watching a secular expansion that accorded with his vision. But like other developments in American secularism, the action did not begin in the executive branch. It began in the Supreme Court.

The moment had been coming for some time. Although the court consistently declined to take another establishment clause case after *Zorach*, in other ways it had been active, especially after the appointment of Earl Warren as chief justice in 1953. Warren had been a moderate Republican governor of California before joining the court. Behind his moderate veneer was a commitment to substantive liberalism waiting to manifest itself. The year after Warren joined the court, he led the other justices in a decision to strike down educational segregation in *Brown v. Board of Education.* That substantive liberalism continued to grow throughout the decade. By the time Kennedy entered office in 1961 the court had signaled a broad willingness to defend rights in a variety of ways, including addressing the question of religion.

The court's return to establishment clause cases began a few months after Kennedy assumed office but it did not immediately yield a secular revolution. The first case involved Sunday closing laws in Maryland, where employees at a discount department store sold floor wax, a loose-leaf notebook, a stapler and staples, and a toy to customers on Sunday. Maryland law allowed only a few items to be sold on the Lord's Day—drugs, tobacco, newspapers, some food. After the employees were convicted and fined, they appealed their conviction all the way to the Supreme Court. They alleged that the law violated the First Amendment.[12]

The case was challenging to the justices. Labor groups supported the law because it allowed a day of rest to workers. And business groups supported the law because it allowed them to shut their doors without having to fear the competition. But the Sunday closing laws in Maryland dated back to colonial times, when Maryland was a Catholic colony. Maryland state code had many remnants of its religious history on its books, including a provision to protect the Lord's Day from secular desecration. In agreeing to hear the case, the court had to decide whether the explicitly religious origin of the law invalidated it in a later era.[13]

During conference, Warren led off the discussion with a frank presumption of the Christian character of American life. It was simply obvious to him that everyone should have one day of rest per week. That was why both labor and business supported the law. And if one day a week could be set aside, why not Sunday? "Picking Sunday only conformed to the usages and habit of most people," Warren said, "and this does not mean an invasion of religious beliefs or a preference for one particular belief."[14]

Nearly all of the other justices agreed, hardly seeing anything to discuss. The one outlier was, surprisingly, William O. Douglas, who had written the majority opinion in *Zorach*. In intervening years Douglas had come to regret his decision. He now saw that the solicitousness toward religion in American life nearly always meant the perpetuation of Christian privilege. That was especially apparent in the case of Sunday Laws.

"None of these statutes comports with the First Amendment," he told the other justices. "I think that we are entitled to our religious scruples, but I don't see how we can make everyone else attune to them. I can't be required to goose step because eighty or ninety percent goose step."[15]

But Douglas's efforts failed to persuade the others. When the court handed down its 8–1 opinion, Chief Justice Warren, writing for the majority, laid out the case in simple terms. He admitted that the laws began as a way to encourage or to compel church attendance. But he thought that the laws had acquired a secular purpose over time to protect the health and well-being of workers. That they originated in religious purpose and that they continued to comport with dominant religious ideals did not undermine the secular effect of the laws.[16]

To Douglas, the court was simply disingenuous in its argument. Unlike his own opinion in *Zorach*, which unapologetically acknowledged state support for religion, the court now sought to obscure its support behind a cloak of secularism. Douglas's dissent was accordingly blunt. "The question is not whether one day out of seven can be imposed by a State as a day of rest," he wrote. "The question is whether a State can impose criminal sanctions on those who, unlike the Christian majority that makes up our society, worship on a different day or do not share the religious scruples of the majority." He thought Sunday laws were an obvious example of religious groups using the power of the ostensibly secular state to compel religious observance.[17]

But, as usual when it came to the subject of religion and secularism, the court soon faced other questions. A few years earlier Leo Pfeffer had been looking for a case that he could take to the court. He came across a story in the Religious News Service about a man name Roy Torcaso who had been denied a license to be a notary public by the State of Maryland because he was an atheist. Maryland law required all officeholders, including notaries, to swear their belief in God. After Torcaso was denied his license, he retained the firm of Sickles and Sickles in Washington to represent him in a lawsuit.[18]

Pfeffer thought he had found his case. He reached out to Torcaso offering help. When Torcaso agreed, Pfeffer worked with Sickles to refine the brief. In the original version Sickles emphasized that Maryland's law violated the establishment clause because it constituted an official endorsement of theism. But Pfeffer, having been burned in the *Zorach* opinion, made Sickles rewrite it to demonstrate that the law violated the equal protection clause as well, since it privileged theists over nontheists, and to argue that it violated the constitutional prohibition of a religious test for office.[19]

Pfeffer pursued the case all the way to the Supreme Court. This time his attempt was successful. When the court handed down its opinion, in a unanimous decision written by Black, the justices agreed with Pfeffer entirely. There was, again, historical evasion in the court's opinion. Maryland law was typical of many state laws dating back to the nineteenth century that required a person to affirm the existence of God in order to appear before a court, to assume public office, and to perform a wide variety of civic functions in several states. But Black ignored the ubiquity of these laws and instead portrayed the United States as historically capacious in its embrace of many religious traditions. Those included nontheistic traditions such as Buddhism, Daoism, and secular humanism, so requiring an affirmation of God's existence both violated the Constitution and ran against the diversity of American religion.[20]

Black's opinion was relatively uncontroversial in the wider public. Protestant liberals, in an indication of their increasingly direct defense of individual rights, hailed the decision as, in the words of the *Christian Century*, "a reaffirmation of a basic American principle of pluralism." But it was hard to square the decision with the court's upholding of Sunday Laws, handed down a month earlier, or even with the *Zorach* opinion's declaration that "we are a religious people whose institutions presuppose a Supreme Being."[21]

The case, in that way, was confusing. The court was prepared to confront outright discrimination in the name of pluralism as it understood it. But it was not fully prepared to roll back mainstream Christian power and privilege, as it showed in the Sunday Laws case. And it was especially reluctant to do anything that would make it seem antireligious, which is part of the reason it listed secular humanism as a religion even though many secular humanists would reject the label. The effect of the court's ruling in *Torcaso* was to secularize law, even though the rhetoric was couched in a protection for religion.

The court would not be able to rely on such prevarication for much longer. Having indicated that it was willing to hear cases again, the challengers would soon materialize, this time around the far more explosive issue of school prayer.

The problem was an old one. Going back to the beginning of public schooling, prayers had been recited in schools, often by the teacher, sometimes by the principal, occasionally by local ministers, and frequently through rote prayers, such as the Lord's Prayer, said by everyone. In New York the Board of Regents of the New York public-school system decided to compose a prayer that would, as the board later explained, teach children "that Almighty God is their Creator and that by Him, they have been endowed with the inalienable rights of life, liberty and the pursuit of happiness."[22]

The prayer itself was fairly anodyne, by design. After the pledge of allegiance, the children were instructed to say, "Almighty God, we acknowledge our dependence upon Thee, and we beg Thy blessings upon us, our parents, our teachers and our Country. Amen."[23]

As the prayer was rolled out in New York schools, it ran into the increasing religious diversity of American life. That diversity had already caused strife. In Nassau County in Long Island, the tension was the result of an influx of newer residents, many of them liberal and nonreligious Jews. The older residents, now often with grown children, were Protestant and Catholic. They had built up a variety of Christian practices in the schools that included Christmas pageants, clergy-offered prayers, and other Christian rites. The Jewish arrivals resented the Christian privilege embedded in the school calendar and in the school day. The older residents resented the influx of children, the need to build new schools, and the refusal to conform to the latently Christian forms of public religion in the area.[24]

The rollout of the Regents' Prayer in Nassau County was the last straw for those who objected to the public role of Christianity. A couple of Jewish parents decided to sue. The ACLU got involved and offered to sponsor the litigation. Jewish residents were verbally attacked by outraged Christian neighbors. Eventually the litigants were joined by others so that the case went forward with five sets of parents: two families of religious Jews, one family of Ethical Culturists, one Unitarian family, and one family with no religious affiliation.[25]

Pfeffer was not convinced that the prayer was obviously sectarian. He also disliked the fact that so many of the parents were Jewish, nonbelievers, or freethinkers of one kind or another. And after getting burned in the *Zorach* case, he wanted to approach the Supreme Court with litigation he was absolutely confident he could win. Pfeffer kept the AJC from explicit support, but he did write an amicus brief for the Synagogue Council of America, whose religious identification helped him affirm the notion that his position was not irreligious. The other major Jewish organizations also shied away from the case because of the obvious anti-Semitic dynamics of the controversy.[26]

The parents' position was straightforward. They asserted that the Regents' Prayer was sectarian because it was theistic; that it was inherently coercive because it made a person self-identify as a nonconformist and therefore violated the privacy of religious belief; and that it involved state support for religion in violation of the establishment clause. The Board of Regents, supported by nineteen state attorneys general, held that the prayer was nonsectarian and entirely in keeping with past educational practices.[27]

During oral argument the justices actively interrogated both sides. They asked the plaintiff's lawyer about the many religious rituals that were ubiquitous in American public life: the use of "under God" in the pledge, Bible reading in schools, prayers before legislatures. The lawyer for the parents, William J. Butler, sidestepped these other practices while pressing the point that the Regents' Prayer was obviously religious and sectarian.

"The reason why this prayer is said every day in the public schools is to inculcate into the children our love for God and a respect for the Almighty," he told the justices.

"Is that a bad thing?" John Marshall Harlan asked.

"I want to make it absolutely clear before this Court that I come here not as an antagonist of religion," Butler responded. "We come here in the firm belief that the best safety of religion in the

United States and freedom of religion is to keep religion out of our public life and not to confound . . . the civil with the religious."[28]

The Board of Regents, by contrast, tried to deemphasize the religious quality of the prayer without entirely denying it. Rather than propagating religiousness, their lawyer Bertram B. Daiker said, the prayer assumed religiousness. The people were religious, so the daily practices of the school would reflect that attitude without an attempt at propagating belief by the state.

"You say it isn't teaching religion to take for granted that which underlies our whole national life," Frankfurter suggested. "You don't promote the air which you breathe."

"That's correct, sir," Daiker responded. "This is an affirmation of all that we have learned since we were youngsters." He pointed out that it was the same thing that happened when the Supreme Court crier said, "God save the United States and this honorable Court."

Earl Warren was not persuaded. "Would [there] be any difference in your mind," he asked, "if we were to require every litigant and every lawyer who comes into this Court, before he receives any recognition from this Court, to deliver the prayer that your children in the schools have delivered?"

Daiker responded that the prayer was not compulsory. This was not a case involving, in his characterization, "a captive child."[29]

But Warren was not so sure. Back in conference he confronted the issue head on. "It is practically conceded that this is religious instruction, and is so intended," he said. As such, the court had no choice. "It is a violation of the church–state rule under the First Amendment. . . . [It] is the camel's head under the tent," Warren concluded.

Everyone agreed but Potter Stewart. "I am still in doubt and not at rest," he told his colleagues.[30]

The case presented a conundrum given the court's historically naïve and frankly convoluted reasoning in earlier cases. But if the justices saw the dilemma, it was not apparent in the resulting 6–1 opinion written by Black. The court found that the prayer was obviously religious and that the establishment clause prohibited the government from composing prayers for anyone. Black offered his usual history lesson about why Madison and Jefferson had thought it necessary to avoid governmental entanglement with religion, which he claimed had characterized American practice. And he defended the court from accusations that it was antireligious. "It is neither sacrilegious nor anti-religious to say that each separate government in this country should stay out of the business of writing or sanctioning official prayers," Black wrote, "and leave that purely religious function to the people themselves and to those the people choose to look for guidance."[31]

Black's opinion was relatively restrained and borderline disingenuous. By shrouding his opinion in a historical lecture on Madison's and Jefferson's thoughts on church and state, he rhetorically made the court into the conservator of American heritage rather than a modernizing force bringing about secular change.

Douglas, writing in concurrence, dispensed with the disingenuous rhetoric. The real issue before the court, in his opinion, was whether or not the state could finance or mandate a religious exercise. "Our system at the federal and state levels is presently honeycombed with such financing," he wrote. He referenced the prayer uttered by the Supreme Court crier, the legislative prayers at both the state and the federal levels, the prayer in schools all over the nation. He would strike them all. "I think it is an unconstitutional undertaking whatever form it takes," he said.[32]

Stewart, writing in a lone dissent, protested the damage being done to "the spiritual heritage of our Nation." He pointed out, like Douglas, that the religious notions embedded in the Regents' Prayer were mirrored in other institutions of American life. They were either all valid or all invalid. Stewart thought they must all be valid.[33]

In spite of Douglas's and Stewart's provocations, the majority of the court had tried hard to avoid taking a stand on other public religious practices. They were really unsure of their direction. But regardless of the avoidance, as the New York Times pointed out, "the clear implication of the ruling," which Douglas had simply articulated, was that any religious ceremony sponsored by the state "would be suspect."[34]

Others saw the implication as well. Public reaction to the decision was immediate and visceral, though it betrayed the usual sectarian split. Some religious groups voiced support. The New York Board of Rabbis praised the decision as correct because prayer in schools was "not in conformity with the spirit of the American concept of the separation of church and state." Dean M. Kelly of the National Council of Churches, the liberal Protestant group, said that Christians should support a decision that obviously "protects the religious rights of minorities." Thirteen prominent Unitarian Universalist ministers issued a statement defending the holding as "sound in respect to principle" and "in the interest of religion."[35]

Many other religious leaders expressed opposition. Catholic bishops were incensed. Cardinal McIntyre of Los Angeles denounced the opinion as "positively shocking and scandalizing." "It is not a decision according to law," he continued, "but a decision of license." Cardinal Cushing of Boston said the court's ruling was a vehicle for communism. "It is ridiculous to have a motto like 'In God We Trust' on our coins and to begin legislative sessions with a chaplain's prayer and at the same time prevent children from opening classes with public school prayer," he said. Cardinal Spellman pronounced himself shocked. A few days later he had more to say. He called the decision "a tragic misreading of the prayerfully weighed words of our founding fathers." He also noted that the church endorsed the prayer. The Vatican itself soon weighed in, supporting Spellman's statements.[36]

Conservative Protestant figures piled on. The evangelist Billy Graham announced that he was disappointed because the court's decision was "another step toward secularism in the United States." Stanley Mooneyham, the director of information for the National Association of Evangelicals (NAE), complained about the focus on minorities. "The only way left for the majority to express their opinion on this matter," he said, "is to have the majority push for a Constitutional amendment."[37]

Former presidents denounced the decision. Herbert Hoover objected to the ruling as "a disintegration of a sacred American heritage." Dwight Eisenhower complained that the court misunderstood history. "I always thought that this nation was essentially a religious one," he said. Of the living ex-presidents, only Harry S. Truman sought to reinforce the court's authority. He reminded everyone that the Supreme Court was "the interpreter of the Constitution."[38]

Congress was apoplectic. In the days after the decision legislative business came to a standstill as one after another congressman rose to deplore the court's ruling. The rhetoric was strident and biting. Representative Frank J. Becker, a Republican of Nassau County, called the decision "the most tragic in the history of the United States." Representative John Bell Williams, a Mississippi Democrat, condemned the decision as "a deliberate and carefully planned conspiracy to substitute materialism for spiritual values." Senator Eugene J. McCarthy, a Democrat from Minnesota, said the ruling was part of a trend toward "not just a secularized Government but a secularized society." Representative L. Mendel Rivers, a Democrat from South Carolina, said that the court had "now officially stated its disbelief in God Almighty." To Rivers, it had shown its true colors in more ways than one. The justices on the court, Rivers said, were "legislating—they never adjudicate—with one eye on the Kremlin and the other on the National Association for the Advancement of Colored People."[39]

The outrage got ugly fast. Representative George Andrews, a Democrat from Alabama, complained that the court "put Negroes in the schools and [has] now taken God out." Many of the Jewish plaintiffs were threatened. Lawrence Roth, one of the parents, was bombarded with messages calling him a "Communist kike" and telling him to "go back to Russia." Frances Roth, his wife, told *Newsweek*, "I have a feeling of sadness because these are so called godly people. If their God teaches them to wish my kids get polio and my house be bombed, then I think he hasn't done a very good job with them."[40]

Inevitably, the press began to report on the religious affiliations of the justices in an attempt to suss out their personal attitude toward religion. Black and Warren were Baptists, reporters announced. Clark, Harlan, and Douglas were Presbyterians (Clark had been a Presbyterian elder for many years; Douglas was a minister's son). White and Stewart were Episcopalians. Brennan was the sole Roman Catholic. Frankfurter, the lone Jew, responded "No comment" whenever asked about his religious affiliation.[41]

Two days after the ruling, with the public still irate, President Kennedy addressed the issue in a press conference.

"Mr. President, in the furor over the Supreme Court's decision on prayer in the schools, some members in Congress have been introducing legislation for constitutional amendments," a reporter told him by way of preface. "Can you give us your opinion of the deci-sion itself and of these moves of the Congress to circumvent it?"[42]

Kennedy was quick in his response. He acknowledged that he had not seen the language of the proposed amendments, but he thought that the Supreme Court decision ought to be supported, even if people disagreed with it. That was especially true of a sub-ject like prayer. "We have in this case a very easy remedy," Ken-nedy said, "and that is to pray ourselves. . . . I would think that it would be a welcome reminder to every American family that we can pray a good deal more at home, we can attend our churches with a good deal more fidelity, and we can make the true meaning of prayer much more important in the lives of all our children."[43]

But Kennedy's response served to inflame the controversy. Pri-vate prayer only advanced the secularizing thrust that so many people decried. The issue, in that way, was not really about the spe-cifics of the Regents' Prayer or the ability of the state to compose prayers for its children. The controversy was symbolic of a wider set of social transformations that some religious people lamented. "What many observers saw last week as an erosion of deep-seated religious traditions," *Newsweek* said, "was actually another sign of America's continuing transition from a primarily Protestant coun-try to an essentially pluralistic one."[44]

Oddly, given that the ruling did not apply to the parochial school system, Catholics were the ones most upset. Many bishops could not let it go. Several months after the decision, Spellman was still criticizing the court. His position had conspiratorial and somewhat hysterical overtones. He saw the court's decision as part of a wider movement, as he put it, "to take God out of the public school and to force the child out of the private school." The result would be "the establishment of a new religion of secularism."[45]

The Jesuits over at *America* thought they understood the leaders of the movement: Jews. *America* had expressed distrust about the Jewish position on church and state for some time. Back in 1953, after the *Zorach* decision, the magazine had run an editorial admon-ishing the AJC for abandoning "the Christian, and traditionally American, position" that religion was essential to society. "Chris-tians have learned from history that absolute separatism is the slogan of anti-religious government," *America* wrote, "the USSR's use of it being the most alarming example today."[46]

A month after Spellman's comments, *America* returned to the issue in an editorial entitled "To Our Jewish Friends." It was an oddly twisting performance. The magazine began by lamenting the spike in anti-Semitism that had occurred since the prayer decision. It took pains to point out that it was not seeking to contribute to that anti-Semitism. But the magazine thought that Jews needed to consider their course carefully. There was a movement to eradicate religion from public life. "Along with the well-publicized Jewish spokesman, Leo Pfeffer, and such organizations as the American Jewish Congress," *America* explained, "responsibility for the concerted opposition to the New York prayer—and to other forms of religious practice in the public schools and in public life—belongs to the American Civil Liberties Union, the Ethical Culture Society, the Humanist Associations, some Unitarians, many atheists and certain other groups with doctrinaire views on the meaning and application of the principle of separation of Church and State."[47]

The problem, as *America* saw it, was that Pfeffer and other prominent spokesmen were pursuing a strategy of secularization that invited backlash. Pfeffer and his allies sought to manipulate public opinion to pressure the court to adopt their absolutist vision. Even moderate Jewish groups sought to create a climate of opinion to further the separation of church and state, which people then blamed on Jews as a whole. The editors thought that "responsible Jewish spokesmen" ought to disavow Pfeffer and other secularizers. They had to think about their self-preservation. "What will have been accomplished if our Jewish friends win all the legal immunities they seek," *America* asked, "but thereby paint themselves into a corner of social and cultural alienation?"[48]

Jewish leaders were inevitably distressed. Pfeffer later explained, with barely concealed disgust, what it was like to be name-checked by the Jesuits at *America*. "In singling me out as the arch villain who exercises Svengalian influence on all the Jewish organizations, rabbinical, congregational, and secular," Pfeffer wrote, "the editors of *America* manifested surprising ignorance of American Jewry." The anti-Semitism of the piece was obvious to Pfeffer and was confirmed by *America*'s decision not to mention two of the more likely villains: the court and the plaintiffs. At the time, Pfeffer decided that the best course was to stay silent.[49]

The burden of response fell on the American Jewish Committee, who wrote the magazine to protest the editorial. The committee pointed out that *America*'s open letter was, in effect, a story of Jewish conspiracy (a classic anti-Semitic trope) dressed up as a warning against anti-Semitism. It demanded that Jews abandon their position on the First Amendment and implied that they were themselves to blame for anti-Semitism if they did not. But if the editors of *America* were actually disturbed by anti-Semitism, they could have warned their readers about the entrance of bigotry into public debate. "Your warning, instead, is issued to Jews," the committee wrote. The effect of *America*'s editorial was to advance the anti-Semitism that its editors supposedly decried.[50]

Christian Century spoke more plainly. Noting the controversy, the magazine denounced *America*'s "thinly veiled threat" issued behind an expression of care. "The purpose of the piece seems to be to frighten Jews into deserting Protestants and other Americans who support the Supreme Court's ruling," *Christian Century* noted. "Do the editors of *America* mean to imply that the only way Jews will be able to forestall anti-Semitic attacks is to maintain silence on issues involving constitutional liberties of all citizens, including Jews?"[51]

America responded, with a certain defensiveness, that the editorial was either misunderstood or misrepresented. They sought only to question Pfeffer's ability to speak for all Jews. Catholic readers had understood the point, they thought, as evidenced by the many Catholic journals that echoed *America*'s call for Jews to take a stand against secularization. Critics had accused them of the anti-Semitism that they were warning against. It was like shouting to a friend about an oncoming truck, they said, and then having the friend turn on you and accuse you of driving the truck.[52]

As the fallout from the school-prayer decision continued, the next bomb was already in the air. In Philadelphia a young Unitarian named Ellery Schempp began a program of silent protest over the school's daily practice of saying the Lord's Prayer and Bible reading. Rather than standing with the rest of the class, he sat silently and read from the Koran. "My homeroom teacher told me I would have to pay attention," he later said. "I replied that in conscience, I didn't think I could." Eventually his teacher excused him from class, allowing him to read elsewhere.[53]

The next year, his senior year, the principal made him come back to the classroom because, he told Ellery, Pennsylvania state law required students to participate in religious exercises. Schempp responded by contacting the ACLU, which eventually agreed to represent him.[54]

Other challenges were also forming. The state of Maryland was experiencing controversy begun by a divorcee named Madalyn Murray. Though she had earlier been somewhat religious, by the 1950s Murray had rejected her earlier religious belief, embraced a somewhat militant form of philosophical anarchism, and had two sons by two men, neither of whom was her husband. In spite of her personal heterodoxy, she kept her irreligious beliefs largely to herself until her eldest son refused to participate in the required religious exercises in school.[55]

The consequences were immediate. He was beaten up repeatedly—Murray alleged over one hundred times—by his Catholic classmates. The torment was so severe that her son was later placed in psychiatric care. But the abuse was not limited to her son. She received constant threatening phone calls. One morning she found her cat strangled and hanging from a tree in the yard. The family received a voluminous stream of hate mail, which she collected and curated. Her idea was to generate a trail should a threat be acted upon. She also had the idea that she might publish the lot under the title *Letters from Christians*. Eventually she decided to sue Baltimore City Schools for requiring the religious exercises that led to the bullying.[56]

If conservative religious leaders could invent an antireligious zealot to lead the secularist cause, that person would be Madalyn Murray. In explaining to city officials her resistance to religious instruction, she told them, "I believe that the Virgin Mary probably played around as much as I did and certainly was capable of orgasm." She later said her ultimate goal was not merely to find a little freedom for herself and her son. She wanted, in her words, "social revolution." "I don't want to die before I have made a revolution in America," she told the journalist Robert Anton Wilson.[57]

As the combined Schempp and Murray cases made their way through the court system, conservative Protestants began to speak out. The evangelical magazine *Christianity Today* referred darkly to the "atheistic and naturalistic forces . . . seeking to foist their partisan prejudices upon our national institutions." It warned that the United States was facing a declension away from God and "into the service of anti-Christ." It predicted that should Murray succeed, the public-school system would become an irreligious vehicle of "widespread skepticism about everything sacred and holy."[58]

During oral argument some of the justices agonized about the same thing. Murray's lawyer, Leonard J. Kerpelman, told the court, "What we have here is a religious ceremony . . . which is sectarian." Baltimore's arrangements amounted to an establishment of religion in which Murray's rights of conscience as well as those of her son were nullified.

Justice Potter Stewart, who was visibly disturbed by Kerpelman's statement, asked whether striking down the practice would not nullify the religious rights of others who wanted it.

Kerpelman responded that one could not establish a religion and call it free exercise. State support for religion was state support for religion. Free exercise involved the individual's right to arrive at his or her own religious ideas, free of state interference. To explain what he meant, he pointed out that although he was Jewish, his young daughter, who attended public schools, believed that Jesus was the son of God. She had gotten the idea through the religious exercises at her school. "I'm not too worried," he told the court. "I think she'll get over it, but I would rather she had never come to this belief."[59]

Thomas B. Finan, the attorney general of Maryland, said in response that the school system was caught in a dilemma. If you ban theism, he said, then you establish atheism. Neutrality was not possible. So what Maryland tried to do was to recognize the long-standing Christian heritage of the country, while excusing any student who wished not to participate. It adopted a religious system that accommodated the irreligious or the religiously different. It did not adopt a secular system.[60]

Similar issues came up during oral argument in the Schempp case, which was scheduled just after Murray's. Ellery Schempp was no longer a plaintiff. During the appellate process he graduated from high school, and the state of Pennsylvania modified its law without doing away with the exercises. Schempp's case became moot. ACLU lawyers switched to his younger siblings as plaintiffs. Their attorney, a Unitarian named Henry W. Sawyer III, told the court that Pennsylvania's practice of prayer and Bible reading was obviously sectarian and so ought to be prohibited.[61]

In response, the deputy attorney general for Pennsylvania, John D. Killian III, stated that the removal of Bible reading from the schools would indicate hostility to religion. It would also "open a Pandora's box of litigation which could serve to remove from American public life every vestige of our religious heritage." But in an indication of the tortuous weakness of the state's position, Killian further proposed that prayer and Bible reading were not really religious. As the school practiced it, he told the court, prayer or Bible reading consisted of "a secular exercise with a secular, that is, moral purpose."[62]

During conference, all the justices but Potter Stewart agreed that the practices were unconstitutional. They violated the establishment clause. Stewart, in response, tried to reframe the issue.

"All of our establishment clause cases are wrong, historically," he said. They upheld the separation of church and state in a way that never existed in the past. Now, he said, the establishment clause had become obsolete. No one really talked about paying churches, which was his definition of an establishment. All the current cases were about governmental support or nonsupport of religion, which was about religious freedom.

What Stewart wanted to do was to have all the religion cases sent back to the states to allow them the opportunity to give every religious sect, including the atheists, their own exercises in the schools. "The state has an affirmative duty," he told his colleagues, "to create a religious atmosphere in schools where anyone and everyone can pray and worship as he wishes." His proposal would become enormously powerful in the future.[63]

But at the time, the others were not convinced. Arthur Goldberg pressed Stewart on the narrowness of his vision. Stewart clearly had not thought this through, Goldberg implied, and he had no real sense of the diversity of American life.

"Schools can't be opened to every sect," Goldberg told Stewart. "How about Black Muslims? How about screwball groups? You can't draw a line that is a viable one. It would mean drawing lines that would interfere with free exercise." The act of drawing a line itself would negate some people's religious beliefs. The way to respect the massive diversity of American religious life was to remove the state from promoting religion in any way.[64]

The resulting 8–1 opinion, written by Tom Clark, said as much, though the court tried to blunt the message. Once the two cases were combined, Murray's lawsuit should have been the controlling opinion. It had been filed first. But the justices instead put the *Schempp* case at the head, and Tom Clark's opinion made repeated reference to the Schempps as an intact Unitarian family, in implicit contrast to the atheistic and libertine Murray.[65]

Clark also tried to downplay the transformative quality of the ruling. Rather than acknowledge that the court was overturning practices dating back to the beginning of public schooling in the United States, Clark again portrayed the Pennsylvania arrangement as aberrant. To the district's contention that Bible reading was not really religious, Clark noted that school officials read from multiple versions of the Bible—the Catholic Douay, the Protestant King James, and what the court called "the Jewish Holy Scriptures." In using alternate versions, the school district implicitly acknowledged the sectarian implications of its practice and the deeply religious, rather than secular, import of Bible reading and prayer.[66]

But Clark did acknowledge that the wall of separation metaphor did not really help much in deciding these cases. So he offered a new standard to determine when a practice violated the establishment clause. His test was twofold. Legislation must have (1) a secular purpose (2) whose primary effect neither promoted nor inhibited religion. The state must be neutral. On that test, prayer and Bible reading in schools were unconstitutional because they did not have a secular purpose and because they promoted religion.

The other justices, though, did not quite agree with Clark's reasoning, an indication of the issue's touchiness. They were slowly beginning to wake up to how far their jurisprudence was pushing them. As a result, they fractured, filing three concurrences. William

J. Brennan Jr., the court's sole Roman Catholic, tried to reframe the issue to confront what he called "an increasingly troublesome First Amendment paradox."[67]

What the court should have seen, Brennan said, was that there was a logical interrelationship between the free-exercise clause and the establishment clause. The two clauses were so connected that allowing free exercise, such as prayer in schools, could be said to create an establishment. Alternatively, striking down the establishment could be said to limit the free religious exercise of those who wish to pray in school. It had not been a problem in the past, Brennan declared without evidence, but it had now become one because of the many religious groups with vastly divergent sensibilities that inhabited the United States. To solve the problem, Brennan began to articulate a doctrine of religious privacy as the only effective solution to the pluralized nature of public schools. That meant, in effect, the expulsion of religion from the public schools, though Brennan did not quite say so. At the same time, he allowed that in other aspects of life there might be some kind of cooperation or accommodation between religion and the government. But given the delicate subject of the education of children, he wrote, religious privatization was the only clean response to the situation.

Goldberg, joined by Harlan, also agreed with the court's conclusion that prayer and Bible reading had to go, but he rejected the test proposed by Clark. It implied, in Goldberg's words, "a brooding and pervasive devotion to the secular and a passive, or even active, hostility to the religious." Goldberg's desire was to avoid the French model of secularism in which the government took no cognizance of religion. So although he agreed with the decision, he, like Brennan, wanted it known that the goal was not a thoroughgoing removal of religion from public life, which is where he thought Clark's test would go.[68]

Douglas, like the others, agreed with the court's conclusion, but he rejected the pose of moderation struck by the court and the further limitation of the decision proposed by the other concurrences. True freedom from religion required not merely striking down prayer and Bible reading in schools but also much more. He declined to specify any limits whatsoever, which tacitly embraced a sweeping sort of secularism that all the other justices would reject.

That left only Stewart to dissent from the actual holding. Again, like Douglas, he pointed out that the government and religion interacted in countless ways. Like Brennan, he predicted that a doctrinaire reading of the establishment clause would violate the free-exercise clause. He had objected to the wall-of-separation language in the past, and he now objected to the attempt by the court to offer a more nuanced test. The problem with the majority was that it always ended in a muddle. The choice really was between Douglas's approach and his, he thought. There was either a thoroughgoing secularism or there was the embrace of religion in public life supported by the state. Either a person rejected religion from public life or a person allowed it and nurtured it so long as it was not coercive. There was no in-between.

The case was, in that way, revealing. In spite of the 8–1 majority the court was at odds with itself and unclear about the secularism that it was unfolding. The court's negative secularism, with the thinness of its liberal commitments, always threatened to tip into other directions or to unravel entirely.

But the justices' disagreement did not matter in the short term, given the core of their agreements. Reporters immediately pointed out the far-reaching effect of the case. The ruling would require changes in 41 percent of school districts in thirty-seven states. Policies requiring prayer and Bible reading were especially common in large districts, and thus the ruling probably affected the majority of American schools and the vast majority of American schoolchildren.[69]

In the aftermath of the decision, Ellery Schempp talked about the case and the hate calls his family received. "They all found in us an example of some group they had a prejudice against," he said. "They'd ask: 'What are you—Jews?' or if we were Catholics, Polish, Arabians. Each person saw in us something he hates."[70]

Catholics and conservative Protestants deplored the decision. The NAE said the ruling "augments the trend toward complete secularization" and "veers away from our national heritage of reverence." Harold Ockenga, a prominent evangelical leader and president of Fuller Seminary, rejected what he saw as the court's evasive reasoning. "A neutral or secular state," he said, "while preserving the nation from dominion by a denomination, leaves America in the same position as Communist Russia."[71]

Cardinal McIntyre of Los Angeles echoed Ockenga. The decision, he said, "can only mean that our American heritage of philosophy, of religion, and of freedom are [sic] being abandoned in imitation of Soviet philosophy, of Soviet materialism, and of Soviet-regimented liberty." Cardinal Cushing of Boston said simply, "The Communists are enjoying this day." Cardinal Spellman of New York said, thunderously, in a sermon, "No one who believes in God, and I say believes in God, can approve such a decision."[72]

But Spellman's homily was subverted by facts. Many religious groups did approve of the decision. The National Council of Churches, speaking for forty million church members, applauded the ruling as a reminder that "teaching for religious commitment is the responsibility of the home and the community of faith ... rather than [of] the public schools." Right Reverend Arthur Lichtenberger, presiding bishop of the Episcopal Church, affirmed the decision as being in line with the court's "responsibility to assure freedom and equality to all groups of believers and non-believers."[73]

The religious division stymied conservatives. Within a year the House held hearings on a constitutional amendment that would have allowed prayer and Bible reading in schools. During the first week many witnesses warned of moral decay, of a marching atheism of the Madalyn Murray variety, and of the denial of the nation's religious heritage. But soon the committee leaders lost control. Liberal Protestant groups demanded that they be included. When they appeared before the panel, liberal leaders spoke against the amendment and affirmed instead that the court's decision rightly acknowledged the diversity of American life. Seeing the religious disagreement, even some conservative groups dropped support for the plan because it might open the door for a scramble to control the school system that they could lose. A few months later the Senate also held hearings on a constitutional amendment to allow prayer and Bible reading back in schools. But by that point they had trouble finding any religious leaders who would support the cause.[74]

The following year *Time* marveled that church leaders now overwhelmingly agreed with the ruling. "Almost every Protestant denomination—ranging from the Seventh-day Adventists to the Episcopal National Council—has gone on record endorsing the decision," the magazine noted. They were joined by virtually every Jewish organization. And even the Catholic bishops had begun to come around, going from visceral opposition to muted acceptance. Some were still staunchly and vocally opposed, notably the evangelicals and some of the Catholic hardliners, but they were outnumbered.[75]

Leo Pfeffer was ecstatic. "It is quite probable that the year 1963 will prove to have been the most momentous year not only in American church–state relations but in interreligious relationships as well since the First Amendment was added to the Constitution in 1791," he wrote. The decisions were so historic because they heralded a true secularism in which, as he put it, "no particular religious faith may any longer impose its culture, its values, and its political and moral standards on the nation as a whole."[76]

But if that was the goal, the court was continually surprised by it. The justices, not really clear about what they were doing, had declared a principle of church–state separation and then found themselves confronting the entire panoply of preferential treatment given to Christianity in American life. The result was a constant shock when confronted with challenges they had not foreseen and were unsure how to address.

Two years after the *Schempp* case the court was brought up short again when a group of pacifists led by Daniel Andrew Seeger claimed exemption from the military draft. None of the litigants belonged to an organized religious body, and none said their objections were explicitly derived from God, though they still avowed some kind of religious sensibility. Federal draft law allowed an exemption only when someone objected to war on the basis of the moral directives of a Supreme Being.

The court was confounded by what to do with the law.

"I have difficulty here," Warren told his colleagues in conference. The justices did not want to strike down the law. But they also did not want to privilege certain religions over others that did not see a religious being. They decided to fudge the issue.[77]

In a unanimous opinion written by Clark, the court expanded religious freedom to include political, sociological, and philosophical reasoning. If a heterodox person could articulate a principled objection to war, then that person could be exempt from the draft. Douglas issued a concurring opinion to say the ruling was applicable to an explicitly irreligious person as well, even though that was not necessarily the case with the current plaintiffs and even though the court had not said as much.[78]

Soon the court heard another case that should have been an obvious application of its jurisprudence but that it was again surprised by. A few years earlier Estelle Griswold, the head of Planned Parenthood in Connecticut, opened a birth-control clinic with the Yale gynecologist C. Lee Buxton. The two women were soon arrested and convicted for violating a Connecticut law that banned contraception. The law was similar to other anticontraception laws around the country, though stricter than the norm. The pair appealed the case all the way to the Supreme Court, demanding that the law be struck down as unconstitutional.[79]

"I am bothered with this case," Warren told his colleagues in conference.

"I am not at rest on it," Black agreed. He thought the policy was bad, but he could not figure out how or whether to strike down the law.

Douglas had no such compunction. He thought the law was an obvious violation of personal rights. The case came "in the radiation of the 1st Amendment," he said. It had been both passed and sustained as a result of Christian—especially Catholic—sentiment.

"I agree with Bill Douglas," Clark said. "There is a right to marry, to have a home, and to have children."

Black regarded the state as able to abolish marriage, so why, he asked Clark, could it not regulate the affairs of a family?

"This is an area where I have a right to be left alone," Clark responded.[80]

The resulting 7–2 opinion, written by Douglas, followed Clark's lead. It overturned the Connecticut law and sought to sum up the jurisprudence of the court. Douglas recounted the constitutional revolution created by the Fourteenth Amendment and the court's subsequent decisions to incorporate aspects of the Bill of Rights into the Fourteenth Amendment. Many of those decisions went beyond the strict text of the Constitution, assuming that the Bill of Rights created "zones of privacy" where the individual was free from governmental scrutiny. The constitutional purpose, Douglas held, was to shield the individual from governmentally enforced moral sanction that would allow individuals to make free choices.[81]

Writing in a dissent joined by Stewart, Black rejected what he saw as the loose reasoning of the court. He could see no way to uphold a right to privacy within constitutional law, even if he was opposed to the legislation personally.

But Black's dissent missed the obvious directionality of the court's decisions. In a sense, the notion of a right to privacy was the logical terminus of the court's rights revolution begun by Brandeis and Holmes nearly fifty years earlier. It involved the privatization both of religion and of formerly public moral norms so that individuals could make choices free from governmental pressure. The pluralization of American public life involved the multiplication of religious, moral, and intellectual authorities. That multiplication made it difficult to choose one over another without wading into a contested religious arena. To avoid religious disagreement and entanglement, the court declined to adjudicate between authorities. It left the decision about contraception to the individual in her or his private life. That still left many issues up for grabs and all the tensions of prior rulings in place.

CHAPTER SEVEN

The Death of God

These developments—the growing assertiveness of civil society groups, the rising prominence of sectarian rivalry, the maturation of the court's rights revolution, and the growing impulse toward inclusion and toward liberalism—were a beginning, not an end. Part of the dilemma was the political philosophy expressed by the Supreme Court. Prior to midcentury many people had operated with the vague sense, as the Harvard political scientist V. O. Key put it in 1942, "that the government is identical with the mass of the population and that by some mysterious process the 'will of the people' is translated into governmental decision and thereby people 'rule themselves.' "[1]

In fact, as the conflict at midcentury showed, society was composed of groups. Politics consisted primarily of group conflict. Policy emerged from disagreement, bargaining, and consensus among groups who, individually, could muster only a plurality within American society. But when several groups worked together, they were able to achieve a stable governing alliance in American life. This is known as the pluralist conception of politics.[2]

The court on some level recognized the political reality and saw itself as part of a pluralistic social and political process. When groups engaged in litigation, they were using suits, the court said

in 1963, as "a form of political expression." "Groups which find
themselves unable to achieve their objectives through the ballot
frequently turn to the courts," it continued. "Under the conditions
of modern government, litigation may well be the sole practicable
avenue open to a minority to petition for redress of grievances." As
a result, the court became a principal place for minorities, religious
or otherwise, to be recognized in American public life.[3]

But the dilemma of pluralism was about to be faced by more
than just the court, in part because the political developments of the
sixties forced a confrontation with the scale and scope of American
multiplicity that had hitherto been unimaginable. It turned out that
midcentury conceptions of diversity were too narrow, which ac-
counted for the justices' continued surprise as groups appeared before them with a bewildering number of affirmations. The narrow
conception of diversity that animated pluralist politics left many
people on the margins of American life, struggling to find ways into
the public debate.

Those other groups soon began to muscle their way more fully
into public political consciousness to decenter white Christian conceptions of the United States. The process had already begun in
1955 with the start of the civil rights movement, though initially the
movement posed no real challenge to the public role of American
Christianity. Movement leaders were mainly ministers who spoke
the language of theology and who called on the American public
to embrace black rights as a matter of Christian religious interest.
For white Christian groups, who viewed themselves as guardians of
American public culture, the religious language of the early civil
rights movement was merely an invitation to extend their custodianship to the acquisition of black rights. It advanced pluralist politics while keeping Christian religious prerogatives in place.[4]

By 1960, though, the cultural and social dynamics that struc-
tured the era would take a turn. David Hollinger has spoken of
two long-term processes that came to a head during the 1960s.
The first, which he calls "cognitive demystification," dated to the
nineteenth century and was the original impetus for Protestant liberalizers to update their faith. It involved the critical assessment of
religious truth in light of modern biological, geological, sociological, biblical, and political understandings. By the sixties a growing

commitment to cognitive demystification led a variety of religious people, especially Protestants, to engage in self-interrogation about their religious beliefs, their social role, and the American political system.

The second process, which Hollinger calls "demographic diversification," proved to be even more convulsive. The growing diversity within American life and the resulting encounter with difference tended to call into question whether the practices and norms of a group were universalizable across an entire society or societies. This dynamic, which also dated back to the nineteenth century, was sparked by the massive migration of various ethnic and religious groups into the United States and the centrifugal force of the American religious scene that always threatened to pull apart the religious center. By the 1960s demographic diversification took on a new and more pronounced form, one that would challenge white Christians.[5]

As usual, many religious leaders were unprepared for what was about to happen. The problem was a set of mental limits that white Christians adopted when thinking about other people. The way leaders tended to talk about religious diversification always presumed that religion-in-general furnished a stable basis for society in spite of religious variance. The white Christian confrontation with otherness was, as a consequence, often somewhat superficial because beneath the experience of difference was the presumption of a sameness rooted in ecumenical faith. If only the underlying sameness-within-difference could be uncovered, then the essentially religious foundations of society could be maintained.

But the experience of the sixties shattered that presumption. It began in 1960 with the formation of the Student Non-Violent Coordinating Committee and a more confrontational approach to protests. As black student groups began to drive the civil rights movement, and as white, disproportionately Jewish students followed their lead into activism, their critique of American society broadened and deepened. Soon the civil rights movement branched out into groups that were often led primarily or even exclusively by young people and that adopted either an overt hostility to religious faith or a belief in the irrelevance of religion to their causes.

The new movements had a similar origin. Often the awakening to activism first involved a personal awakening, a kind of self-discovery

on the part of people whose sense of themselves fell outside the normalizing categories regnant within American culture. The terminus of
that self-awakening was what would soon be called identity politics, a
pejorative term in some circles today but a revelation back then. As
the intellectual historian Andrew Hartman has said, to people coming
of age in the 1960s "identity was something to be stressed; it was
something to grow into or become. Only by becoming black, or Chicano, or a liberated woman, or an out-of-the-closet homosexual—and
only by showing solidarity with those similarly identified—could one
hope to overcome the psychological barriers to liberation imposed by
discriminatory cultural norms."[6]

The discovery of identity outside mainstream categories led to a
doubling down on that sense of self as the basis for protest. Activists
soon launched a wide-ranging assault on American political culture
that promoted women's rights, campus free speech, Black Power,
Latino worker protections, Chicano liberation, native American autonomy, antiwar dissent, and gay rights. Protest was often exponen-
tially radical, as the goal or goals became ever more transformative.
The centrifugal thrust of sixties politics became dizzying in scope,
intensity, and omnidirectional dissent. Wave after wave of increasingly angry remonstrations became the norm in the United States.[7]

The immediate effect of the identity-based movements was to
force the American public to confront the actual scope of diversity
in the United States and the ways in which such diversity had been
suppressed or ignored in the past. Affiliation with the subgroup
and differentiation from the wider society pushed the logic of pluralist politics to its obvious conclusions. Identity politics was, in
that sense, an extension of pluralist politics that simply sought to
produce an awakening in the American public consciousness about
the true scope of American multiplicity. As Stokely Carmichael and
Charles V. Hamilton put it in *Black Power: The Politics of Liberation*
(1967), "Group solidarity is necessary before a group can operate
effectively from a bargaining position of strength in a pluralistic
society."[8]

Sixties activism would eventually change the American secular
order. It led nearly every religious group to confront the astonishing diversity of the human family that could be found in American

life. And it profoundly destabilized Christian leaders, who regarded themselves as guardians of the nation. Custodianship became more difficult to sustain given the press of diverse claimants in the 1960s and the rejection of white Christian privilege articulated by many activists.

No religious group experienced the change more suddenly, or more surprisingly, than the Roman Catholic Church. The hierarchy had long depicted the church as a fortress that stood firm amidst the chaotic maelstrom of the modern world. The church remained faithful to its values, anchored to the rock of doctrine, and committed to its catholic and apostolic tradition. The self-conception of the hierarchy as promoters and articulators of an unchanging Truth had suggested to some critics an indifference to the contemporary world, an increasing detachment with which church leaders surveyed global affairs. To the prelates, though, their steadiness of leadership was a necessary component of the church's office as the explicator of an unchangeable God.[9]

Yet in spite of their public face of imperturbability, the currents of modern life were buffeting church leaders. It had been a vexing several decades for the hierarchy. By midcentury Catholic prelates looked around and began to observe the limited appeal of the church's formulations to many within Western societies. Those countries were growing more open to non-Western religious traditions or were turning away from religious traditions entirely. The erosive social dynamics, some within the leadership began to acknowledge, threatened the stability of the church unless it shored up its intellectual foundation.

Their discomfort came to a head in 1958, when Pius XII died. Although conservatives had remained in firm control of the hierarchy, the Catholic cardinals found themselves unexpectedly at odds. They were divided on a variety of issues and uncertain about the best way forward. Their division made it difficult to appoint a successor to Pius. After eleven ballots they finally settled on Cardinal Angelo Giuseppe Roncalli, a sweet old man. He was seventy-eight years old and was expected to be a short-lived caretaker pope until the cardinals could work out their divisions. But to everyone's surprise Pope John XXIII, as Roncalli called himself, immediately announced his intention to open a Second Vatican Council. His goal, he said, was to bring "the modern world into contact with the vivi-fying and perennial energies of the gospel."[10]

The opposite would more likely be the outcome, but in the early months of preparation no one could be quite sure what would happen. When the Vatican called for proposals on topics that the council might address, American bishops promptly sent their ideas. Two-thirds of the responses dealt entirely with internal church mat-ters. Many said nothing about the social, economic, and political challenges facing the church. And although some did propose that they take up questions of church and state or of religious freedom, many bishops went to the council entirely unprepared for what was to take place.[11]

John Courtney Murray, though, was hopeful. His status had been ambiguous in the years since his silencing. Just before Pius XII died, it seemed as though the Holy Office, the seat of conservatism in the Catholic church, had won explicit papal rejection of Murray's views. Murray's attempts to clarify the matter were shot down. But the condemnation stalled. Pius's sudden death, John's enthronement, and the call for a Vatican council offered new possibilities.[12]

Murray soon found vindication. When Pope John opened the council in 1962 he noted the many challenges the church faced. Their gathering offered the opportunity to address the challenges and to update Catholic tenets for the contemporary moment. To be sure, John went out of his way to defend the unchangeableness of doctrine. But, he said, "the whole world expects a step forward." The council offered an opportunity in which traditional beliefs "[could] be studied and expounded through the methods of research and through the literary forms of modern thought." The Truth would remain the same, John said. But the manner in which truths were expressed could vary.[13]

Murray immediately saw that John had endorsed his formula-tion. As he later said, "The council moved the church squarely into the world of history." That sounded simple, but it was far-reaching. It involved a series of interlocking propositions affecting the nature and understanding of truth. One must acknowledge, Murray said, that truth was part of history, that it had to be apprehended by an individual human person, and that it finally had to be experienced or lived by real people in the modern world. Bringing the church into the realm of history meant confronting the inherent subjectivity and the historical mutability of truth. That, in turn, undermined certainty, questioned authority, and required a reworking of the entire edifice of Catholic doctrine. Murray's thinking was deeply radical.[14]

The council went a long way toward working out that radicalism. By the time the council closed in 1965 the bishops had approved sixteen total documents that reformed nearly every aspect of church life. It especially changed how the church related to the world and to everyday affairs. The bishops allowed for greater participation of the laity during Mass and permitted the Mass to be conducted in the vernacular languages or languages other than Latin. It brought the Mass within the ordinary experience of the people.[15]

The council also drafted a statement on the relationship of the church to non-Christian religions. Rather than emphasizing the exclusive truth of Catholic beliefs, the bishops now spoke of "what human beings have in common." All people shared a religious sense and all religions—Hinduism, Buddhism, even folk traditions—contained aspects of truth. Speaking to the monotheistic religions, the council looked "with esteem" on Muslims and absolved Jews from guilt for Jesus's death. The statement eased the ability of Catholics to interact with non-Christians.[16]

Murray drafted the most far-reaching change of the council. After being shut out of the first session—disinvited, Murray complained, by some of his Vatican enemies—he received an invitation to the second one. Rather than stepping lightly, he drafted a statement on religious freedom. Because it altered the political theory of the church, it immediately became a point of conflict.[17]

The source of controversy, as Murray saw it, was not the notion of religious freedom per se or, rather, not just the notion of religious freedom. The deeper problem was the pattern of thought that was required to support religious freedom in the first place. The church had essentially stopped thinking about the subject with the encyclicals of Leo XIII. For hardliners within the church, Leo had articulated a long-standing Catholic position that was further systematized by subsequent canonists. It held forth the Catholic confessional state as a transhistorical and unquestionable ideal.[18]

But Murray pointed out that an alternative ideal of religious freedom had been growing among the political democracies of the

West as they confronted the level of religious dissimilarity that existed within their societies. To hold to the classical position of the church entailed a hostility toward modern constitutional law and a posture of nearly constant reaction toward its rulings. If one thought instead that doctrine could change and that that growth could occur not primarily through the church but through natural revelation that was available in the world, then there was no real reason to believe that doctrinal development ceased with Leo XIII. This was in keeping with what Murray called a proper historical consciousness.[19]

In the statement on religious freedom itself, Murray sought to further his point by making a distinction between the ecclesiastical and the political orders. Politically, Murray wrote, all people ought to seek the truth, but they can fulfill their duty to seek that truth only when protected from civil coercion. He acknowledged the plural nature of modern societies and the diversity of opinions within contemporary democracies. Given the markedly perspectival ways that people responded to truth, modern democracies seemed to require political freedom as individual people worked out their own beliefs. But the church had not historically recognized political freedom; in fact, it had rejected it. Yet it had now come to see that political freedom, in Murray's words, "[left] untouched traditional Catholic doctrine on the moral duty of men and societies toward the true religion and toward the one Church of Christ."[20]

The point was simple but profound. Political rights and religious duties were not identical. Accepting the distinction between the political and the religious allowed the church to acknowledge religious freedom in a political sense, Murray pointed out, while continuing to affirm the exclusive truth of the Catholic position in a religious sense. It also allowed the council to affirm contemporary religious freedom without explicitly disavowing any of the positions of the past. Those prior notions were true, Murray wrote, but limited to the ecclesiastical realm in a specific historical moment. The modern embrace of religious freedom was a fuller truth that allowed the church to speak to contemporary constitutional development.

When the council approved the statement, at the end of the final session in 1965, observers were amazed. It was the only con-

ciliar document addressed to the entire world and could rightly be
seen as a concession to the pluralistic realities of modern political
democracy. Joseph Fletcher, a Protestant ethicist, confessed his
astonishment that Catholic liberals had managed to drag their
church's ethics into the twentieth century. Paul Blanshard, a fierce
anti-Catholic journalist, wrote in the *Nation* that after Vatican II
Catholicism could "no longer be described as a monolithic glacier
of reactionary thought." To the man and woman on the street all of
this came as a shock. It showed that, contrary to everything that
had been taught, the Church Immutable could change.[21]

But even as Catholicism renewed itself, its reformist energies were
far outstripped by what was happening within Protestant circles.
Protestant leaders responded to the tumult of the 1960s with a
level of self-interrogation that is, even now, remarkable in its ex-
tensiveness. Their interrogation worked along the two tracks that
Hollinger has identified: demystifying the tenets of Protestant belief and confronting the dizzying diversity that emerged through
sixties politics.

   Among liberal Protestants there had long been a desire to rework
the categories of theology in light of modern, scientific knowledge.
By the 1960s the desire was intensifying. In 1961 Gabriel Vahanian, a
Princeton-educated theologian teaching at Syracuse University, published *The Death of God*. Borrowing from the nineteenth-century
German philosopher Friedrich Nietzsche, Vahanian dismissed the
picture of God that emerged from the Bible. "The essentially mytho-
logical world-view of Christianity," he wrote, "has been succeeded by
a thoroughgoing scientific view of reality, in terms of which either
God is no longer necessary, or he is neither necessary nor unnecessary: he is irrelevant—he is dead."[22]

   Vahanian's work began a movement toward what its proponents
called a secular theology within Protestantism. Two years later, as
the Supreme Court was striking down Bible reading in schools, Paul
Van Buren of the University of Texas followed Vahanian with his
book *The Secular Meaning of the Gospel*. Like Vahanian, Van Buren
rejected traditional Christian doctrines and urged religious leaders
to strip Christianity of supernatural elements in order to become
believable again.[23]

In 1965, as the court was declaring a right of privacy, Harvey Cox of Harvard Divinity School added to the literature with *The Secular City.* En route to urging a radical ethical commitment upon the church, Cox dismissed many traditional religious subjects. Doctrinal issues, cultic worship, pietistic devotion, the stuff of historical Christian life, these were all distractions from the wider work of, as Cox put it, "liberating the captives." The book was wildly successful, selling over a million copies.[24]

Others wrote in quieter, more personal ways. Thomas J. J. Altizer of Emory University spoke frankly of the corrosive power of modern scientific knowledge and the effect that that knowledge had on church life. "Lament as we may its vanished glory," he wrote in 1965, "the whole established order of Christendom is eroding about us. As its foundations disappear into the dark ocean of the past, we can experience only the receding ripples of its dying waves. Theology has met this challenge by a heroic if futile attempt to establish an island of faith, an impregnable fortress fully shielded from the dangers outside it, but a fortress containing a lighthouse that would direct a saving beacon to the surrounding darkness." Unfortunately, he wrote, the waters had now swallowed both the land and the fortress on the island of faith, leaving a lonely lighthouse that plunged directly into the water. "Having vanished from our historical present," Altizer continued, "its beacon has become a mirror reflecting the vacuity of a faith that would claim to stand upon thin air."[25]

The sense of loss among these writers was palpable. William Hamilton, a theologian at Colgate Rochester Divinity School, spoke frankly of his own creeping experience of bereavement. He first lost the language of theology, then any feeling of transcendence, both of which finally terminated in his lack of God. But the bereavement, Hamilton said, was paired with a sense of liberation from now-obsolete creeds.[26]

The movement was not without tension. Cox complained of the imprecise language that others used. What exactly caused the absence? he asked. "Is it the loss of the experience of God, the loss of the existence of God in Christianity, or the lack of adequate language to express God today?" Others questioned Cox about his desire to jettison God-talk while doubling down on Christian ethics.[27]

The *New York Times*, trying to figure out what united all the efforts, decided that they shared two basic stances. First, according to the *Times*, death-of-God theologians acknowledged the unreality of God. Second, they affirmed the mundane world as the source of spiritual and ethical inquiry. Both claims fed into the same ethical impulse common to liberal Protestantism. But the formulations dispensed with any pretense that they still believed the old truths, even if they could not quite abandon Christianity itself. The resulting theological mode could at times seem self-stultifying. Daniel Day Williams, a process theologian at the University of Chicago and a death-of-God critic, put a fine point on the tension when he said that death-of-God theology could be reduced to a relatively simple position. "There is no God," he said, in the voice of death-of-God theologians, "and Jesus is his only begotten son."[28]

The uproar remained fairly localized, in spite of press coverage, until Easter 1966. That year *Time* magazine decided to highlight, in its words, "the visibly growing concern among theologians about God and the secularized world of the mid-1960s." It had already run several articles about the theologians, but unlike past efforts it decided to address the issue in a cover story. After a back-and-forth the editors realized that no cover image could convey the message. After all, part of the radical theologians' position was that God defied adequate representation because in the lives of modern people he had ceased to exist. So *Time*, in a first, dispensed with a cover image. Using red lettering on a black background, the editors asked simply, "Is God Dead?"[29]

The decision caused a sensation. Unlike the cover, the actual article discussed the religious confusion and cacophony of the 1960s. But readers took their cues from the question posed on the front of the magazine. The letters to the editor continued for weeks.

They often consisted of strongly worded statements offering the usual Christian apologetics, on the one hand, or atheistic triumphalism, on the other. *Time* also received a large number of appreciative responses from Protestant ministers of many persuasions.[30]

The controversy spilled beyond the pages of *Time*, in ways that stunned the theologians. Hamilton later complained, "The reaction overwhelmed the original event." It became a "pseudo-event . . . in which angry men were fighting non-existent enemies, and people

were reacting to things never spoken." He received a variety of letters from readers. They ranged from the taunting ("I heard that
you have lost a dear friend"), to the nasty ("You dirty commie atheist homosexual bastard"), to the Christian nationalist ("You are a
communist working in the international conspiracy against Jesus
Christ and Christians").[31]

He soon started receiving death threats. Friends began to dis-
tance themselves. Gene E. Bartlett, the president of Colgate Rochester, said in response to Hamilton's provocations, "We do not
accept his views. We debate them and affirm the opposite." Bartlett
took Hamilton's basic course in theology away from him, and,
within a year of the *Time* article, Hamilton left Colgate Rochester
to teach religion at New College in Florida.[32]

The reaction raised an obvious question: Why all the fuss?

Looked at in one way, the death-of-God debate was not all that
novel. It simply repackaged older theological developments. But
the newness of the controversy was not the issue, at least not the
main issue. All of the theologians tended to speak of their project in
the same way. They began by questioning their personal beliefs and
conceptions of God. Then they moved to the impossibility of finding an adequate image or metaphor for God in modern, technological society. And, finally, they crept up on the real issue, which was
the social significance or insignificance of the Christian religion in
contemporary American life. Their declaration that God was not
just meaningless but unnecessary seemed to reinforce the broader
secularizing thrust of American political culture in a way that many
people found either liberating or unacceptable.[33]

In that way the death-of-God theologians popularized and main-
streamed ideas that had long circulated in intellectual circles. Paul L.
Holmer, a professor of theology at Yale, complained that "the neo-
Protestant intelligentsia" was simply promoting the "theme of the
avant-garde," that is, echoing the radically anti-Christian thinkers who
believed that the theological thought of the church was an anachronism. To those who saw Protestant Christianity as already standing on
an insecure social foundation, the death-of-God theologians were
committing a strategic error.[34]

But while Holmer and others were complaining about van-
guardist themes among Protestant writers, other Protestants began

to confront the fact that their custodial posture toward American culture was no longer tenable. This was the more profound discovery, the encounter with difference that sixties politics provoked. The dawning realization of diversity and the corresponding loss of custodial confidence did not happen overnight. As late as 1964 the National Council of Churches was urging Christians not to withdraw their explicitly religious voice from public affairs because doing so would "create a vacuum" that would "be filled by secular religions or by secularistic philosophy."[35]

The council's statement would prove to be one of the last public expressions of guardianship from mainline Protestants. Many within the liberal Protestant community simply dropped the posture as not just unviable but positively nefarious. John C. Bennett, the president of Union Theological Seminary, spoke for many when he said that "the ecumenical Christian community" needed to actively reject the idea of Christian America. The declaration that the United States had a Christian foundation was simply not ecumenical enough. It confused the religious community with the nation as a whole. It was latently sectarian. Sixties politics had revealed American society as too diverse to be subject to Christian leadership. Only by dropping the pretensions of a Christian America, Bennett asserted, would liberal Christians be able to collaborate with others in a secular regime for the betterment of American life.[36]

The liberal Protestant position was helped along by a creeping demographic weakness. By the 1960s many politically active young adults started to conclude that the churches were unnecessary in the political and ethical work they wished to pursue. Other young adults, though they tended to be much fewer in number, decided that liberal churches no longer stood for historical Christianity and migrated into conservative denominations. Soon the big Protestant denominations that had long dominated American life went into demographic free fall, the result of the low ecumenical birthrate and the loss of their children to other organizations or, more often, to no religious affiliation at all.[37]

These challenges caused other groups associated with Protestantism to transform. Protestants and Other Americans United (POAU) began to fall into a crisis of self-awareness. At its height in 1964 the organization had two hundred thousand members, fifty

full-time staff in ten cities, and hundreds of part-time and volun-
teer workers. But while the National Council of Churches was still
urging Protestants into the public arena, the POAU began to shed
its Protestant identity and its self-congratulation. As Franklin H.
Littell, a professor of church history at Chicago Theological Seminary, told *Newsweek*, "It is one of the myths of Protestantism that
we had religious liberty in the past and that this was a Protestant
contribution." In fact, the religious liberty was somewhat limited,
and Protestants, as a result of their position in public life, often set
the limits that were experienced by others. Once POAU had inter-
nalized the historical reality, the organization dropped the explicit
Protestant reference from its name and became instead Americans
United for the Separation of Church and State. The shift—from
Protestant to American—demonstrated the wider Protestant embrace of diversity that emerged in the era.[38]

Yet the biggest challenge of sixties politics had not quite fully presented itself. It was one thing to accept pluralized democratic practice, to grant that many groups existed in society that had political
rights. But it was harder to acknowledge that once these groups
came fully into the American political process the consensual moral
norms which had long been taken for granted could no longer be
upheld. The revelation of plural moral worlds required a much
fuller embrace of difference and a much more consequential rejection of Christianity's protective role over American culture.

The challenge soon became apparent, as sixties politics merged
with the counterculture and affirmed that personal authenticity
often terminated in sexual and social liberation. The slogan often
heard at New Left rallies, "It is forbidden to forbid," expressed the
antinomian impulse. As the New Leftist Theodore Roszak said in
1968, "The counterculture is the embryonic cultural base of New
Left politics, the effort to discover new types of community, new
family patterns, new sexual mores, new kinds of livelihood, new aes-
thetic forms, new personal identities on the far side of power politics, the bourgeois home, and the Protestant work ethic."[39]

Once the counterculture became more prominent, its cultural
displacement of latently Christian norms became more powerful.
All that had formerly been agreed upon seemed to be up for recon-

sideration. In place of established mores or values many people within American culture were forced to consider that the normative embrace of heterogeneity, which they had willingly undertaken, required a corresponding cultural, ethical, and even intellectual relativism. Politically speaking, such relativism tended to terminate in secular liberalism, which privatized religious beliefs about proper behavior and accepted that individuals could determine their own standards. This is what John Courtney Murray described, skeptically, as "the secularistic tradition of the autonomous man."[40]

The directionality of countercultural politics toward relativism was especially clear in the aftermath of the *Griswold* decision, which declared a right to privacy. One of the central preoccupations of religious groups up to that point had been how to promote a public morality. That was why so many liberal Protestants had spoken of the importance of religion as the basis of society. It offered a collective moral compass that pointed people in the direction they should go. But *Griswold* made social and moral regulation much harder. The political philosophy that the court affirmed was essentially what Betty Friedan had offered in her 1963 classic *The Feminine Mystique*, when she declared that "[women] must live their own lives again according to a self-chosen purpose." Individual people—individual women—were free to choose their own directions rather than having society lay out the path for them.[41]

The emphasis on personal autonomy and freedom from societal, cultural, and religious constraint confounded religious leaders who still saw a place for public morals in American life. Catholic leaders were especially perturbed. It turned out that even though liberals had won a battle within the hierarchy during Vatican II, many conservatives had not yet conceded the war. They continued to affirm that God established morality, that the church sought the protection of moral norms, and that even those who rejected the church's authority were still subject to what Catholics considered natural law.

The idea of natural law was vital to conservative Catholic thinkers who sought to preserve the place of religious norms in public culture. The concept presumed a morality that was publicly available rather than privately determined, that was objective rather than subjective, and that was, because it came from the natural revelation of the world, available to everyone, not just Catholics. But, in practice, natural law comported entirely with Catholic doctrine.

Catholic natural law became especially critical after *Griswold*, as the feminist movement began to push for greater sexual autonomy for women. Technological developments in birth control, especially the development of the birth control pill, raised the specter of a sexual ethics that profoundly upset conservative Catholic leaders. Sexual liberation and medically controlled birth ran up against a cluster of Catholic beliefs that had a long history in clerical pronouncements and were tightly interwoven. This cluster entailed several notions: first, that a natural law existed; second, that contraception violated natural law; third, that God determined the purpose of sex, which was procreation; fourth, that God determined the limits and meaning of life; fifth, that if a person suffered through disease or deformity or for any other reason during the course of life, that suffering must have meaning because God allowed a person to come into being, allowed the suffering to continue, and sustained his or her life in the midst of suffering for however long God chose. The comprehensiveness of Catholic doctrine committed the church to a variety of positions that were all well known: birth control was bad; doctors and patients should err on the side of the preservation of life; medical technologies that allowed choice were evil, in that they fostered the autonomous illusions of modern secularism.[42]

Their pro-life doctrines placed the hierarchy in opposition to many revolutionary components of movement politics, but the American Catholic leadership became especially hardened after contraception activists turned to the issue of abortion. As women's groups associated with second-wave feminism began to lobby for a loosening of abortion laws, Catholic clerics turned frantic. The apparent success of feminists made the American Catholic leadership, conservative though it had been to that point, consider the unthinkable step of making alliances with non-Catholics. After several legislatures took up bills on the issue, Cardinal Cushing of Boston called "all persons of goodwill to unite in opposition" to the revision of antiabortion statutes. "I have viewed with ever-increasing alarm the efforts currently being made in parts of the country either to repeal or to render ineffective . . . the laws condemning the crime of abortion," he said.[43]

Cardinal Cushing was not alone. Nearly the entire hierarchy rejected the legalization of abortion as a violation of public morality that had profound significance. A human embryo was human, they believed, and so it was a nascent person in the eyes of God. To kill that person was murder. The social acceptance of the practice undermined support for the sanctity of human life. To hold firm on abortion, in the hierarchy's view, was to hold firm to the notion that our lives are bound by objective moral standards and that something existed above either the individual or the state. By contrast, to embrace or to allow abortion would be to declare, as the Jesuit Robert I. Gannon said, "God is dead and our right to life comes from the state." If that happened, said the hierarchy, systematic extermination would soon follow.[44]

But the tumult of the 1960s made the hierarchy's position harder to defend because other religious leaders simply rejected it, thereby undermining the notion that their views were an expression of natural law. In New York, Rabbi William F. Rosenblum dismissed abortion opponents as "medieval-minded." Rabbi Joachim Prinz, the chairman of the Conference of Presidents of Major American Jewish Organizations, told a congressional hearing that the Catholic hierarchy was making an issue out of nothing. "We are discussing the legalization of the removal of a fetus, a nonperson, an undeveloped organism," he said.[45]

Protestants tended to agree with the rabbis, at least in part. They were more likely than Jewish leaders to express moral qualms about abortion. But in keeping with the trend in Protestantism toward self-interrogation and a reluctance to exercise cultural authority, many simply expressed their uneasiness while simultaneously affirming that abortion should be legal. Nearly all of the Protestant denominations accepted that it was an issue of private morality that ought to be kept out of civil law. To think otherwise would make it allowable, as Governor Nelson Rockefeller of New York put it, "for one group to impose its vision of morality on an entire society."[46]

Catholics even had a difficult time forming a united front among themselves. A few Catholic thinkers began to question the official position on contraception, drawing on the statement of religious freedom from Vatican II. The most prominent dissenter was Robert F. Drinan, a Jesuit priest and U.S. representative from Massachusetts.

Drinan concluded that the bishops were not thinking about the issue from the proper social and political standpoint. They needed to be strategic, he suggested. If a person were against abortion, the goal ought to be to reduce it as much as possible within a society. But it was unreasonable to expect that it would be curtailed entirely, and it was especially irrational to expect that the passage of a law would eliminate the practice. Abortion, like gambling, adultery, or prostitution, was necessarily surreptitious, having to do with private moral behavior and a woman's body that was not easily controlled through the force of law. The question was how to mitigate fetal death. When put in those terms, it was not at all clear that prohibiting the procedure would curtail it in any way or that outlawing the procedure would be the best way to limit it. Drinan speculated that legalizing abortion might result in the greatest decline. Legalization would, at the very least, give some sense of how widespread abortion was by bringing it above ground, so that the causes could be both understood and addressed. Abortions might thereby be minimized over time.[47]

Others echoed Drinan, using the pronouncements from Vatican II to advance a distinction between moral law and civil law. In June 1965, after the court handed down the *Griswold* decision, *Commonweal* declared that the ruling was long overdue and speculated that it had been put off by the determined activities of the Catholic leadership. The prelates, in *Commonweal*'s view, sought wrongly to embed their moral ideas within the coercive apparatus of the state. Likewise, William F. Buckley Jr., a Catholic conservative, wrote in *National Review* that the hierarchy's obstruction on the contraception issue failed to follow its own conciliar ideas. "Surely the principal meaning of the religious liberty pronouncements of Vatican II is that other men must be left free to practice the dictates of their own conscience," he wrote.[48]

These statements emanating from lay voices showed that the radicalism of Vatican II had permeated deep into Catholic life in ways that the prelates had not anticipated. The council's accommodation with modern democracy seemed to allow people in pluralistic societies leeway to choose their own course, to have the benefit of a private morality, which included the right of private immorality. Some post–Vatican II writers thought that the function of civil law was not to proscribe everything that was immoral, in contrast to the assumption of the hierarchy. Secular law sought to create the rules by which individuals could take the responsibility of moral choice upon themselves.

But the abortion issue ultimately showed the limits of Catholic religious freedom. In 1968 Pope Paul VI issued *Humanae Vitae*, a reaffirmation of the Catholic prohibition against "artificial" birth control. The encyclical tended to tighten Catholic debate and only increased the divide between the Catholic leadership and the laity. A *Newsweek* poll in 1971 showed that 58 percent of American Catholics believed that a person could ignore the church position on contraception and remain in good standing.[49]

All of this conflict occurred within a wider context of institutional religious decline. By the early seventies millions were rejecting traditional, organized religion, and they were not just liberal Protestants. Church attendance and financial contributions to religious institutions declined across the board. Opinion polls showed that what were once considered orthodox beliefs—the affirmation of God, personal salvation, heaven and hell—all showed large drops. That left the Catholic hierarchy struggling to sustain its position not just with its members but among the wider public.[50]

Inevitably, it also shaped the response of the court. After the *Griswold* decision, activists sought to bring cases on appeal that would overturn the nation's abortion laws. It took a few years but finally, in 1971, a case made it to the Supreme Court: *Roe v. Wade*. The justices predictably groped for a response, as they did with many of the issues that dealt with the public role of religion and morality. During conference the majority seemed inclined to strike down the Texas abortion law but without any clearly agreed-upon reasoning. The case had to be reargued the next year. During conference after the second hearing the justices were again bewildered. The issue of abortion raised tricky constitutional, moral, and religious considerations.[51]

Eventually they found their bearings. The resulting opinion, in a 7–2 majority written by Harry Blackmun, struck down many abortion laws in the United States. His reasoning was genuinely historical. Blackmun noted that in the late eighteenth century and much of the nineteenth state laws tended not to prohibit abortions

conducted before the first felt movements of the fetus, its quicken-
ing. Those laws tightened in the late nineteenth and early twentieth
century with, though he did not say so, Catholic emigration to the
United States. But because the laws were of relatively recent origin,
Blackmun reasoned, antiabortion statutes could not be justified by
deep constitutional precedent.

Having dispensed with the historical issues, Blackmun shifted
to the moral ones. Religious and moral authorities tended to dis-
agree about abortion, he pointed out. Their divergence manifested
itself in the political arena, where some voices urged prohibition
and others legalization. But a woman's right to privacy, which the
court had declared in the *Griswold* decision, meant that the state
had no business making a moral decision for her about whether or
not to abort a fetus. The right to privacy carved out a space for individuals to make moral choices within a wider context of societal
and religious disagreement.

Blackmun did acknowledge that the state had an interest in
protecting human life. The right to privacy, like other rights, was
not absolute. Once the fetus became viable outside the womb,
which Blackmun located in the third trimester of pregnancy, the
state could regulate or even proscribe abortion because that fetus
could be considered more fully a person in his or her own right.
Before then, women could make the choice for themselves.[52]

The remarkable thing about the opinion was its detachment.
Even though he was treading through a hotly contested moral issue,
Blackmun used a consistent vocabulary of personal choice, individual medical consultation, professional judgment, and the right to
make a difficult decision within a private mental and moral space.

Shortly after the ruling the legal scholar Laurence H. Tribe un-
packed the court's strategy in the *Harvard Law Review*. The court
faced problems in deciding the case, Tribe pointed out. The foundational problem lay in defining the characteristics of a human being.
Doing so necessarily involved religion and therefore questions about
abortion involved the court in a religious form of reasoning. The legislation itself was shaped within the context of religious controversy.
For the court to weigh into the debate was inherently to take part in
a religious dispute, just as the laws themselves were an outgrowth of a
religious disagreement. The court could not make substantive deter-

minations on the issues without violating the Constitution. So it focused on, in Tribe's words, "who should make judgments of that sort." It had to determine who possessed decision-making authority within a wider context of public religious controversy but avoid entering the disagreement. The Catholic leadership had declared that the state, responding to religious leaders, ought to make the decision. But the court decided that the moral authority to choose lay with the woman in consultation with her doctor.[53]

In that way the court followed the logic of its own jurisprudence, tortured though it sometimes was, toward its endpoint of religious and moral privatization. The court acknowledged the pluralization of ethical norms that occurred in the 1960s. It recognized the impossibility of adjudicating those norms without becoming a party to a religious dispute. It conceived of the individual woman as a point of pure moral self-determination and left the choice to her. At the same time, the court announced an abandonment of the role of the state in defining and defending an official morality. The abandonment entailed a repudiation of the social significance of religion in determining moral norms at the hands of the state. Religion could no longer fulfill that role given the diversity of moral and religious opinion in the United States and the resulting religious conflict that the court had observed over the past thirty years.

With *Roe*, in other words, American secularism reached its apotheosis.

PART THREE

Instabilities

CHAPTER EIGHT
The Personal Is Political

Political scientists speak of the emergence of regimes or orders that are, at bottom, successful configurations of power at certain moments. The American secular order at the time of *Roe v. Wade* was one such regime. It emerged in an almost accidental arrangement, the result of layered social conflict. And it relied upon divergent assumptions, norms, and laws with various and sometimes variable rationales.

Part of the tension within the arrangement came from the available political vocabulary. Privacy, religion, secular, public, freedom, conscience, democracy, liberalism, and pluralism—all offered the material to rework public life. The peculiar shape of secularism at mid-century was the result of a constant reframing of terms and concepts within the American political tradition. At the beginning of the secular arrangement, these words took their meaning from the way that Christian bodies exerted influence over public culture in an often-illiberal social space. The expansion of civil liberties, the embrace of cosmopolitan pluralism, and the protection of individual privacy went hand in hand with a rejection of even the mildest forms of public religious authority. The constellation of words emerged through the work of many people, a number of whom were religious.

But the terms of the secular order had already begun to shift by the time of *Roe v. Wade*, either the beginning of a breakdown or

the assumption of an as-yet-unrecognizable form. The trend continued in the subsequent decades, as the vocabulary took on fresh
meanings. The legal forms of secularism became especially fluid.
Because the secular order emerged out of the language of civil liberties, it was subject to a highly volatile application that drew upon
other concepts. One of the main sources of instability, which would
grow over time, originated as a conceptual disagreement between
liberals and leftists over one of the key notions of American secularism: privacy.

The dispute can be difficult to understand because in contemporary journalistic parlance "liberal" and "left" are often used as syn-
onyms in a way that makes the historical disagreement between the
two groups illegible. But among midcentury American leftists the
enemy was what they called the establishment or what historians call
the liberal establishment. Leftists objected that the liberal establishment focused narrowly on the individual and that the liberal tradition itself too often exalted freedom over equality. Liberalism's deep
attentiveness to political liberty, leftists thought, rendered it unable
to elaborate a theory of the good society, and therefore lacking in
any positive, purposeful vision through which to pursue change. In
contrast to liberals, then, leftists saw themselves as articulating a conception of the collective that thereafter could be expressed in new
laws, cultural standards, and social and institutional arrangements.[1]

Their hostility to liberal individualism made many leftists skeptical of the pillars of American secularism, the doctrine of privacy
especially. In creating the secular order, the liberal establishment decentered the dominant place of Christianity and relegated religion
to the private realm along with other moral issues that an individual
might confront. The goal, as in other disputes, was to minimize social conflict and to maximize personal freedom. But the line between
public and private had always been somewhat problematic in a variety of domains—from schooling to presidential politics—and by the
1960s and 1970s, even as the court was drawing upon the language,
the distinction between public and private was beginning to break
down.

Leftist hostility to the concept of privacy started early. Back in
1959, C. Wright Mills, the radical sociologist who was a guiding light
to many New Leftists, had predicted that people would soon connect

"personal troubles to public issues." The civil rights movement had already been doing that, lambasting the racism found in private activities and spaces. Discrimination at lunch counters, by transportation companies, in employment, and in real estate were central subjects of the movement's concern. Civil rights protestors pointed out that private decisions to exclude based on race reinforced the public power of white supremacy. As the movement mobilized against discrimination, it demanded political protection against what had formerly been considered personal acts or instances of non-state oppression. The efforts finally came to fulfillment in the 1964 Civil Rights Act, which prohibited discrimination in public spaces even if those public spaces were privately owned.[2]

Others questioned more than just the property-based conception of privacy. They began to interrogate the liberal ideal, put forward by Brandeis, of privacy as the guarantor of an inviolate personality. Brandeis's mature version of the notion had looked to personal development and individual self-expression as essential components of American diversity. Individual people, unfettered by government regulation, could and would grow in varying ways that furthered the kaleidoscopic patterns of American life. The court's jurisprudence in the 1940s and 1950s had drawn upon the notion, culminating in *Griswold v. Connecticut* (1965) by declaring that all individuals could order their private lives as they saw fit.

But looked at from another angle, privacy caused a divided, rather than inviolate, personality. It presumed that certain behaviors or ideas were not subject to political oversight and ought to be kept out of the public eye. Many in the New Left began to assert that only by rejecting the distinction between public and private, only by transforming formerly private matters into issues of public relevance, could a new social order be brought into effect. As early as 1962, the Port Huron Statement spoke of creating a form of politics that would allow individuals to find "meaning in life that is personally authentic" through public struggle. In the leftist conception, politics became a mechanism for unifying the fractured self in an attempt to find personal and psychic wholeness. The liberal concept of privacy stood in the way.[3]

As the feminist movement began, the impulse to interrogate privacy expanded. Women's rights activists pointed out that so-called private phenomena such as the woman's role in the home and in child-rearing were public issues that demanded political responses. The right to privacy in the context of the women's rights movement took on a less salutary connotation. The concept accepted a demarcated realm in which the state was impotent and simultaneously relegated women to that realm, subject to the whim and control of their husbands. Viewed through the feminist framework, in the words of the theorist Catharine MacKinnon, "A right to privacy looks like an injury got up as a gift." Women's rights activists, in response, destabilized the public–private distinction by maintaining, as Carol Hanisch put it in the title of her 1969 essay, "The personal is political."[4]

Cultural, intellectual, and political innovations followed. Because many sixties activists presumed that privatization was a psychic burden to be overthrown, people should "let it all hang out," to use an evocative phrase of the period. Young people rejected the notion that public comportment was necessarily formal, while private matters could be informal. The informal—the private—was the real and needed to be brought into public. Dress became casualized with the proliferation of bell-bottoms, the rejection of bras, the shortening of skirts, and the lengthening of hair in both men and women. Television began to show what had formerly been considered private and therefore taboo: Characters spoke of menopause. Shows depicted the process of childbirth. Mild curse words and flushing toilets became allowable on television. The standards separating public and private behavior began to break down.[5]

The court itself contributed to the breakdown even as it continued to invoke the right to privacy, and in that way it displayed an ambivalence within the liberalism it espoused. In 1969, in *Stanley v. Georgia*, the court invalidated many obscenity laws on right-to-privacy grounds. The state of Georgia claimed that in banning obscene material it was merely trying to uphold a public morality. But the court rejected the state's position. Speaking for his unanimous brethren, Justice Thurgood Marshall alleged that Georgia, under the veil of morality, sought "the right to control the moral content of a person's thoughts." "If the First Amendment means anything," he wrote, "it means that a State has no business telling a man, sitting alone in his own house, what books he may read or what films he may watch."[6]

But in spite of the court's rhetoric, the effect of the decision was not just to allow individuals to view obscene material in the privacy of their homes. Because it defined freedom as the freedom to do something or to show something, as the historian Lee Ann Wheeler has explained, it allowed "images, messages, and behaviors once considered private" to "saturate public culture." The liberal freedom to depict the obscene overwhelmed the public's freedom from obscenity. Freedom to, rather than freedom from, became a controlling understanding on the court.[7]

The doctrine of privacy began to shift in other ways. As the momentous changes of the period began to compound, many people had trouble accommodating themselves to the emergent reality. Religious conservatives, who tended to join or conflate the nation with their church, especially resisted. The nation was a repository of the ideals of the religious community, they thought. If those ideals declined in national life, the nation itself would decline. The actions of the court, the drift of American society, the transformation of mainline Protestantism into an agent of secular liberalism—all the developments were upsetting to Christian conservatives who saw their religious ideas as integral to national health.

But as conservatives became increasingly agitated by sixties innovations, the destabilization of privacy generated another change. As the sociologist Robert Wuthnow has pointed out, between 1950 and 1970 American religion underwent an extended restructuring. At the beginning of the period, religious groups were riven by sectarian controversy, unable to come to agreement about basic matters of public life. The divisions between the Protestant denominations or the more basic division between Protestants and Catholics led to sectarian infighting that the courts had to manage. By the end of the period, as New Left activists began to question the terms of political debate, the denominational divisions or even the basic division between Protestants and Catholics had given way to a new arrangement. What mattered was no longer a denominational or sectarian identity but whether a person was a liberal or a conservative practitioner of a religious tradition. If a person was liberal, he or she tended to support the direction of the court, the liberalization of American politics, and the expanded freedom within American society. If a person was conservative, the legal, political, and social developments of the previous thirty years were appalling. Suddenly it became apparent that conservative Catholics and conservative Protestants had more connection between themselves than they did with liberals who were in their own tradition.[8]

As with the emergence of the New Left, the restructuring of American religion began with the civil rights movement in the 1950s. In response to the movement, almost all religious denominations, even in the South, passed explicit statements against racism. But liberals and conservatives divided on the exact strategy to bring about the end of white supremacy. Those who advocated direct action against racism, and especially the liberal clergy who joined civil rights protests, embraced an ethics of social justice that united them across the denominational divide. Those who declined activism and who decried the civil rights protests for what they saw as the protestors' lawlessness began to align as conservatives who feared that a long-term decline of Christianity was under way within the social order.[9]

The controversies over religion and school prayer furthered the realignment. At the beginning of the period, Protestants were united in their opposition to Catholics and vice versa. But Protestants began to fracture over church–state separation as the court excluded religion from the public schools. Liberals accepted the growing secularism as a reasonable extension of their principles. Conservatives thought that religion was essential to any education worth the name and that therefore religion must remain in schools. Observers noted in the aftermath of the first school-prayer decision that many of the strongest critics of the court were southern segregationist leaders who first objected to the court's desegregationist policies and then rejected church–state separation.[10]

Both conservative responses resulted in a flight from the public schools and a strategy of quasi-privatization. In the South, when the court forced the integration of schools in the 1960s, racial conservatives began to withdraw their children from the public-school system and formed private segregation academies where they could continue the racial status quo. In many cases these private schools were simply a reconstitution of the formerly white public school. In Holmes County, Mississippi, white enrollment in the public schools went from 771 to 28 in the first year of desegregation. The next year the number of white children enrolled fell to zero.[11]

Christian conservatives were also reconsidering the public-school system. In 1963, after the court struck down Bible reading, Bishop Fred Pierce Carson, the president of the World Methodist Council, predicted a "new movement among Protestants and Catholics for parochial education to protect their children from a growing secularism which now seems to have invaded the courts." His prediction turned out to be accurate. In tandem with segregation academies, Christian day schools emerged all over the nation. These schools featured conservative religious teaching and the regular religious devotion that was now disallowed in the public schools.[12]

Because the two developments occurred in tandem it was sometimes difficult to separate them. Some segregation academies were also private Christian day schools. Some were not. If plotted on a Venn diagram, the overlap between the two kinds of schools in the South would have been large. In other parts of the country, perhaps less so. American policy makers wanted to suppress the segregation academies while not necessarily discriminating against religious schools. But it was not always clear how to do that.

In the late 1960s the U.S. Commission on Civil Rights, an independent commission of the federal government, recommended that segregation academies be denied tax exemption as a way to restrain their growth. Shortly after the commission issued its recommendations, a group of black parents in Holmes County, Mississippi, filed suit. They demanded that the Internal Revenue Service (IRS) change the status of the segregation schools in the state.[13]

After an initial hearing, the U.S. District Court for the District of Columbia temporarily enjoined the IRS from granting tax exemptions to private Mississippi schools that had discriminatory policies. It then permanently enjoined the IRS from doing so.[14]

The agency followed up by formalizing its policy disallowing tax exemption for segregation academies. The decision raised questions about the status of other nonprofit, private organizations. In the past the courts had ruled that tax exemption involved indirect aid, not direct aid, to an entity. But in ruling against segregation academies the IRS and the district court seemed to suggest that excusing an organization from the burden of taxation offered direct aid to nonprofit organizations. That had disturbing implications for churches and religiously run institutions like hospitals in that it

construed tax exemption as public, governmental support for private, religious institutions. If that was true, then it could be said that
such aid violated the establishment clause of the First Amendment.[15]

The government tried to resist the implication. When announc-
ing the policy, IRS Commissioner Randolph W. Thrower went out
of his way to say that a church-run school would not come under review as a result of the rule. Churches had a separate status. The IRS's
position was further affirmed the next year when the U.S. Supreme
Court rejected a challenge to tax exemptions for religious bodies. In
an 8–1 opinion the majority again said that such accommodations offered only indirect aid and helped to avoid entanglement between
church and state. Douglas, writing in dissent, complained, "I would
suppose that, in common understanding, one of the best ways to 'establish' one or more religions is to subsidize them, which a tax exemption does."[16]

The IRS's statements and the court's affirmation seemed to
create a safe harbor for those seeking to privatize the school system. The decision drew segregation academies and Christian day
schools still closer together. Observers began to predict that, as
Jonathan Spivak and Tom Herman put it in the *Wall Street Journal*,
some segregation academies might "seek church sanctuary" as a
way to avoid public scrutiny.[17]

The actions of the IRS also strengthened a rhetorical realignment
between segregationists and Christian conservatives. When segregationists complained about an overweening federal government, their
complaints mirrored conservative Christian outrage about the secularist thrust of that same government. Even for conservative Christians who were not racist or who did not want to think of themselves
as racist, their shared rhetorical enemy drove the two together. What
they supported, both said, was the ability of individuals to freely associate and to privately order their communities. They came up against
a public order that was, variously, antiracist or anti-Christian or both,
and they sought to dissent from that cultural consensus through the
maintenance of private institutions.[18]

Put succinctly, when the court invoked the right to privacy in *Roe v.
Wade*, the public–private idea was going in two directions. Those
on the left sought to break down the distinction in an attempt to

create a more liberatory and authentic politics that used the state as an agent of transformation in private life. At the same time, conservatives began to withdraw from public spaces and sought refuge in private ordering and private institutional life that was governed by their own sense of values. The court's decision in *Roe* further complicated these developments in ways that defied neat categorical distinction.

The immediate effect of *Roe v. Wade* was to further the denominational realignment. After the court handed down its decision, conservative Protestants joined Catholics in denouncing the ruling as a violation of moral values and of the basic obligations of the state to protect innocent life. The fundamentalist Billy James Hargis created a pro-life organization, Americans Against Abortion, soon after *Roe*. Articles with titles like "Murder of Babies: It's a Major Issue in New York," "Does a Woman Have a Right to Murder?" and "The Sacrifice of Human Life Goes On" appeared in conservative Protestant publications. The NAE issued a statement in the immediate aftermath of the ruling. "We deplore, in the strongest possible terms," the statement read, "the decision of the U.S. Supreme Court, which has made it legal to terminate a pregnancy for no better reason than personal convenience or sociological considerations." *Christianity Today* announced that "Christians should accustom themselves to the thought that the American state no longer supports, in any meaningful sense, the laws of God, and prepare themselves spiritually for the prospect that it may one day formally repudiate them and turn against those who seek to live by them."[19]

Legislators immediately began to work through the implications. In light of the court's ruling in *Roe*, conservative religious organizations, notably those that had private hospitals as part of their ministries, feared that they might have to perform abortions. The Catholic church had already prepared for the possibility that the procedure would be made legal. In 1971, as *Roe* was making its way through the system, the Catholic Health Association was alarmed that previous directives from the bishops were beginning, in its words, "to be interpreted more liberally in certain dioceses" to allow abortive and sterilization procedures. The National Conference of Catholic Bishops responded with a revised version of its "Ethical and Religious Directives for Catholic Health Care Services." The new statement clearly prohibited all abortions and sterilizations. After ensuring its doctrinal consistency, the Catholic leadership began to lobby legislators.[20]

Their efforts bore fruit immediately. Senators Frank Church and Adlai Stevenson, both supporters of legalized abortion, sponsored legislation granting doctors and institutions exemption from the procedure if they could invoke their conscience. The legislation was an amendment to the Hill–Burton Act of 1946, which offered federal grants and loans to hospitals if they agreed to abide by rules that were designed to benefit the public. Many private religious hospitals had taken the money and now feared that it bound them to offer abortions or sterilizations as part of their obligation of public benefit. Support for the freedom of conscience amendment swelled from all directions, even from people who were otherwise political enemies. *Commonweal* explained, "Some are attracted by the basic anti-abortion features of the resolution, but some also see it safeguarding religious freedom and civil rights and perhaps heading off efforts in the direction of a Constitutional amendment."[21]

A careful observer would have noticed the shift in the debate. The actual position of religious conservatives was that their ideas were correct and ought to be broadly adopted. But when faced with collective hostility to their principles, and given the dominance of the American secular order at the middle of the twentieth century, conservative leaders turned to the only strategy available to them, namely, appropriating parts of the secular political vocabulary to forestall other uses. They turned to a politics of preemption—the phrase comes from the political scientist Stephen Skowronek—that sought to rearrange the regnant words and ideas into novel forms and thereby open policy avenues not previously available.[22]

The broad support for the conscience amendment marked a transformation within the Catholic church in particular. The Catholic hierarchy had long been suspicious of a declaration of conscience, seeing it as a Protestant and individualist notion that led to the privatization of religion. When John Courtney Murray first drafted the Statement on Religious Freedom in 1964, he told Pope Paul VI that he sought to bracket the concept of religious freedom from the freedom of conscience because the latter concept was dangerous. But during the debate over the Church Amendment, the Catholic hierarchy had come to see that conscience could be used as a defense against secularism, as a privatizing move that opened space for continued religious privilege.[23]

Liberals stumbled over the amendment. They saw their concepts being appropriated to ends they opposed but in a way that they were powerless to resist. The ACLU's somewhat tortured deliberation was instructive. The organization wanted to support conscientious exemption as a matter of principle because such accommodations had been crucial to excusing young men from going to war in Vietnam. But the ACLU Reproductive Freedom Project pointed out that conscientious objection to abortion would constrain access in many ways and would accordingly limit reproductive freedom for women. The freedom to have an abortion collided with the freedom from having to perform an abortion. Freedom to and freedom from again did not work together.[24]

After much internal discussion the ACLU came out against the amendment. Its reasoning turned on a set of categorical distinctions between individual and corporate conscience and between public and private institutions, all of which were already growing tenuous. The ACLU Women's Rights Project explained, "Our position is that any institution which serves the public and receives public funds becomes, in effect, an arm of the state and therefore should be required to provide health services to everyone who needs them. . . . Rather than 'denying freedom of conscience' we are proposing that institutions supported by public funds are not in fact private and must, therefore, serve the public. This position in no way contradicts the ACLU's long standing defense of first amendment freedoms, but rather reinforces our position against the establishment of any religion." The ACLU's fear was that, by granting private institutions an exemption based on religious doctrine, the proposed legislation would, in effect, privilege the rights of institutions over the rights of individual women. It would also bestow public approval to private religious expression.[25]

Other critics began to object that the amendment acknowledged only the conscience of antiabortionists. Doctors who worked in religious hospitals and whose conscience allowed or compelled them to perform the procedure received no such protection. Neither did women whose sensibilities allowed them to have an abortion. Nor did taxpayers who demanded public support for the procedure as a matter of social welfare. In congressional debate Senator Jacob K. Javits and Representative Bella Abzug both pointed out the highly selective accommodation that the amendment offered.[26]

In spite of these objections the Church Amendment was passed by the U.S. Congress in 1973. By the end of the next year twenty-eight states had enacted similar resolutions. In 1977 the U.S. Congress passed the Hyde Amendment, which prohibited public money from being used to pay for abortive procedures. The Hyde Amendment privatized and individualized support for abortion while raising the conscience claims of those who objected to it into a controlling position in matters of public policy.[27]

In educational desegregation efforts, the public–private confusion went in parallel directions. The state commitment to antidiscrimination also found conservatives pointing to conscience in support of their right to privately order their institutional lives. Critics saw these moves as disingenuous attempts to project their commitments back into the public realm while continuing their racial control. In 1974, a year after *Roe*, the U.S. Commission on Civil Rights criticized the IRS for still inadequately responding to discrimination in private schools. The following year the IRS issued two changes to address the issue. First, the agency decided that a school had to make a statement rejecting discrimination in its hiring and admissions process. Second, it placed religious schools in the same category as nonreligious schools. "The First Amendment," the IRS ruled, "does bar governmental interference with mere religious beliefs and opinions, but it does not affect the legal consequences otherwise attending a given practice or action that is not inherently religious."[28]

In response, black parents from Holmes County, Mississippi, again sued the agency. They pointed out that the IRS, in spite of its rule changes, continued to award tax exemption to racially discriminatory schools. The U.S. Commission on Civil Rights enumerated at least seven segregation academies in Mississippi that were still receiving tax exemption.[29]

By 1978 the agency agreed that it was not doing enough. It took a step back to assess its performance and soon issued still more guidelines. It now created two classes of schools, reviewable schools and nonreviewable schools. Reviewable schools would be scrutinized over their tax-exempt status. Nonreviewable schools would not. The IRS defined a reviewable school as one that was established around the time of desegregation and had an insignificant number of minority students, which would include many Christian day schools. Once the agency placed a school in the reviewable category, school administrators had to demonstrate that it was not a segregation academy. They also had to show that they had taken steps to attract and to secure minority students. To be finally moved out of the reviewable status a school needed to have a significant number of minority students, which the agency defined as 20 percent of the student body. If it could not overcome the presumptive burden that it was a vehicle for discrimination, the school risked loss of its tax exemption.[30]

Conservative Protestants were outraged. They realized that the agency's commitment to desegregation would infringe upon their rights to privately order themselves in a religious sense. Over the previous decade they had started Christian day schools at a rate of two per day. The rules threatened their institutional viability. They were further upset that the IRS placed many Catholic schools, Jewish day schools, schools for Muslims, and schools for the Amish in the nonreviewable category, partly because they had been created much earlier. Congress received over four hundred thousand letters complaining that religious freedom was being infringed. The IRS received one hundred twenty thousand letters of protest. The agency's press officer Ellen Murphy admitted, "The response is more than we've ever received on any other proposal."[31]

Richard Viguerie, the conservative direct-mail pioneer, later said that the rule change "galvanized the Religious Right. It was the spark that ignited the religious right's involvement in real politics." Robert Billings, who would soon become a spokesman for Christian schools in their lobbying, agreed. "The IRS ignited the dynamite that had been lying around for years," he said. The reason it did so, as the conservative political activist Paul Weyrich later said, was that the rule change "shattered the Christian community's notion that Christians could isolate themselves inside their own institutions and teach what they pleased."[32]

Jerry Falwell Sr., the founder of Lynchburg Christian Academy and Lynchburg Baptist College (later Liberty University), was among those shaken by the ruling. Both Falwell's academy and his college had been overtly segregationist, church-based organizations, founded as extensions of his Thomas Road Baptist Church. By 1978, when the IRS changed its rules, Falwell had relaxed his segregationist stance, but the academy still enrolled only 5 black students out of the 1,147-member student body. He saw immediately that the IRS threatened his growing educational empire.[33]

The next year, in 1979, Falwell formed the political action group the Moral Majority. The express purpose of the group was to mobilize, in Falwell's words, "an army of 'nonbelievers,' " which included Catholics, Mormons, and many others with whom Falwell disagreed religiously but who could nevertheless support what he considered "God's Will for the Nation." Shortly before the 1980 election Falwell further explained his purposes: "I am seeking to rally together the people of this country who still believe in decency, the home, the family, morality, the free-enterprise system, and all the great ideals that are the cornerstone of this nation."[34]

Others quickly signed on, seeing the potential power of the new organization. "We have together, with the Protestants and the Catholics, enough votes to run the country," the Christian broadcaster Pat Robertson said. "When people say, 'We've had enough,' we are going to take over."[35]

To work effectively, though, the Moral Majority needed a political leader. Falwell cast about before eventually settling on the actor-turned-politician Ronald Reagan as their standard bearer. It was not, at first glance, an obvious match. Reagan was religiously illiterate, divorced, and an infrequent churchgoer. But he had a long history of supporting the causes Falwell championed. In 1964, after the school prayer and Bible-reading decisions, he endorsed constitutional amendments to bring both back to public schools. In 1967, after being elected governor of California, he pledged at a prayer breakfast that "trusting in God for guidance will be an integral part of my administration." In 1976, while running for president (unsuccessfully), he told a Christian talk-show host that he had "had an experience that could be described as 'born again.' "[36]

He spoke their language in another way as well. An essential part of Reagan's political persona was his lamentation of decline.

He had long perfected the jeremiad, declaring that the United States had betrayed its principles at some point in the past. The exact moment differed—it was either the 1930s or the 1960s or a long, progressive slide—but he decried again and again the loss of principle as a national disaster. His story worked perfectly with the conservative Christian feeling of political decay, even when he did not specifically invoke God.[37]

During the 1980 election Reagan sensed the emerging power of the Religious Right and courted them assiduously. In January, before the South Carolina primary, he appeared at Bob Jones University, a fundamentalist college that had been fighting with the IRS since 1971 over its reluctance to admit nonwhites as students to the school. The leaders of the university believed that the Bible forbade interracial dating, marriage, and sex. Because their racial policies were grounded in religious belief, Bob Jones thought that IRS rules interfered with religious practice and violated the First Amendment.[38]

But the university began to change its policies under pressure. Prior to 1971 it had prohibited nonwhites from enrolling in the school. Between 1971 and 1975, after the IRS began to threaten action, the university admitted married black students, but then only if they had married another nonwhite student. Finally, in May 1975, it removed its discriminatory admissions policy entirely. The administration instituted in its place a rule that prohibited interracial dating and marriage. It also promised to expel any student who violated the policy, advocated a change in policy, or even affiliated with any group that advocated a change. In 1976 the IRS rescinded the university's tax-exempt status. The university sued.[39]

The agency said in response it was only following earlier court rulings that regarded tax exemption for nonprofits as an expression of the common law concept of charity. A nonprofit demonstrated its charity by generating some kind of public benefit as a justification for its status. Racially discriminatory schools by definition did not offer a public benefit, the IRS said, and operated contrary to public policy. Bob Jones University and other schools like it were therefore properly denied tax exemption. But the university convinced the U.S. District Court of South Carolina that because its racial policies reflected its religious belief it was immune to the rules for nonreligious, private schools. The District Court set aside the IRS's determination.[40]

The government appealed the case to the Court of Appeals for the Fourth Circuit. It had not yet been argued when Reagan decided to speak at the university as part of his 1980 campaign. Reagan used the occasion to address the many religious schools that objected to federal interference. He denounced the actions against Bob Jones, signaling the general solicitousness toward private religious rights that he promised would be a hallmark of his administration. The audience so loved his speech that it gave him, in the characterization of the *New York Times*, "one of the warmest receptions of his . . . campaign."[41]

Reagan systematically worked conservative religious issues into the Republican Party platform. At the Republican National Convention the delegates promised to "halt the unconstitutional regulatory vendetta launched by Mr. Carter's IRS commissioner against independent schools." Party officials were annoyed to discover that the action had actually begun under the Republican Richard Nixon, not the Democrat Jimmy Carter, but the point was made regardless. The platform also denounced abortion and promised to appoint judges who would "respect traditional family values and the sanctity of innocent human life." When he first read the platform Jerry Falwell said with satisfaction that the document "could easily be the constitution of a fundamentalist Baptist Church."[42]

Shortly after the convention Reagan appeared before fifteen thousand conservative church leaders in Dallas. He continued his courtship by assuring them that he supported the attempt to bring their ideas into the public. "When I hear the First Amendment used as a reason to keep traditional moral values away from policymaking, I am shocked," he told them. "The First Amendment was not written to protect the people from religious values, but to protect those values from tyranny." His succinct disparagement of, in effect, the last forty years of jurisprudence, communicated to evangelicals that he had their back.[43]

The sweeping nature of his statement surprised news outlets. The *New York Times* pointed out that before he spoke Reagan sat in the audience as religious leaders railed against the government and the direction of society. He applauded frequently, including during a sermon by the Reverend James Robison, who told the crowd, "I'm sick and tired of hearing about all of the radicals and the perverts and the liberals and the leftists and the Communists coming out of the closet. It's time for God's people to come out of the closet."[44]

The Catholic church began to mobilize too. In September Humberto Cardinal Medeiros, archbishop of Boston, issued a pastoral letter that was read from the pulpit at many Catholic churches during Sunday Mass. The letter condemned politicians who "make abortions possible by law." "If you are for true human freedom—and life—you will follow your conscience when you vote," the letter said. "You will vote to save 'our children, born and unborn.' "[45]

Howard Phillips, the head of the Conservative Caucus, was jubilant when he heard about the letter. "Cardinal Madeiros has joined the Moral Majority," he told reporters. Richard Viguerie also lauded the letter's effect in mobilizing the Christian voter. "It certainly gives legitimacy to the whole process," he said.[46]

Two weeks later Reagan appeared at the National Religious Broadcasters Association in Lynchburg, Virginia, where he condemned the expulsion of God from the classroom. Not quite prepared to believe he was being sincere, reporters began to press him about his alliance with the Religious Right. They asked about his statements to the broadcasters, querying him about his position on church and state. In response, he said that he supported church-state separatism. But what that meant was that he opposed state-mandated prayer. He thought voluntary, nonsectarian school prayer was perfectly fine.[47]

Liberal Christians were especially troubled by Reagan's alliance with conservatives, but they had no effective political response. News reports began to take note of the organizational difficulties in mainline churches, especially the drop in membership and what the *New York Times* characterized as a "loss of cohesive purpose." The best that liberal religious leaders could do was to complain that conservatives regarded themselves as the one true church, which was ironic because that charge had formerly been made by Protestants against Catholics. Now liberal Protestants were saying the same thing about their conservative Protestant counterparts.[48]

On election night liberal despair would deepen. Reagan won in a landslide. Forty of the forty-three congressmen endorsed by the Moral Majority won their races. Several congressmen targeted by the organization, including George McGovern (D-SD), Birch Bayh (D-IN), and Frank Church (D-ID), lost their seats.

Christian conservatives were jubilant. It was, from their point of view, a complete electoral vindication. Gary Jarmin, the political director of the advocacy group Christian Voice, said that Reagan's victory "points to the beginning of a new era." Jerry Falwell called the election "the greatest day for the cause of conservatism and American morality in my adult life."[49]

Reagan could not agree more. In his inaugural address he went out of his way to reinforce conservatives' optimism. He told the crowd that the long period of national decline was coming to an end. The past leaders of the country had forgotten that "we are a nation under God." He promised to govern in a way that recognized the proper role of the Christian deity in human affairs. Recommitting to God would change moral direction. "Let us begin an era of national renewal," he said.[50]

Reagan's election was obviously a watershed, but it was not exactly clear at first what the policy goals were. Often Reagan's rhetoric seemed to point in opposite directions at once. He sometimes spoke in defense of private ordering, asserting that communities and individuals ought to be able to control their lives as they saw fit, free of governmental interference. Other times he spoke of the importance of religious values in public policy determinations, in effect claiming that personal religious ideas were justifiably brought into public life to establish moral and political norms. His rhetorical inconsistency mirrored that of the Religious Right, whose leaders could invoke religious freedom from public policy in one sentence and in the next lament the naked public square in which religion no longer formed a protective canopy. The notions of public and private, in conservative rhetoric, became manipulable, even fungible, depending upon the situation.

The court system in the meantime tried to come up with some coherent public-private standard without much success. Shortly after the election the Appeals Court for the Fourth Circuit handed down an opinion against Bob Jones University. The majority upheld the IRS's decision to change the college's tax status. Because tax exemption offered a kind of monetary subsidy, it constituted a form of governmental support. If an educational institution contradicted a central component of public policy, such as nondiscrimination, the government could withdraw its support. The court dismissed the university's insistence that First Amendment rights were being violated. Because taxation necessarily involved some kind of entanglement with religious institutions, the government would be involved in religious life whether it granted or denied tax exemption. Given the conundrum, the agency ought to err on the side of equality.[51]

Bob Jones immediately appealed to the U.S. Supreme Court. A wide coalition of groups filed amicus briefs urging it to accept the case. The grouping showcased the coalition of the Religious Right. It included the National Association of Evangelicals, the Church of Jesus Christ of Latter-day Saints, the Center for Law and Religious Freedom of the Christian Legal Society, and the Church of God, a Pentecostal group.[52]

All tended to make overlapping points. The case offered an opportunity to the NAE to counter the "ominous threat" that had risen from governmental policy. The Church of Jesus Christ of Latter-day Saints fretted that enforcing national policy through tax law would erode the rights of religious organizations under the First Amendment. "This question goes to the heart of the very existence of religious organizations," the Mormons' brief pointed out, because "the power to tax" included "the power to destroy."[53]

For all of the groups the case allowed them to clarify the limits of religious freedom, which they thought should be minimal. Their definition privileged institutional autonomy over individual liberty. That was why the Center for Law and Religious Freedom believed, as it said in its brief, "This issue of racial discrimination is but the thin end of the wedge." If sustained, the rule would allow governmental intrusion into religious institutions for any number of reasons. Likewise the NAE complained that the lower court's notion of a "compelling state interest" might lead to a situation in which the right of religious liberty was "totally eclipsed" and religious institutions would become subject to state control.[54]

After reading the briefs, the court agreed to hear the case. It combined the Bob Jones appeal with a similar petition from Goldsboro Christian Schools, Inc. Located in Goldsboro, North Carolina, the school was established "to conduct an institution or institutions of learning . . . giving special emphasis to the Christian religion and the ethics revealed in the Holy Scriptures." The IRS had denied tax-exempt status to the school because it had a racially discriminatory admissions policy. It justified the practice by using the so-called Son of Ham interpretation of the Christian scriptures, which held that the races could be traced to Noah's three sons. His son Ham produced Asians and Africans. His son Shem produced the Hebrews. His son Japheth produced Caucasians. In the Genesis account, Noah put a curse on his son Ham after Ham saw Noah's nakedness. The darker skin of Asians and Africans was supposed to be a mark of the curse. In Goldsboro's interpretation, the mixing of these races, especially between the sons of Ham (Asians and Africans) and the others, violated God's commandment.[55]

Once the Supreme Court accepted the case, House minority whip and Republican from Mississippi Trent Lott decided to get involved. He filed an amicus brief in support of Bob Jones and Goldsboro, but he also worked behind the scenes. He contacted officials in the Reagan administration, urging them to change policy. When officials briefed Reagan on Lott's position, the president agreed with Lott. The Department of the Treasury revoked the earlier IRS rule and sought to re-award tax-exempt status to the Christian segregation academies. As the shift in position began to leak out, the administration justified itself by contending that tax policy ought not be used to foster "social aims."[56]

Critics erupted. Benjamin Hooks, the president of the NAACP, said the administration's decision "panders and appeals to the worst instinct of racism in America." The *New York Times* editorialized that Reagan supported "tax exempt hate." In the critical news coverage observers cited two prominent motives: the administration was either racist or it was paying off the Religious Right or both.[57]

The administration soon informed the court of its intended rule change. It said that the IRS did not possess the authority to remove tax exemption from racially discriminatory, private religious schools. Because the government was now in agreement with Bob Jones, it asked the court to dismiss the case as moot.[58]

Amicus briefs in support of the government's former position flowed into the court. The ACLU, the NAACP, and several Jewish organizations, including the AJC and the Anti-Defamation League, urged the High Court to reject Bob Jones's argument and that of the administration.

Many of the briefs simply echoed the opinion of the lower court. But the NAACP's brief went further. It feared that to accept Bob Jones's position would be to affirm a sprawling definition of religious freedom that would have profound consequences in public life. Institutional religious autonomy would allow schools "the right to expand racial discrimination into their secular educational business, a private enterprise they have set up to compete with the public schools." There was no reason to believe it would stop there. To agree with Bob Jones's ideas would be "to extend the most stringent forms of First Amendment protection to a religious organization's conduct of a normally secular business," including hospitals, charities, and any number of other concerns. The effect would be to allow private religious imperatives, backed by law, into large portions of public life.[59]

The issues were dense. The court was confused. After oral argument the justices had a hard time agreeing on what the case was about. Was it about religious freedom? Equal protection? Legislative authority? They were all over the map.[60]

Finally, Chief Justice Warren Burger took the case for himself. Writing for the eight-person majority, he explained that the lower courts were correct in denying tax exemption to the two schools because such institutions must confer public benefit. Since tax exemption affected all taxpayers, who became "indirect and vicarious 'donors' " to the tax-exempt entity, "the institution's purpose," Burger wrote, "must not be so at odds with the common community conscience as to undermine any public benefit that might otherwise be conferred." And because "racial discrimination in education involves deeply and widely accepted views of elementary justice," Burger continued, the state's interest in ensuring equality was a compelling national interest.[61]

Conservatives were incredulous and decried the decision as the logical extension of secularism, especially the court's invocation of a "common community conscience." Rather than allowing the privatization of faith in religious communities, the court now penalized the elaboration of religious commitments in separate institutions if those commitments conflicted with public policy or with some overarching national conscience that was simply handed down from on high. Here, they complained, was a positive secularism that established a new orthodoxy and sought to regulate religious commitments even when they occurred in a private setting.

Beverly LaHaye, a prominent Christian activist and head of Concerned Women for America, spoke for many when she said that the case was in keeping with a much longer trend in which "the secularists have been cleverly using the First Amendment to suppress religious freedom." She connected the case with the decisions about school prayer, Bible reading, obscenity, and other liberalizing decisions. With the court's affirmation that the government could use taxes to penalize religious institutions, the way was now open for a variety of things that LaHaye found objectionable. What would stop the government from requiring the church to hire homosexuals to maintain tax exemption? What if pedophilia became public policy? What if a suit were brought by the North American Man-Boy Love Association that wanted a doctrinal change internal to a church? Was it not obvious, she asked, what the court would decide?[62]

Others also criticized the court, not always from the perspective of the Religious Right. In the *Harvard Law Review* the Yale legal scholar Robert Cover wondered if the court understood what it was doing. In any kind of community, he pointed out, there was an operative set of norms and values, a regulatory principle in social life that Cover considered a kind of law. Inevitably in a pluralistic society these forms of law and these social rules had to be trimmed, pruned, or even killed by the courts. The diverse, wild profusion of cultural values and norms made the procedure both painful and necessary since their unrestrained growth would make national life and national law impossible. The conflict between norms made cases like the one involving Bob Jones an inevitable outcome of pluralistic society, which required careful consideration of the purposes of constitutional government to resolve.

But in the *Bob Jones* case Cover thought the court had failed to act decisively enough on any discernible principle and without any clear purpose. The problem was the old one of conflicting rights. Insular communities wanted the space to practice their own way of life, a right that was in principle threatened by the court's decision and left the communities open to intrusion by the state. Racial minorities, by contrast, wanted the court to adopt a redemptive constitutionalism that would prohibit the state subsidization of racism through private organizations. The court satisfied neither group. It allowed that the IRS's actions were permissible, but it refused to say that the loss of tax exemption was mandated by the Constitution. It declared that IRS regulation was possible simply because Bob Jones and schools like it violated the common community conscience upon which public policy was constructed. By ruling that Bob Jones violated public policy and thus was rightly denied tax exemption, the court left a variety of privately ordered institutions open to the vagaries of change, while not producing a constitutional ruling against the state-subsidization of racism.[63]

The problem was again traceable to the court's ambiguous commitments and uncertain priorities. When faced with a case that turned on the distinction between public and private and the freedom of religion, the court seemed unable to resolve its many contradictory imperatives. It found itself at odds and adrift on past opinion and without any kind of constitutional agreement. Unlike the Warren court, with its substantive liberalism, the court under Burger began to labor under the breakdown of categories and the loss of cohesive philosophy. It was a predicable outcome of the somewhat tortured jurisprudence the court had created over the past forty years.

Postsixties activists working toward gay rights also steadily obscured the line between public and private. By the early eighties, gay activists had been aiming for fifteen years to normalize alternative sexualities and alternative arrangements. They had had some success, mostly cultural. Their first task had been to remove the stigma of homosexuality by coming out as gay. Howard Brown, a former New York health commissioner, explained that the act of coming out had social implications. It would, in his words, "help free the generation that comes after us from the dreadful agony of secrecy, the constant need to hide."[64]

Because the focus was on normalizing various sexual identities, gay activists joined feminists in their suspicion of the public–private distinction. "It is primarily our *public* existence, not our right to privacy, which is under assault by the right," one gay activist explained in 1982. So long as gay people conducted their lives behind closed doors, they were not likely to be harassed. To hold hands or to kiss in a public space, by contrast, involved not just social disapproval but often the threat of arrest or violence.[65]

Yet some within the gay community thought they saw in the court's privacy jurisprudence an opening wedge to advance the cause. The primary target from a legal standpoint was the rejection of antisodomy laws, statutes that were once common in many places and were in the 1980s still present and enforceable in about half the states. These laws had various provisions, but they usually forbade anal and oral sex, even in the privacy of a home, sometimes limited to same-sex intercourse or sometimes forbidding any anal or oral sex, even among heterosexual partners. In 1986, three years after *Bob Jones*, gay activists finally got a case to the U.S. Supreme Court with the contention that antisodomy violated their privacy.

It began a few years earlier, when Michael Hardwick was cited by an Atlanta police officer for throwing away a beer can outside the gay bar at which he worked. The officer thought he had been drinking in public, which violated a local ordinance. Through a clerical error Hardwick missed his court date. A warrant was issued for his arrest. Although the error was quickly corrected and Hardwick paid his fine, the original officer who issued the citation went to Hardwick's home to serve the now-invalid warrant. He discovered Hardwick having oral sex with another man. Georgia antisodomy law prohibited both oral and anal sex, though it did not distinguish between homosexual and heterosexual sodomy. The officer arrested Hardwick after observing what he characterized as Hardwick's belligerent attitude and booked him for violating the antisodomy statute. The district attorney chose not to pursue the case since he did not believe that consensual sodomy ought to be a prosecutable offense and, even if he had thought so, the warrant had already expired when the officer entered the residence. But Hardwick was incensed at the entire episode. He sued Michael Bowers, the attorney general of Georgia, in an attempt to get the sodomy law overturned. Eventually the ACLU offered to represent Hardwick in his appeals.[66]

In oral argument before the U.S. Supreme Court, the attorney for Georgia, Michael E. Hobbs, was forthright about the state's reasons for defending the sodomy law. Up to that point the court had acknowledged only a few forms of private association that were protected by the right of privacy and were therefore immune from intervention by the state. Hobbs warned that if the court struck down sodomy laws based on a right to privacy, then the family itself would face a redefinition because gays and lesbians would be seen as having the ability to create their own families outside of a heterosexual union. There was the potential, Hobbs said, "for a reshuffling of our society, for a reordering of our society." The change would make the Constitution an engine of revolution rather than of ordered liberty, and it would undermine the traditional conceptions of family life that had guided the nation. This was again a case of "the collective moral aspirations of the people" and "the collective conscience of our people," Hobbs told the court. His language echoed that of Chief Justice Warren Burger in the *Bob Jones* case.[67]

By the time the case got to the Supreme Court, Hardwick was represented by the Harvard law professor Laurence Tribe, who pressed the court to uphold the principle of its prior opinions. He rejected Georgia's framing of the case. The state made an issue of the family structure, Tribe told the court, when what they were talking about was sex. The sole issue under dispute was the ability of the state to control the intimate associations of consenting adults. The right to privacy ought to cover those associations.

The justices pressed Tribe on his understanding, notably more skeptical of his position than of Georgia's. They thought the state had the legitimate ability to regulate moral conduct inside the home, comparing homosexuality with other moral offenses like incest or polygamy. If the state could ban incest, they asked, why could it not ban homosexual liaisons? Tribe responded that there was no agreed-upon harm in homosexual liaisons between consenting adults. And even if there was, they were consenting adults, so they had the liberty to conduct their lives according to their own lights. This was the moral relativism that had been an obvious component of postsixties politics. But several justices continued to be apprehensive about how to limit Tribe's reasoning. They spoke of a slippery slope that would require them to strike down all moral regulation.

During conference it was apparent that the majority was set to uphold sodomy laws. A minority of justices sought to point out, in Harry Blackmun's words, "the thought control aspects and the religious underpinnings" of the statutes. The frankly theocratic quality of antisodomy meant that the court should strike down the laws to protect secular liberty, Blackmun said.[68]

The five-person majority simply waved away Blackmun's warning and denied that the right to privacy applied to homosexual acts. Gay sex, the court wrote, had no connection to family, marriage, or procreation, which was the whole point of the right to privacy in the majority's understanding. Since the right did not apply to Michael Hardwick's sex life, the state was perfectly free to pass laws that expressed moral positions or that grew out of moral principle.[69]

But in spite of the majority's claims, the court's ruling was a departure. In Brandeis's original conception, the right to privacy was a right of the individual in recognition of an inviolate personality. In *Roe* the right to privacy allowed the individual woman to make a moral determination in consultation only with her doctor, freed from the moral constraints of those around her and without regard to her marital status. But now the court construed the right to privacy as a collective right within the family that those who remained outside the bonds of a heterosexual union could not access.

The court's opinion left Blackmun, the author of *Roe v. Wade*, dismayed. In his dissent he chided his colleagues for their abandonment of both privacy and secularism. "That certain, but by no means all, religious groups condemn the behavior at issue gives the State no license to impose their judgments on the entire citizenry," he wrote for the four liberal justices. "The legitimacy of secular legislation depends, instead, on whether the State can advance some justification for its law beyond its conformity to religious doctrine. . . . A State can no more punish private behavior because of religious intolerance than it can punish such behavior because of racial animus."[70]

To gay activists, the ruling further turned them away from asserting privacy. It was now clear, as Sarah E. Igo has put it, that the right was "just another form of discrimination." The way forward, according to the literary scholar Deborah Nelson, was the abandonment of privacy and the attempt instead to form "queer publics" and a "transformed public space where identities form, communities are built, and individuals are recognized in new ways."[71]

By the middle of the 1980s, in short, both the Religious Right and the postsixties Left had become convinced that private ordering was of no compelling use to their political projects. What both the *Bob Jones* case and the Georgia sodomy case showed was that each group had only one option left. If the personal was political, all that remained was a battle over culture, an attempt to get the norms of public life to conform to one's personal ideals; in other words, a culture war.

The culture wars of the 1980s and 1990s are often remembered as a series of angry shouting matches, which they were. But they were shouting matches in the absence of any way to privatize disagreement. They involved, as the sociologist James Davison Hunter has said, "our most fundamental ideas about who we are as Americans," but they were made possible by a belief that who people are as Americans ought to be the same as who they are as individuals. They turned on a suspicion of privacy and a conflation of privacy with a kind of shame or falseness.[72]

The court itself was impotent to help as the culture wars began to make themselves felt in law as well. The justices confronted past opinions, their own political divisions, and the divides of the citizenry in the cases that came before them. Part of the problem they faced was the old one of diversity, now made worse and more confounding in the postsixties era. The loss of a cultural center made it especially difficult to understand or to create religious determinations, to decide what counted as religious.

The befuddlement about what was and was not religious had been long-standing but was heightened by sixties activism. Many countercultural figures had long been attracted to an alternative religious orientation that the psychologist Abraham Maslow described in 1964 as "peak experience." The idea was that there were certain moments when a person's rational calculation was overwhelmed by a hallucinatory emotional release, often in the context of religious worship and ritual. New Age religions from the 1960s onward sought to find avenues into peak experience, for example, through meditation, incantation, Native American ritual, or mind-altering chemicals.[73]

As the counterculture went mainstream, religious categories began to expand and in some sense to break down as people of all types began to dabble in formerly fringe ideas and behavior. Gone was the time when Associate Justice Arthur Goldberg could dismiss, as he had in conference in 1963, Black Muslims and "screwball groups" as being outside the parameters of constitutional protection. Given the often-weird, the sprawling, and the bewildering variety of the many religious groups that spun out of the sixties maelstrom, the court increasingly labored with its own sense of real and fake religion.[74]

Shortly after the court ruled in the Georgia sodomy case, another suit began to make its way through the system, one that would, again, cause problems for the strategy of privatization in a secular political order. The case began in the 1980s as a result of the so-called War on Drugs, which was itself a response to the counterculture. Although federal policy makers began to target the illicit use of marijuana, narcotics, and hallucinogens in the early 1970s, by the time of the Reagan administration the War on Drugs had become connected to a variety of conservative policy initiatives.[75]

The plaintiff in the case making its way through the courts was a native man named Al Smith, born in 1919 on the Klamath Indian Reservation at the foot of the Cascade Mountains in Oregon. On the reservation as a child, government authorities prohibited Smith from engaging in native ritual or tradition. They instead issued directives that required native children to enroll in Catholic school. Once he graduated from high school, Smith left the reservation, joined the army, and eventually faced dishonorable discharge as a result of his alcoholism. By the time he was forty he had become sober and worked in drug and alcohol treatment centers for the Bureau of Indian Affairs, a section of the Department of the Interior.[76]

Here is where the problems began. As part of his recovery he began to reconnect with native culture, and he joined the Native American Church, an intertribal and syncretic Christian group that used peyote as a sacrament. A powerful hallucinogen, peyote was listed as a Schedule 1 drug, meaning that the Drug Enforcement Agency considered it highly addictive and medically inutile. It was therefore illegal to use peyote or prescribe it, which brought it into the ambit of the federal government's War on Drugs.

In 1982, as the *Bob Jones* case made its way to the U.S. Supreme Court, Smith got a job with the Douglas County Council on Alcohol and Drug Abuse Prevention and Treatment Center. He was required to remain drug free as a condition of his appointment and was warned by his superiors not to ingest peyote. He did so anyhow, within the context of the religious ritual of the Native American Church. When his boss found out, he was in trouble. His superiors asked for his resignation. Smith refused. They offered to let him participate in an Employee Assistance Program for substance abuse. He refused again. He later said, "I did not need rehabilitation for going to church." In the face of his repeated refusals to address his supposed drug problem, he was fired. And because he was let go with cause, he was denied unemployment assistance by the state of Oregon.[77]

Smith sued for unemployment benefits, and, initially, he won. At this point, the state attorney general, Dave Frohnmayer, got involved. "We saw it almost completely as a drug case," Frohnmayer later told the religious studies scholar Carolyn N. Long. He continued,

> We knew that there was a First Amendment issue related to it, because it was a religious practice, but it seemed anomalous that someone would be able to use the First Amendment as a sword, not merely as a shield. That is to say, that belief and action may well be protected against some form of criminal prosecution, but the notion that someone can affirmatively claim unemployment compensation, that is, to claim money from taxes that are coercively exacted from other people, for engaging in activity which for anyone else not of that religion would actually violate criminal law, seemed almost nonsensical.[78]

Led by Frohnmayer, the state appealed all the way to the Oregon Supreme Court, which also ruled in favor of Smith. The state decided to appeal to the U.S. Supreme Court. In his petition to the court, Frohnmayer put the constitutional issue front and center. "Does the Free Exercise Clause compel a state to award unemployment benefits to a drug rehabilitation counselor who agrees to refrain from using illegal drugs as a condition of his employment and is fired for misconduct after illegally ingesting peyote as part of a religious ceremony?" he asked. In putting the issue so starkly, Frohnmayer raised again the question that had bedeviled the court since the Jehovah's Witness cases and had reemerged in the Bob Jones controversy. What were the limits of religious freedom, and how did those limits function in a pluralistic society?[79]

After an initial round of briefing and oral argument the High Court remanded the case to the Oregon Supreme Court with a further question. Since the case was about Oregon unemployment compensation, did the sacramental use of illegal drugs violate the state's drug laws, not just those of the federal government?

The Oregon Supreme Court ruled that Oregon law did prohibit the sacramental use of illegal drugs, but then it struck down that law as violating the free-exercise clause of the First Amendment. The state appealed to the U.S. Supreme Court, which agreed again to hear the case. This time, the court marshaled a 6–3 majority written by the conservative jurist Antonin Scalia.[80]

The opinion sought to break through the categorical confusion about public and private by departing from past opinions. The court had earlier ruled that the government needed a compelling public reason to infringe on religious practice because religious freedom was a fundamental right. The nondiscrimination policy in the case of Bob Jones University was one such example of a compelling reason. But Scalia rejected that standard. If the government needed a compelling reason to infringe upon religion, then, given the diversity of American religious belief, it would be courting anarchy. Ruling in favor of Al Smith, he wrote, "would open the prospect of constitutionally required religious exemptions from civic obligations of almost every conceivable kind." Such exemptions might include compulsory military service, health and safety regulations, compulsory vaccination laws, drug laws, traffic laws, social welfare legislation such as minimum wage laws, child labor laws, animal cruelty laws, environmental protection laws, and equal opportunity laws. "The First Amendment's protection of religious liberty does not require this," Scalia wrote.[81]

His position was startling, given his reputation as a Catholic religious conservative. Scalia put forth a vision of American secularism that privatized religious practice and privileged the power of the state. A state might accommodate religious belief. Or it might not. But that was to be left to the relevant legislature to decide. It could not be constitutionally mandated. The crucial thing was that an individual ought not be allowed simply to hold a religious conviction and then make himself exempt from relevant public law. Scalia even quoted Felix Frankfurter to the effect that "the mere possession of religious convictions which contradict the relevant concerns of a political society does not relieve the citizen from the discharge of political responsibilities." Scalia's vision was, like Frankfurter's, one that saw the power of the secular state and the disintegrative possibilities of religious convictions.[82]

But within Scalia's reasoning was a presumption of religious privilege that ran against the substantive secularism that Frankfurter supported. "It may be fairly said," Scalia acknowledged in the opinion, "that leaving accommodation to the political process will place at a relative disadvantage those religious practices that are not widely engaged in." That was, he said, "an inevitable consequence of democratic government." His position, which he would later put more explicitly, was that the government was permitted to disregard atheists, polytheists, and New Religion practitioners. Their religious expression was not, for the purposes of the Constitution, considered religion. It was the monotheists that the Founders had in mind when they sought to constitutionally protect free religious exercise.[83]

His presumption of Judeo-Christian privilege was part of the reason that secular liberals who might otherwise have supported the decision came out against it. To many liberals and leftists, the majority's reasoning amounted to a denial of Al Smith's identity as a native American and therefore ran against the embrace of diversity and pluralism that had been so central to the development of liberalism since the 1920s, if not before. The fact that Smith was demanding positive privileges from the state that were not afforded to other nonreligious people, as the Oregon attorney general first pointed out, seemed not to enter the calculations of many who protested from the left of center. Had Smith been a white evangelical Christian, it is likely that they might have seen the matter differently.

Religious conservatives, by contrast, immediately saw the threat of the *Smith* decision to their movement. They had been demanding public accommodation, even support, for private religious sentiment since the *Bob Jones* case, if not before. If the *Smith* decision stood, they would necessarily have a harder time using the law and the courts for their political project.

A groundswell of criticism soon emerged against the decision from all sides. A coalition of liberal and conservative religious groups began to come together to uphold religious freedom as a key constitutional value. The heterogenous character of the critics was astonishing and ought to have been disquieting. The coalition included homeschoolers, church–state separationists, the National Council of Churches, the NAE, the U.S. Catholic bishops, and major Jewish organizations. Overall, sixty-eight religious and civil liberties groups joined the cause.[84]

The Coalition for the Free Exercise of Religion began to lobby both the states and the federal government. Politicians took notice. A few months after the *Smith* decision Representative Stephen Solarz (D-NY) introduced a bill entitled the Religious Freedom Restoration Act (RFRA). The prospective act required that "governments should not substantially burden religious exercise without compelling justification." The primary purpose was to restore the protections of religious freedom that were in line with the court's earlier jurisprudence. The bill required the courts to use a balancing test to decide between religious freedom and competing government interests.[85]

When the act was introduced Solarz commented on just how universally people seemed to support it. "It is perhaps not too hyperbolic to suggest that in the history of the Republic, there has rarely been a bill which more closely approximates motherhood and apple pie. . . . In fact, I know, at least so far, of no one who opposes the legislation." The universal acclamation, in the midst of an otherwise bitter culture war, might have given secularists pause had they thought it through. In the end only a few Catholic and anti-abortion groups, fearing that a woman might invoke a right of conscience to get an abortion, mounted any opposition. The bill's sponsors made a few changes, none of them substantive, and the bill proceeded through the legislative hurdles before being passed by both houses of Congress.[86]

In 1993 President Bill Clinton signed the RFRA into law. Nineteen states also passed state-level RFRAs. At the signing ceremony for the act Clinton mentioned the rare bipartisan coalition that had come together to pass the bill. "The power of God is such that even in the legislative process," Clinton said, "miracles can happen."[87]

CHAPTER NINE

Religious Freedom

Those hoping that the RFRA would mark an end to the culture wars were bound to be disappointed. There was a certain naivete on the part of many of the act's boosters, a longing for a consensual order that had passed. It soon became apparent that the freedom being restored was an essentially contested concept, in keeping with the wider political disagreements that beset American life. In the case of religious freedom, those disagreements had been long-standing. Going back to the Jehovah's Witnesses cases, the courts, politicians, and citizens had worked to define and limit it. The resulting jurisprudence had created divisions over how to protect individual conscience while simultaneously upholding a political order that did not privilege any one religion.

In the *Smith* decision part of the dilemma was the way that pluralism and conscience seemed to work against secularism. In the early development of the American secular order, pluralism had been a way of decentering the demands of Christianity. The normative embrace of diversity rejected Christian privilege and power in a variety of domains, usually through privatizing difference and religious belief. But the breakdown of public–private as a stable conceptual distinction shifted the configuration of terms. Now, pluralism could be used to demand the public recognition of private religious belief via the language of religious freedom.

That would be especially useful for the Christian Right. In May 1994, about a year after Clinton signed the RFRA into law, a group of conservative theologians and leaders published a carefully crafted statement entitled "Evangelicals and Catholics Together" (ECT). It noted that the past several decades had seen the convergence of and cooperation between the two groups as they fought, in the words of the statement, "for the truth that politics, law, and culture must be secured by moral truth." "More specifically," the statement continued, "we contend together for religious freedom."[1]

To the signers of the statement, contending for their shared liberty meant not merely the right of individual belief or private religious expression. It also required the recognition that religious groups had a responsibility to order civil society. Their duty of public ordering relied on the concept of morality, a shared domain that ought to be recognized by everyone. "We reject the notion that this constitutes a partisan 'religious agenda' in American politics," they wrote. "Rather, this is a set of directions oriented to the common good and discussable on the basis of public reason. While our sense of civic responsibility is informed and motivated by Christian faith, our intention is to elevate the level of political and moral discourse in a manner that excludes no one and invites the participation of all people of good will."[2]

Many liberal critics were not so sure. But given the way that old categories seemed to be shifting, their proper response was not entirely clear. Among those seeking to understand the changing dynamic—eager to clear up the definitional confusion—was the philosopher John Rawls, a towering figure in Anglo-American political thought whose influence went far beyond academia. When the ECT statement invoked "public reason," it used a Rawlsian concept to its own ends.

Rawls had long worried about the challenge that religious disagreement posed to the survival of constitutional democracy. It is not too much of a generalization to say that his entire career as a political theorist had been influenced by such a concern. In his early work he had sought to circumvent religious disagreement and the challenge of pluralism by finding some universal reasoning procedure that could be accepted by all parties in a political dispute. His goal was to avoid the divisiveness of religious thought that he associated with the Protestant Reformation, the Wars of Religion, and the Catholic Counter-Reformation. The search for an alternative language that subverted religious disagreement reached its fullest expression in 1971 when Rawls published *A Theory of Justice*, his first masterwork.[3]

By the 1980s and with the advance of the Religious Right, Rawls had begun to reconsider whether such a universal reasoning procedure was feasible in a democracy, whether it was possible to circumvent the language emerging from disparate and often antagonistic traditions in the way he had attempted. It was not that he departed from his earlier position. He was simply forced to admit that his philosophical and ethical commitments amounted to only one theory among many in American society. He recognized that his search for, in William A. Galston's words, a "transcultural, truth-based political evaluation" would not have the effect he hoped for in any actual, living democracy. There was an ongoing, inescapable amount of moral, ethical, and religious disagreement that necessarily fed into the political process.[4]

So as he watched American debate become polarized by moral and religious questions, and as he observed the culture wars driving American democratic practice, Rawls began to ask even more foundational questions, ones that went to the heart of democratic theory. How, he wondered, did someone accept a law as legitimate and authoritative in a society? Under what conditions would they follow a law, even when they thought that law was unjust? How did a political order maintain legitimacy in the face of deep difference, given that laws were always going to be opposed by somebody? How did that political order command allegiance?

To parse the problem, Rawls made a series of distinctions that implicitly criticized both the New Left of the 1960s and the Religious Right in the 1980s. The most important distinction was between what he called a comprehensive doctrine and a political doctrine. A comprehensive doctrine was often a religious, moral, or philosophical persuasion that offered a deep view of human life. It was personal, necessarily. A political doctrine was something else. Rawls believed that the personal was not ever political. In a political democracy, Rawls said, people will have many kinds of comprehensive doctrines that necessarily contradict one another. To place one version of truth over others within a political system would involve an intolerable level of coercion. So a political doctrine could not be justified solely by one's comprehensive views, Christian or otherwise, if the political system was to be liberal in the broad sense of the word.[5]

This much was obvious, Rawls thought, or should have been, but categories had become confused in the years since the 1960s. The identitarian politics of the New Left and the tendency of its successors to conflate the personal and political had overlooked how such a conflation was dangerous to the political order in a diverse society. Public political ordering required a broader foundation than comprehensive personal views. It was not that such views were irrelevant, but that they were not enough on their own. In a properly functioning democracy, Rawls decided, public policy ought to rely on what he called an overlapping consensus between groups that held fundamentally rival views but who could agree on specific policy proposals. Rawls was careful to say that the overlapping consensus did not extend very far. It covered only what he called "the domain of the political," which was, again, a tightly circumscribed arena that affected all citizens in a liberal constitutional polity.[6]

The key task of the democratic process was to find an overlapping consensus. In Rawls's explanation, it emerged through a process of uncovering. The idea was that there was some kind of latent agreement in a society if that society was in any way functional but that it must be realized and brought into effect through political deliberation. If the perpetuation of their common political project was to be realized, people needed to adopt a form of political self-discipline that avoided their comprehensive doctrines while seeking to meet one another halfway. They ought to rely on what he called "public reason."[7]

In making an argument against abortion, for example, a person ought not quote from the Bible as though that settled the question because not all members of the society believed that the Bible was the word of God or understood the sacred status of the Bible in the same way or even interpreted the Bible in similar fashion. Instead, a person needed to use reasoning that would be recognized by other members of the public who shared political space but not similar religious views. The use of public reason recognized the shared nature of the political project by emphasizing the commitments of citizens in a democracy and by avoiding comprehensive doctrines likely to drive disagreement.

The question was whether or not the signers of the ECT statement, in spite of their claims to do so, abided by the rules of public reason. When they declared, "Politics, law, and culture must be secured by moral truth," they asserted their belief in an absolute set of moral rules that bound all members of society. The rules were operable, or ought to be, on everyone regardless of how many people subscribed to the view of moral truth put forward by conservative Christians.[8]

But at the same time they made gestures to public reason by using the constitutional language of religious freedom. That language had been central, if somewhat problematic, to the emergence of American secularism, and it had likewise been part of the conservative Christian strategy of preemption since the civil rights movement. By promoting their own religious freedom rather than, say, the absolute truth of Christianity, they were in some sense comporting to the secular rules of public debate.

As Rawls watched that debate unfold through the 1990s he came to the conclusion that the notion of public reason needed a greater degree of clarification than he had previously offered. The "public" part of public reason had, in spite of Rawls's efforts, continued to crumble. And the ECT statement revealed that many private religious questions did seem to have political import because something like religious freedom was a political concept that related to a person's comprehensive views.

After being criticized by religious thinkers, Rawls modified his theory. He announced that political discussion could originate in a citizen's foundational religious commitments. He accepted even that those commitments could be expressed in public discussion. "Any comprehensive doctrine, religious or secular, can be introduced into any political argument at any time," he later said, "but I argue that people who do this should also present what they believe are the public reasons for their argument." To do so would be to acknowledge that the political relation was fundamentally not one of agonistic combat but "one of civic friendship." If a person was unable to articulate his or her position in terms of public reason, that indicated the sectarian and therefore illegitimate nature of his or her political project.[9]

Still, he faced deep levels of resistance to his formulations, which exposed the wider difficulty of uniting around a common political liberalism in the postsixties era. The breakdown of categories made even one-on-one conversation hard. Shortly after Rawls began to modify his position, the Catholic philosopher Bernard Prusak, in an interview in *Commonweal*, questioned him about his recent thinking. Prusak's main point was that he understood civic friendship differently than Rawls. Prusak's conception was based on a Catholic notion of the common good. It was fundamentally a religious idea. That idea could not be bracketed in quite the way that Rawls seemed to want. He pressed Rawls on his terms.

"How do you think, in your work, the idea of the common good is revised?" Prusak wondered. "Is there still a common good? How would we speak of it in a liberal constitutional democracy where pluralism is a fact? Is it thrown out, or is it reconceived?"

Rawls responded that the common good in a liberal democracy consisted of "the means provided to assure that people can make use of their liberties." That was what made it liberal; it was focused on the individual.

"So the common good would be the good that is common to each citizen, each citizen's good, rather than an overarching good?"

Prusak was, in effect, contending that Rawls had smuggled a conception of the secular, autonomous individual into the rules of debate that he was offering. Rawls was shaping the debate through his rules. But Rawls refused to concede that his project was simply about maximizing liberal, secular autonomy. All the individuals in a polity had a common project that required one another for their individual and collective well-being.

"In my language," Rawls responded, "they're striving toward one single end, the end of justice for all citizens."[10]

While Rawls sought to clarify the debate and his own position, other thinkers began to pick up the problem by different handles. In 1989, at the high point of the culture wars, the pragmatist philosopher Richard Rorty published a collection of essays that tried to break through the dilemmas of solidarity in the postsixties era. Rorty's perspective as a philosopher, like that of Rawls, made him uniquely attuned to the role of language in these disputes. But by the late eighties he had come to the conclusion that the way analytic philosophers used language was flawed. Rorty no longer believed that offering a proper set of distinctions or adequately defining one's terms, as Rawls sought to do, would allow a person to arrive at clear thought that could solve the debate. Language just did not work that way, Rorty concluded.

Instead, human beings drew on vocabularies that were unique to time and place. These collections of words expressed certain sensibilities, values, and political projects. The American political tradition offered one such vocabulary. It came down to the present as a result of past use, and to the extent that it continued to be drawn upon it was because it continued to be useful. But there were always tensions in any vocabulary because words are inevitably imprecise, metaphorical at bottom, and definable only by reference to other words. That was not a problem for Rorty, as it was for Rawls.

The flexibility of language and its slipperiness in debate actually created an opportunity, Rorty thought, not for clarification but for political mobilization. The tensions in the American political order opened a space for action through rearrangement and negotiation of inherited concepts. One had to ask what kind of state of affairs a vocabulary helped to bring about. For instance, what did a focus on religious freedom do when deciding a political question? Answering that query required, in turn, considering other possible words, concepts, and categories in an extending exercise of compare and contrast. Rather than religious freedom, for example, what might a focus on equal treatment lead to? Linguistic analysis became not a question of definition but of strategy. "Does our use of these words," Rorty asked hypothetically, "get in the way of our use of those other words?" If so, some words or concepts had to go. Again, the point of asking the question was not to arrive at logical or definitional consistency. The goal was to find words that would create solidarity around a common political purpose.[11]

Although Rorty dispensed his lessons as an avowed member of the Left, it was the conservatives who put his ideas into practice with greatest effect. They exploited the tensions within the secular order and the conceptual confusion emerging out of sixties to stunning effect. Their appropriation of formerly secular words and their coining of ostensibly secular phrases allowed them to achieve a set of religious ends they sometimes forthrightly acknowledged and sometimes did not. And they slid in and out of alternate vocabularies as it suited their political purposes.

The RFRA soon became central to their efforts. The ECT statement had rightly pointed to religious freedom as a foundational interest of both Protestants and Catholics. Leaders within the two groups used the secular language of religious freedom to overcome their sectarian animosities and to organize for political success.

Their mobilization became more urgent at the end of the Clinton presidency, as gay rights activists also began to have some successes. In the aftermath of the Georgia sodomy case, the focus of gay activists had shifted to finding other ways of recognizing gay and lesbian civil liberties. By 1993, when Clinton signed the RFRA, some municipalities and corporations had responded to activists' pressure by creating domestic partner benefits and other arrangements that acknowledged same-sex unions. The time seemed ripe for another legal challenge. Casting about for a test vehicle, the gay and lesbian civil rights organization Lambda Legal heard about an incident in Texas involving a man named John Geddes Lawrence Jr.

Both Lawrence and his friend Tyron Garner had been arrested after the police were called to Lawrence's apartment. Lawrence was white, Garner was black. The police alleged that they found the pair having sex. Lawrence and Garner were charged and pled no contest to a misdemeanor violation of the state's antisodomy law. Lawrence later said that the two were not having sex and had never had sex. They were seated fifteen feet apart from one another when the police came in. The sexual and racial dynamics of the incident, combined with the potential of police misconduct, demonstrated how sodomy law intersected with other cultural disagreements. The episode had all the elements of a good appellate case.[12]

When it finally got to the Supreme Court in March 2003 Christian conservatives grew nervous. During oral argument Antonin Scalia asked Lawrence's attorney, Paul M. Smith, how "flagpole sitting" could be considered a fundamental right? After all, condemnation of homosexual behavior had grown out of what Scalia characterized as "a 200-year tradition of a certain type of law" that allowed the state to protect a public morality. Other conservatives on the court joined Scalia in pressing Smith on what exactly had changed over the past two hundred years.

Obviously, much had changed over that time, not least the constitutional revolution of the Fourteenth Amendment and the court's determination that certain parts of the Bill of Rights were incorporated into it. The moral condemnation toward gay sex had also begun to change. Smith decided not to lecture the justices on the law. But he did tell the conservatives that their history was selective. The case was not about public morality but about protecting, in his words, "the privacy of couples ... in their home." The fact that three-quarters of states no longer had sodomy laws implied that something had shifted. The vast majority of states had concluded that prohibitions against specific kinds of sex were, as Smith put it, "not consistent with our basic American values about the relationship between the individual and the State."

"Well, it depends on what you mean by our basic American values," Scalia responded.[13]

Conservatives were soon disappointed. In a 6–3 decision Anthony Kennedy struck down sodomy laws. The ruling advanced the religious privatization and the pluralization of moral values that the court had begun in *Griswold* and that had, in recent years, seemingly broken down. Kennedy ignored recent history and summarized what he saw as the long-term direction of the court. The majority had come to a general recognition of the right of the individual to be shielded from governmental intrusion in his or her life choices. He acknowledged that many people objected to gay sex on religious grounds, as was their right. But he noted that their beliefs about the immorality of homosexuality did not enable them to regulate the conduct of others through the coercive apparatus of the state. Antisodomy laws were, therefore, unconstitutional and should have been struck down when the court last ruled on the issue.[14]

Scalia, writing in a dissent joined by William H. Rehnquist and Clarence Thomas, was confounded. The court's decision, he wrote, opened the door to full-fledged moral licentiousness. It called into question, in his words, "laws against bigamy, same-sex marriage, adult incest, prostitution, masturbation, adultery, fornication, besti-

ality, and obscenity." If the court followed its own directive, American society was set for a massive upheaval. But he took some
comfort in the idea that if the court was going to overrule its own
precedents so quickly, as it did in *Lawrence*, then maybe *Roe v. Wade*
would be next. And unlike the reversal on gay sex, he pointed out, a
dismantling of *Roe* would simply revert to "the regime that existed
for centuries before 1973."[15]

Scalia had reason to be disquieted. The ball seemed to be roll-
ing toward the ultimate recognition of gay rights. Within a few
months the Massachusetts Supreme Court declared that marriage
discrimination on the basis of sexual orientation violated the state's
promise of equality. Gay marriage became legal in the state. Other
states followed.[16]

After the court's decision and the subsequent victories in state
courts, gay rights joined abortion as one of the central issues in the
culture wars. Christian conservatives were at first unsure how to respond, but they quickly gathered themselves, shifted their rhetoric,
and mobilized the full language of Christian power and triumphalism. Sandy Rios, the president of Concerned Women for America,
announced on her radio program that she needed her millions of
listeners to get involved in the effort to fight gay rights. "We will
equip you, we'll help you organize to fight back on this issue," she
said. "The time is now. If you don't do something about this, then
you cannot in 20 years—when you see the American public disinte-
grating and you see our enemies overtaking us because we have no
moral will—you remember that you did nothing."[17]

Christian Right activists succeeded in getting constitutional
amendments prohibiting same-sex marriage on the ballots of many
states. Others began to drive their base to voting, if not activism,
using gay rights as a whip. James Dobson, the head of Focus on the
Family, sent out an email to his 2.5 million subscribers explaining
the stakes. "The homosexual activist movement is poised to adminis-
ter a devastating and potentially fatal blow to the traditional family,"
he wrote. "And sadly, very few Christians in positions of responsibility are willing to use their influence to save it."[18]

The effort was enormously vitalizing. Richard Land, the president of the Ethics and Religious Liberty Commission of the Southern Baptist Convention, told the *New York Times*, "I have never seen

anything that has energized and provoked our grassroots like this issue, including *Roe v. Wade*."[19]

Their activism came out of a sense of betrayal. Up to that point many Christian conservatives had been feeling pretty good about where they were. Since George W. Bush's election to the presidency in 2000 they had experienced a solicitousness toward their priorities that was unparalleled, even under Reagan. Bush was one of their own, an avowed evangelical. He ran in 2000 on a platform of compassionate conservatism, an idea put forward by the writer Marvin Olasky, who wanted to bring back a pre–New Deal form of welfare to the United States. Olasky had persuaded then-governor Bush to roll back Texas's regulatory oversight of what he called faith-based groups, a seemingly neutral and descriptive concept encompassing many private organizations with charity missions, and to redirect existing welfare monies to those programs after the limits were removed. The point was to help the poor through private or nonprofit charities supported by public money.[20]

En route to the presidency, Bush promised to broaden the initiative by apportioning eight billion dollars in federal funds for faith-based programs to fight poverty. The emphasis was on the public good of the programs delivered, not on the financial support of private groups. But on the ground many of the groups, who were overwhelmingly Christian and conservative, focused as much on promoting faith as on delivering welfare. The *New York Times* had no difficulty finding examples of taxpayer money being used for explicitly religious activities that had hardly any welfare component. Bill Stanczykiewicz, who worked directly under Bush's top domestic advisor for the campaign, admitted he was not overly scrupulous about making sure that public money had public purposes. "I encourage them to play a shell game," he told the *New York Times*. The groups accepted the cash and held faith rallies or proselytizing missions or whatever. Money was fungible, so it was not easily kept from an organization's more sectarian activities. The program seemed to offer a path to renewed Christian relevance, if not power, and until 2003 it appeared to be working.[21]

But after the court's ruling in *Lawrence*, many Christian conservatives began to feel a creeping sense of insecurity. Their alliance with Bush had not saved them from the ruling. The president tried to reassure them of his support without coming across as an anti-gay bigot. He was quickly pushed into it anyhow. Antigay Christian activists began to float the idea of a federal constitutional amendment limiting marriage to heterosexual unions. Bush announced in response that he was committed to protecting "the sanctity of marriage."

Diane Sawyer of ABC News asked him what exactly that meant. Did it mean that he would support the federal marriage amendment?

"If necessary, I will support a constitutional amendment which would honor marriage between a man and a woman, codify that," he responded. But he also seemed to open the door for same-sex civil unions, if some states wanted to go that route.[22]

His calculations further energized the conservative base, driving them to the polls. On election day Bush triumphed largely owing to the votes of the Christian Right. Seventy-eight percent of evangelicals and 52 percent of Catholics voted for him. The *Economist* estimated that 3.5 million more evangelicals voted in 2004 than in 2000. Karl Rove, the president's chief political advisor, announced that moral values had carried Bush to victory, and he promised that politicians ignored the interests of Christian voters at their peril.[23]

But Bush's reelection did nothing to redress the larger cultural shifts that were occurring and that conservative Christian leaders had begun to sense. Pollsters had already begun to take notice of what they called the God gap, the overwhelming tendency of the most religious to support Republicans rather than Democrats. That tendency had resulted in electoral triumph in 2004. But there was a corollary that Rove's focus on religious Republicans tended to obscure: a sizable and growing number of the least religious people voted Democratic. In some sense it was a continuation of a much longer development that had just begun to accelerate and that many observers initially missed.

Seen from that perspective, the demographic trend was ominous for the long-term success of the Christian Right. By 2004 the number of white Christians in the United States had begun to plummet. The decline was considerable among liberal Christians, but the institutional rot had begun to hit conservative and evangelical groups as well. As the number of white Christians dropped, the nation saw a dramatic rise in the "nones," those who claimed either no religion or no specific denominational affiliation. In 2007, 15 percent of Americans reported no religion. By 2012 one-fifth of American adults and one-third of those under thirty declared no religion. In the three years between 2012 and 2015 the numbers rose several points further. Put in real numbers, between 2012 and 2015 around 7.5 million people abandoned their religious affiliation. Their rejection was connected to other shifts, equally profound. The number of Americans who revealed they rarely, if ever, attended religious services and who said they rarely, if ever, prayed rose dramatically. Other markers of religiosity likewise went down.[24]

These changes were beginning to be apparent in 2004, and they implied problems for the Religious Right. People who attended church least regularly, professed the loosest religious commitments, and displayed the lowest levels of religiosity as measured by social scientists were the most likely to vote Democratic. And their numbers were growing rapidly, whereas the number of those with the highest levels of religiosity, who were most likely to vote Republican, was shrinking with equal speed.[25]

Faced with the dawning realization of their cultural and political weakness, conservative Christians saw their project skid toward crisis even after the 2004 electoral victory. Their sense of catastrophe grew in 2006, when Democrats swept into a majority in the Senate and the House. Up until that point conservative religious leaders continued to believe, deep down, that they possessed majority status. Jerry Falwell called his organization the Moral Majority for a reason. Conservatives expected to mobilize their numbers to achieve electoral success and to overcome the subversion of a secularist minority in the courts. But the rapid acceptance of gay rights, the growth of non-Christian and anti-Christian sentiment, and their loss in 2006 presaged that, in the long term, their ability to succeed electorally was in doubt.

In response the Christian Right shifted the rhetoric. They continued to complain about the triumph of secular values while falling back on the language of religious freedom. When confronted with regulations that required adoption agencies to place children with gay and lesbian couples or when facing employment and disability regulations that required agencies to refrain from discriminating against such couples, conservative Christians promoted religious exemption from otherwise applicable law. Rather than assuming the power to shape public morality, as they had done in the past, religious conservatives demanded the space to practice their faith within an increasingly wide range of activities.[26]

Looked at in one way, this rhetorical shift was a concession to political trends. But looked at in another way, it was an adjustment in tactics to achieve the same ends they always sought. Christian conservatives had already laid the statutory groundwork for the move with the passage of the religious freedom acts at the state and federal levels. They also began to lobby their representatives to accommodate their religious-freedom claims in more specific ways. A 2006 *New York Times* report found that in the United States religious organizations enjoyed widespread exemptions from normally applicable rules. They ran the gamut from tax law to disability law, employment law, regulations of childcare centers, pension law, and land-use regulations. Legislators created the exemptions, sometimes through anonymous amendments of unrelated legislation. The strategy relied on an invocation of religious freedom to opt out of rules that undermined religious autonomy.[27]

But there was an ambivalence in conservative Christian efforts that the rhetoric of religious freedom tended to obscure. The groups did not want just exemption from otherwise applicable laws. They sought a way to live out their faith without the disruption of alternative perspectives. A pluralized social morality had long required the privatization of a person's fully orbed religious ideal. It demanded living in an earthly frame in which a person's life took acknowledgment and even tacit acceptance of alternative views rather than living one's life entirely in a biblical or heavenly frame, which relied fully upon an individual's religious belief. The demand to live in an earthly frame ran against the desire of Christian conservatives who wanted to live their lives with an unbroken religious integrity, as they understood it. It was impossible to do that entirely in a secular political order, which is why even as they began to speak the language of pluralism and of freedom they continued to demand public recognition of their moral and religious position.

Conservative Christians soon found ballast for their troubled project. In the early aughts, just as the Religious Right skidded toward crisis, a group of antiliberal writers began to interrogate secularism as a political, intellectual, and moral value. Soon conservative Christians and antisecularist academics began to come together in a variety of institutional channels—often supported by private charitable foundations—which helped set the terms of public debate.

In 2007, as the Democratic majority was settling into office, the Catholic philosopher Charles Taylor published what promised to be his capstone book, *A Secular Age*. The purpose was to understand the strictures of modern life from Taylor's religious perspective. To do so, Taylor defined secularism differently from what others might have done. Secularization to Taylor was not reducible to the privatization of religion and its expulsion from public spaces or to the decline of religious belief and practice. It required an underlying, more comprehensive development that gave rise to the age of his title. Taylor characterized the change as a shift in the conditions of belief so that religion and a transcendent order was just one option among several.[28]

He wanted to know how such a change came about. But he equally sought to reject the notion that the advance of human civilization ultimately, and ineluctably, terminated in the death of God. The claim had been circulating since the 1960s, if not before, and it had recently gained prominence at the hands of a group of polemicists known as the New Atheists. Starting in 2004, with the publication of Susan Jacoby's *Freethinkers* and Sam Harris's *The End of Faith*, the New Atheists began to attack all religious belief as a personal and political pathology. A flurry of books soon followed: Daniel Dennett's *Breaking the Spell* (2006), Sam Harris's *Letter to a Christian Nation* (2006), Richard Dawkins's *The God Delusion* (2006), and Christopher Hitchens's *God Is Not Great* (2007). Their efforts sought to defend secular political arrangements and ideas by cataloging the diminution of rights that, they said, often occurred in nonsecular regimes.[29]

Taylor regarded their position as impossibly tendentious. It relied on a narrative strategy that he called a subtraction story, which depicted both modernization and secularization as involving, in his words, "human beings having lost, or sloughed off, or liberated themselves from certain earlier, confining horizons, or illusions, or limitations of knowledge."[30]

The subtraction story was flawed because, as Taylor saw it, the development of secularism involved not merely liberation but a set of substantive commitments and an array of self-understandings and practices that could not necessarily be considered good. In the premodern era, human beings had what Taylor characterized as a "porous self" that was embedded in a wider set of social and natural relations. The porous self was awake to the changes in the cosmos in a way that made it finally receptive to God. But the advance of modernity did away with the porousness of the premodern self and created what Taylor called a "buffered self," which tended toward personal autonomy and an ethic of self-responsibility. The buffered self created wider social shifts characteristic of the modern world that relied upon this autonomous individual. Life for people was now lived in an immanent frame that remained indifferent, even hostile, to the transcendent frame that characterized premodern existence.[31]

Taylor had previously written with admiration about the cognitive and social changes that had emerged in the modern era, but his new writing had an air of lament. The immanent frame of modern life seemed to preclude many possibilities that he thought were essential. The buffered self especially allowed, in his words, "an escape from faith." It was to resist and to critique the flight from belief that Taylor wrote. He took issue with secularism's boosters, who saw it as a political liberation and claimed instead that the secular age embodied a cultural state in which life is "empty, flat, devoid of higher purpose." Its triumph is, Taylor wrote, "a victory for darkness."[32]

His work, at bottom, was a jeremiad that worked perfectly with that of Christian conservatives. A few early critics noticed the lamentation. Writing in the *New Republic*, the philosopher Charles Larmore pointed out, "This is not just a book written by a Christian for Christians. It is a book written by a Catholic for Catholics." In the *New York Times* the intellectual historian John Patrick Diggins observed that the book was less about secularism than about solidifying the defense of, as Diggins put it, "the religious values that may save us from the temptations of our selfish desires."[33]

But the critical voices were soon overwhelmed by a crescendo of approbation. *A Secular Age* won the lucrative Templeton Prize for research discoveries in "Spiritual Realities." In Taylor's prize biography, the Templeton Foundation praised his interrogation of, in its words, "so-called objective reasoning" and his reaffirmation of the possibilities of faith.[34]

Taylor, in his public comments, was forthright about his essentially religious purposes. In his acceptance speech, held at the Church Center for the United Nations in New York City, Taylor spoke of the "spiritual rediscovery" he sought to promote. He especially lamented the "series of forgettings" and the loss of things like God and faith that went along with the creation of the modern world.[35]

The Templeton Foundation was hardly alone in its praise. The Social Science Research Council, with funding from the Henry Luce Foundation and the Fetzer Institute, was so taken with Taylor's work that it set up a digital forum, *The Immanent Frame*, with the goal of publishing work on religion, secularism, and the public sphere. Taylor's book was subjected to a three-month-long discussion on the platform that, in the end, included over sixty substantial responses from scholars and a variety of rejoinders from Taylor.[36]

The Immanent Frame soon became a gathering place for critics of secularism, not just Catholic writers but also those who spoke the language of Foucauldian postmodernism and who were critical of what they considered the Western, Enlightenment stories about the emancipatory power of secular values. The most prominent standard bearer of the postmodern critics was Talal Asad, who rejected secularism as a kind of hegemonic fairy tale that touted liberation while instituting more far-reaching forms of oppression.[37]

Others took Asad's perspective and pressed it further, especially the cultural anthropologist Saba Mahmood. In questioning the narratives of secularism, Mahmood took issue expressly with the notion that it was a solution to the problem of religious antagonism or that it promoted toleration. She wrote at length about secular regimes in the modern Middle East that were almost universally oppressive and antidemocratic. Her assertions were astonishingly sweeping. In her view there was no real difference between a liberal secular regime like the United States and an authoritarian secular regime like Egypt. All shared a fundamental trait: they embodied a universalizing project that subjected alternative religions to domination under the rhetoric of church–state separation.[38]

Several writers took this critical project and used it to interrogate the entire direction of American politics and law over the past seventy-five years. They pointed out that the rhetoric of church–state separation empowered the court and the government to make religious determinations about what did and did not qualify as a religion. It did not matter that the court rarely seemed inclined to make such a determination and often sought to avoid it. The justices had to define religion, and the act of definition is an act of regulation. "It is crucial to recognize," the legal scholar Peter G. Danchin wrote, "that such entanglements are not deviations from secularism but an expression of the underlying power that makes secularism possible, a power that generates religion itself as a category and views it through a particular modality of suspicion."[39]

Conservative legal scholars used the work to redirect the course of law. One of the central moves of the revisionist thinkers was to echo the Catholic hierarchy that liberal secularism was essentially a form of Protestantism. The secular privatization of religion drew upon a religious ethos that accorded with the Protestant structures of belief and feeling, they said. Philip Hamburger, one of the leaders of the effort, produced a fat book seeking to show how church–state separatism historically emerged out of skepticism toward Catholic ecclesiastical authority and out of a derisive posture toward the communal ethos of an immigrant church. The resulting institutionalization of church–state separation, in Hamburger's view, turned the First Amendment into an instrument of discrimination against people who wish to bring their faith into public life.[40]

These intellectual and political agendas reinforced one another. Conservative political mobilization found intellectual heft in the Taylorian lamentation about the loss of faith, the Foucauldian interrogation of secular power, and the revisionist examination of church–state separatism. The political and intellectual streams tended to reinforce the conservative modification of American secularism and called for the reinvigoration of corporate religious bodies under the rhetoric of religious freedom.

Still, the way forward was not entirely apparent until 2009, when the Democrat Barack Obama was elected president. He entered office with Democrats holding even firmer majorities in both the House and the Senate. The cultural weakness of the Christian Right was by now so apparent that magazines like *Newsweek* were publishing cover stories about "the decline and fall of Christian

America." Although Barack Obama spoke as a liberal Christian and welcomed religious perspectives in public life, he did not in any way cater to the anxieties of Christian conservatives.[41]

Conflict began as soon as Obama took office. After some discussion the first order of business for the newly empowered Democratic majority became health-care reform. Despite months of controversy, Congress finally passed the Patient Protection and Affordable Care Act in 2010 (known more familiarly as Obamacare). The law took years to go fully into effect because numerous regulations were required to flesh out the already substantial provisions of the bill.

It was around freedom of religion that much of the controversy developed. Even before the Obama administration began to roll out its rules Christian conservatives were uneasy. They objected to the administration's provisional directive that organizations over a certain size had to purchase health-care coverage for their employees. Those health-care plans had to meet minimal standards. Female employees had to have access to birth control as part of their plan. Conservative Christian groups wanted exemption from the contraception mandate because they regarded forms of hormonal contraception (such as birth control pills) as abortifacients.

As the Obama administration pondered its final regulations, the court, now firmly under the control of Christian conservatives, began to make the rhetoric of religious freedom more inviting. It did so by strengthening the rights of religious organizations in a case involving a teacher named Cheryl Perich. At one time she had taught at the Hosanna-Tabor Evangelical Lutheran Church and School, where she received positive evaluations from her bosses. After several years in her position she began to suffer narcolepsy and missed the first part of the academic year. When she finally gained control of her condition she wanted to return. But the school informed her that the position had been filled. It urged her to resign. When she refused, the school fired her.[42]

In response Perich filed a charge with the Equal Employment Opportunity Commission (EEOC). After an investigation the EEOC decided that the school had violated the Americans with Disabilities Act, a 1990 law that prohibits discrimination against a person on the basis of a physical or mental impairment. The church and school declared that they had fired Perich because she consulted an outside attorney and threatened to sue. Church doctrine required that members resolve their disagreements internally. The EEOC rejected that justification and determined that the school used religious doctrine as a pretext for firing Perich for her illness.[43]

When the school refused to budge, the EEOC brought suit against Hosanna-Tabor. In court filings the school proposed a broad ministerial exception to applicable law. Hosanna-Tabor considered Perich, in its designation, a "called teacher" who functioned as a minister in her work at the school. By accepting the position, the school maintained, she had waived her rights under the Americans with Disabilities Act.

The EEOC countered that Perich was not an actual leader or minister. She taught religious subjects for at most forty-five minutes a day. Her position was a nonreligious one, but even if it were not, the EEOC did not wish to grant that there was such a thing as a ministerial exception.[44]

The court, in a unanimous decision, sided with Hosanna-Tabor. Writing for the court, Chief Justice John Roberts ruled that the First Amendment offered "special solicitude to the rights of religious organizations." The ability to hire its ministers and to run a congregation as it wished was a foundational component of a group's rights.[45]

That was in effect the meaning of religious freedom, Roberts held. To the EEOC's position that Perich was a secular teacher who barely taught religious subjects, Roberts responded, "The issue is not one that can be resolved by a stopwatch." Perich disseminated the doctrine of the church and furthered its mission, regardless of how exclusively or nonexclusively she taught religious subjects. There was no clean or clear distinction between secular and nonsecular subject matter. And a congregation itself had the ability to determine who was and who was not one of its ministers. That was an essential component of the First Amendment.[46]

The ruling was, accordingly, sweeping. The EEOC had earlier posited that if the court found for the school, it would allow widespread abuse by religious organizations and would undermine the rights of individuals. But Roberts denied that there would be any negative effects from his ruling. He dismissed the EEOC's warnings as "a parade of horribles" without any basis in fact.[47]

When the court announced its decision the *New York Times* denounced it as an aggressive expansion of religious rights. The ruling abandoned, in the paper's words, "the longtime practice of balancing the interest in free exercise of religion against important governmental interests, like protection against workplace bias or retaliation."[48]

Nine days after the court handed down its ruling the Obama administration finalized its rules under Obamacare. The administration's directives continued the same exemption controversy in an another register. The White House acknowledged that religious groups had certain rights and needs that ought to be honored. It exempted churches and houses of worship from the contraception mandate. But the administration also determined that religiously affiliated employers such as schools or hospitals would not be exempt. They had a public, secular function, not a private, religious one. They would have one year to bring themselves into compliance with the regulations.[49]

Conservative religious groups immediately mounted a campaign. "In effect," Archbishop Timothy M. Dolan of New York announced, "the president is saying we have a year to figure out how to violate our consciences." The Catholic bishops soon released a statement that placed the issue in terms of religious liberty. "We address an urgent summons to our fellow Catholics and fellow Americans to be on guard, for religious freedom is under attack," the bishops claimed. Their conception of their rights meant that they possessed organizational autonomy and the ability to act upon their faith without the hindrance of law. The contraception mandate undermined their prerogatives.[50]

Evangelicals lined up alongside Catholics. The NAE defended the right of religious employers who, it said, "will be forced to pay for services and procedures they believe are morally wrong." The group of scholars behind the ECT statement, which now was nearly twenty years old, came together again to draft another statement, this time defending the ability of believers to bring their faith into the public sphere as an expression of religious freedom. The statement lamented the attempt "to define religious freedom down, reducing it to a bare 'freedom of worship.' "[51]

The resurgence of religious freedom rhetoric marked a shift in American political culture. Gone was the appeal to public reason and the overlapping consensus that could be found in the first ECT statement. In its place was a staunchly religious form of argument that was mixed with the language of constitutional rights. The privatization of faith, the statement said, violated "the order of creation" because "human freedom, and especially religious freedom, reflects God's design for creation and his pattern of redemption."[52]

A careful observer would have noticed that their concept of religious freedom was a distinctly limited one. The individual religious conscience of employees did not factor into conservative religious rhetoric. What mattered was the autonomy of religious institutions operating under the authority of their leadership. The religion scholar Elizabeth Castelli has observed that in contemporary Catholic argumentation, "religious freedom emerges as nothing more than a mode of shoring up the authority of the Magisterium of the Bishops." The same could be said of conservative Protestant churches.[53]

Nevertheless, the rhetoric had real power. Since the *Smith* decision religious freedom had become institutionalized in such a way that a gesture to religious conscience granted nearly automatic exemption from law. And the new politics of religious freedom offered much more than a selective accommodation. It demanded church sovereignty over and above that of the state. The resulting accommodations began to look, as the legal scholar Winnifred Fallers Sullivan has put it, "a lot like what might once have been considered 'established' or 'sectarian' religion in an earlier American parlance."[54]

The Obama administration sought to resolve these dilemmas. After three weeks of controversy it issued a rule to mollify religious critics. It wanted to honor religious organizations' conscience, but it also could not just waive the contraception requirements. Given the extensive public–private partnership in health care, to eliminate the mandate would create massive holes of coverage for the American public. In addition, many people who worked in religious organizations did not share their employers' religious beliefs—hospitals were a prime example. Waiving the contraception requirement would privilege the employers' rights of conscience over the employees' equally valid rights of conscience. After much consideration, the administration announced what it seemed to consider a brilliant fix. Religious organizations would not have to pay for conception coverage, but they would still have to offer it. The costs would be borne by insurers.

Some groups were appeased but many others were not. As the faith-based effort of George W. Bush had shown, money was fungible. Somebody would pay for conception coverage, and those costs would be passed along to religious bodies whether they liked it or not. "We are still afraid that we are being called upon to subsidize something that we find morally illicit," Archbishop Dolan said. "There is still no attention to what you might call the deeper philosophical issues, namely, 'What right does a federal bureau have to define the who, what, where, and how of religious practice?'" This was the question that had been percolating ever since the *Bob Jones* case.[55]

Several groups, including for-profit corporations, filed suit in federal court, making similar arguments. They based their appeal on the RFRA. As the cases began to make their way through the system, conservative judges responded positively. By the time the appeals got to the Supreme Court many liberals started sounding the alarm. Representative Jerrold Nadler of New York, who cowrote the RFRA, complained to the progressive cable channel MSNBC that Christian conservatives were ignoring the purpose of the law. "It was never intended as a sword as opposed to a shield," he said. A few days later he issued a statement elaborating his point: "When we passed RFRA, we sought to restore—not expand—protection for religion."[56]

Other critics began to point out that RFRA became law as the result of a large coalition of groups who supported religious freedom. It now seemed to aid only Christian conservatives, which undermined support for the idea among the general populace. "If anyone had ever come up with a scenario like what's been proposed," said Barry Lynn of Americans United, "that coalition would have exploded like someone hitting a watermelon with a shotgun. There would have never been a Religious Freedom Restoration Act."[57]

Liberal fears were soon confirmed when the court, with a five-person majority, affirmed the conservative demands for religious autonomy. Writing for the court in *Burwell v. Hobby Lobby Stores Inc.* (2014), Justice Samuel Alito ruled that the RFRA required a nearly

absolute right of exemption from otherwise applicable law. To sustain
his position, he had to elaborate a couple of claims. First, he ruled
that closely held corporations—that is, those run by a small group of
individuals, usually a family—had religious rights. Second, he held
that RFRA sought to create a new trajectory in the law of religious
freedom that granted rights to religious organizations of all types.[58]

The result was a monumental decision. Rather than restoring
religious-freedom law to the balancing tests the court had used before the *Smith* decision, Alito freed conservatives to rule as they
wished in the future. "The Roberts Court is now unconstrained by
precedent," a group of law professors writing in *Slate* observed
after the ruling.[59]

Liberals on the court were aghast. In her dissent Justice Ruth
Bader Ginsburg decried the "startling breadth" of the majority
opinion. It promoted, she said, a vision of society in which corporations could control large numbers of people. Unlike nonprofit religious organizations that, when small enough, drew upon a shared
theological or moral perspective, for-profit corporations employed
people from all walks of life. They were bound together only by
the goal of making money. And closely held corporations were also
not always Mom-and-Pop operations with few employees. Hobby
Lobby, a closely held corporation run by the religious family who
brought the case, employed thirteen thousand people. Mars, Inc.,
another closely held corporation, grossed $33 billion a year and had
seventy-two thousand employees. Cargill, Inc. grossed $136 billion
a year and had one hundred forty thousand employees. All were
closely held corporations who could be exempt from the law.[60]

The majority ignored all such considerations, Ginsburg wrote.
In doing so, it allowed a small group of individuals who ran these
huge companies to make medical and moral choices for others, to
impose their religious beliefs upon a much broader group of people whose religious views were rendered irrelevant. It also opened
up a myriad of ways, Ginsburg explained, by which corporations
could "opt out of any law (saving only tax laws) they judge incompatible with their sincerely held religious beliefs."[61]

To Barry Lynn, the effort revealed a wider strategy of Christian
conservatives that betrayed a bad faith. Rather than merely carving
out an autonomous space, in Lynn's interpretation, they sought to

use RFRA as a Trojan horse to continue their cultural and political power. The next steps were already being talked about, he alleged. Characterizing conservative Christian strategy and discussion, Lynn said, "Let's go after equal pay, let's go after the civil rights acts, let's just go after everything that every religious right group doesn't like and doesn't want to obey."[62]

But there was an underlying component that Lynn did not quite see. Christian conservatives had learned the language of the New Left. If the personal was political, then the privatization of faith would be its trivialization and impotence. So in turning to the language of religious freedom, they resuscitated their political project under the banner of constitutionally protected language. They no longer spoke using the consistent vocabulary of Christian triumphalism, though that might still have motivated their actions. They learned to ask, as Rorty had suggested, "Does our use of these words get in the way of our use of those other words?" When it did, they dropped the language of Christian triumphalism and turned to other claims, a tacit accommodation to the rules of the American secular order that still allowed for the advancement of their interests.[63]

They did not always win, though, and defeat only reinforced their sense of beleaguerment. Their biggest anxieties were often related to sex and especially gay rights. By 2014, when the court handed down its *Hobby Lobby* decision, the gay rights movement had made astonishing gains. A majority of Americans supported equal treatment for gays and lesbians. Cases were making their way toward the Supreme Court with the aim of legalizing same-sex marriage rights. Conservatives opposed gay rights, but when the courts required them to submit nonreligious justifications for their opposition, they were unable to come up with anything persuasive. In response, they began to move forward religious freedom bills in several states. These bills allowed people with an objection to homosexuality to deny food service, employment, adoption services, hotel accommodations, and more to gay people. "In this new up-is-down world, anti-gay religious folks are 'practicing their faith' when they're baking cakes or renting out hotel rooms to travelers," Evan Hurst of Truth Wins Out complained in *Mother Jones*.[64]

Christian conservatives redoubled their efforts in 2015 when the Supreme Court, in another 5–4 decision, legalized same-sex marriage. The decision seemed to be the logical extension of the legal and political movement that had swept across the country. Nearly all of the 2016 Republican presidential hopefuls denounced the decision in bitter terms. Many made the trip to Liberty University, where they lambasted the administration and decried what they saw as a war on faith. Ramesh Ponnuru, an editor at *National Review* and a conservative Catholic, told the *Wall Street Journal* that "there's the sense on the part of social conservatives that we need protections of our liberty as dissenters."[65]

Then-candidate Donald Trump happily promised that if he were elected they need not be dissenters anymore. He had long telegraphed his appeal to conservative Christian voters by promising that his enemies would be their enemies. Those enemies included more than gay activists. At a December rally in 2015 he said that the Obama administration had been soft on terrorism because, as he had long implied, Obama was a closet Muslim. As president, he would do more. "Donald J. Trump," he announced, referring to himself in the third person, "is calling for a total and complete shutdown of Muslims entering the United States until our country's representatives can figure out what the hell is going on."[66]

Critics pointed out that a ban on Muslims would likely violate the establishment clause of the Constitution and could be said to infringe on religious freedom. But Trump's strategy was clear. He sought to appeal to the sense of cultural estrangement that Christian conservatives professed and to offer them a route back to privilege, if not dominance. So even as he decried the dangers of Islamic terrorism, and even as he warned darkly of the establishment of Sharia law in the United States, he looked for ways to strengthen the place of Christian institutions in American life. In January 2016, at a small Christian college in Sioux Center, Iowa, Trump was explicit. His speech became infamous for his declaration that, in his words, "I could stand in the middle of Fifth Avenue and shoot somebody and I wouldn't lose any voters, OK?" But the purpose of his visit was to curry that kind of devotion in his Christian disciples. To do so, he made them a promise.

He said to the crowd, "Christianity is under tremendous siege, whether we want to talk about it or we don't want to talk about it." In his view Christians made up the overwhelming majority of the country—which was erroneous, given the demographic shifts that had taken place in the past forty years—but Christians had been sidelined in spite of their numerical superiority. That would all change if he were elected president.

"Christianity will have power," he assured them. "If I'm there, you're going to have plenty of power, you don't need anybody else. You're going to have somebody representing you very, very well. Remember that."[67]

The next month at the National Prayer Breakfast he added a concrete proposal. He promised to "get rid of and totally destroy" the Johnson Amendment, which prohibited tax-exempt organizations from participating in or trying to influence political campaigns. The implication seemed to be that the limitation on religious organizations had resulted in a lopsided political contest that he was going to right.[68]

Once he secured the Republican nomination he added to the ticket Mike Pence, an evangelical governor of Indiana best known for signing the state's RFRA after the legalization of gay marriage.

The entire campaign might have smacked of political opportunism, given Trump's lukewarm religious sensibilities, but Christian conservatives warmed to him. Their support helped him secure the election. After assuming the presidency Trump made good on his promises. One week after being sworn in he issued an executive order banning national entry from several Muslim-dominant nations. This was the promised Muslim ban, now a reality. A raft of lawsuits soon began making their way through federal courts, and judges began suspending or striking down portions of the order. Because it had been issued so quickly and sloppily it contained numerous problems. The administration was forced to retract the first order and issue another one. When similar challenges were brought against that order and judges again began striking it down, the administration had to retract it to issue a third order.[69]

Trump also quickly issued a directive to the IRS to use "maximum enforcement discretion" in deciding when the Johnson Amendment applied to churches and religious nonprofits. His order did not get rid of the amendment, which could be done only by a congressional act, but it did seek to cripple it. At the signing ceremony, held on the National Day of Prayer, Trump said he was simply restoring religion to its proper place in public life. "We will not allow people of faith to be targeted, bullied or silenced anymore," he said.[70]

The Trump administration went out of its way to make sure that a diverse group of religious officials was at the signing. Trump was flanked by orthodox Jews, a Sikh, two nuns who were currently suing the federal government for exemption from the Obamacare contraception mandate, and a priest, alongside evangelical leaders. The optics implied a conservative ecumenical movement united around the principle of religious freedom. But the actual effect of the order was first and foremost to strengthen Christian priorities in public life, as Tony Perkins of the Family Research Council acknowledged in his statement praising Trump's action. "The open season on Christians and other people of faith is coming to a close in America," he said, "and we look forward to assisting the Trump administration in fully restoring America's First Freedom."[71]

The White House put out press releases touting its work in similar terms. The administration said that in addition to allowing greater political speech for religious groups, Trump had modified Obama's health-care law to allow even more exemptions when someone invoked conscience. He supported the religious liberty bills that spared Christians from offering services to gays and lesbians. And as part of Trump's hyped religious freedom initiatives, the administration sought to preserve "the sanctity of life" by stopping the attack on prolife policies.[72]

The courts had to sort out what was legal and what was not. A commitment to religious freedom rather than to Christian freedom might have imperiled the administration's Muslim ban. But when the question came before the Supreme Court the conservative majority went out of its way to disregard the religious animosity that Trump had displayed. Writing for the court, Chief Justice John Roberts said, "The Proclamation is expressly premised on legitimate purposes: preventing entry of nationals who cannot be adequately vetted and inducing other nations to improve their practices. The text says nothing about religion."[73]

Others on the court were outraged. Associate Justice Sonia Sotomayor, in her dissent, cited a catalogue of oral and written statements showing Donald Trump's fervent desire to keep Muslims out of the country. "Islam hates us," he had said. "We're having problems with Muslims." He called for surveillance of mosques. The list of Trump's statements filled pages of Sotomayor's opinion. "Based on the evidence of the record," Sotomayor wrote, "a reasonable observer would conclude that the proclamation was motivated by anti-Muslim animus." That should have been enough to strike down the executive order. But, she continued, "the majority holds otherwise by ignoring the facts, misconstruing our legal precedent, and turning a blind eye to the pain and suffering the Proclamation inflicts upon countless families and individuals, many of whom are United States citizens."[74]

In a way the court's ruling made certain things clear. In the hands of Christian conservatives both in the Trump administration and on the court, religious freedom tended to mean conservative Christian freedom and privilege. But if there was any confusion, it evaporated in the fall of 2019 when Trump's attorney general, Bill Barr, gave a speech ostensibly on the topic of religious liberty at the University of Notre Dame Law School. His topic in reality was an extended criticism of secularism that seemed to echo, in a distinctly Catholic idiom, what the academic critics had been saying about the failures of secular governance.

Barr told a story about the United States that followed the usual forms of lamentation. The Founding Fathers, he said, had created the nation to uphold Christian values. They recognized the importance of religious ideals to American society because they themselves were Christians and had the view of human nature drawn from, in Barr's words, "the classical Christian tradition." What that meant was that the Founders knew that man was capable of great evil and that self-government was possible only through the disciplining process of the Judeo-Christian tradition and the moral culture it fostered. Religious freedom was essential to the creation of that moral culture. But as a result of the sixties, Barr announced, American moral sensibility and its religious foundation had gone into decline.[75]

"I think we all recognize that over the past 50 years religion has been under increasing attack," Barr told his audience. "On the one hand, we have seen the steady erosion of our traditional Judeo-Christian moral system and a comprehensive effort to drive it from the public square. On the other hand, we see the growing ascendancy of secularism and the doctrine of moral relativism."[76]

To Barr, the tendency was clear and unidirectional. Secularism was always positive and substantive, the result of sixties radicals who sought to displace the Judeo-Christian faith. Those who opposed the place of Christianity in American public life were not seeking to make room for diversity. They were setting up an alternative religion. As a result, in Barr's interpretation one could not be a Christian and a secularist at the same time because secularism was always hostile to religion and sought to contain, cripple, and eliminate, if possible, religious influence in American society.

"Secularists, and their allies among the 'progressives,' have marshaled all the force of mass communications, popular culture, the entertainment industry, and academia in an unremitting assault on religion and traditional values," Barr said. They "affirmatively promote secular orthodoxy" and "drown out and silence opposing voices." The result for the nation was a calamity of truly biblical proportions. He pointed to the rise of illegitimate births, the increase of violence in society (violent crime had actually declined dramatically since the 1990s), and the general moral decay of American life as the bitter fruits of secularism. The only alternative to continued national degeneration was the use of law to pursue what Barr characterized as a "moral renewal."[77]

To that end he promised a vigilance in the Department of Justice against state and local governments who sought to limit Judeo-Christian religious freedom. His department would work to allow public monies to be used for private, religious schools. He also promised support for a variety of exemptions: for Christian parents, from sex education in public schools; for private schools, from nondiscrimination laws in employment; and for a variety of private, religious institutions, from many otherwise applicable laws even when they received public money.[78]

"As Catholics, we are committed to the Judeo-Christian values that have made this country great," he said in conclusion. "I can assure you that, as long as I am Attorney General, the Department of Justice will be at the forefront of this effort, ready to fight for the most cherished of our liberties: the freedom to live according to our faith."[79]

For a sitting attorney general the speech was remarkable in its forthrightness. Critics complained that the rhetoric was dangerous.

Liberal Catholics noted that Barr was drawing on an ultraconservative and doctrinaire form of Catholicism in his work at the Justice Department. C. Colt Anderson, a theologian and professor of religion at Fordham, told the *Guardian* that Barr's extreme conservatism threatened to use law to penalize all those who disagreed with his view of Catholic doctrine. In that way, Barr looked a lot like other ultraconservative Catholics who were using religious ideas to crack down on free speech and to purge judges in increasingly authoritarian nations like Poland.[80]

Other critics used his statement to point out the disingenuousness of the Christian Right, whether Catholic or Protestant. In the *New York Times*, the journalist Katherine Stewart and the past president of the American Constitution Society Caroline Fredrickson wrote, "This form of 'religious liberty' seeks to foment the sense of persecution and paranoia of a collection of conservative religious groups that see themselves as on the cusp of losing their rightful position of dominance over American culture. It always singles out groups that can be blamed for society's ills, and that may be subject to state-sanctioned discrimination and belittlement—L.G.B.T. Americans, secularists and Muslims are the favored targets, but others are available. The purpose of this 'religious liberty' rhetoric is not just to secure a place of privilege, but also to justify public funding for the right kind of religion."[81]

Yet none of the criticism slowed the momentum. As the Trump administration, with the aid of Senate Majority Leader Mitch McConnell, continued to fill the federal court system with conservative judges, cases about religious freedom continued to flow up to the Supreme Court. Christian conservatives on the court happily accepted them. In January 2020 the court agreed to hear arguments against the Trump administration's decision to allow more religious freedom exemptions from the Obamacare contraception mandate. Brigitte Amiri, a lawyer with the ACLU's Reproductive Freedom Project, told the *New York Times*, "Allowing employers and universities to use their religious beliefs to block employees' and students' birth-control coverage isn't religious liberty—it's discrimination."[82]

That same month the court accepted a case in which the Montana Supreme Court struck down a voucher program that sent public money to private religious schools. The Montana Constitution had an amendment that prohibited public support of sectarian education, which led to the lower court's decision. But conservatives on the U.S. Supreme Court seemed ready to strike down the provision of the Montana Constitution and of any other constitution that had similar language. At the same time, Secretary of Education Betsy DeVos proposed a $5 billion federal tax credit program to encourage similar voucher systems in other states. The goal was to allow private religious groups access to public money while simultaneously exempting them from otherwise relevant laws.[83]

All looked to be flowing in the direction that conservatives wished. But before these cases could come to fruition, the court faced another gay rights case over whether LGBT people were protected from workplace discrimination by the 1964 Civil Rights Act. In a surprise 6–3 opinion written by the Trump appointee Neil Gorsuch, who felt bound by the text of the statute in spite of his personal opinion opposing gay rights, the court held that gay and transgender people were protected by the law. When asked about the ruling, Donald Trump said to reporters, "I've read the decision, and some people were surprised, but they've ruled and we live with their decision."[84]

Others were not so reticent nor resigned. Associate Justice Samuel Alito, writing in dissent, warned that the majority's decision "will threaten freedom of religion, freedom of speech, and personal privacy and safety." Russell Moore, the president of the Ethics and Religious Liberty Commission of the Southern Baptist Convention, amplified Alito's statement. He decried the decision as an erosion of the freedom and autonomy of religious organizations. The ruling, he said, "will have seismic implications for religious liberty, setting off potentially years of lawsuits and court struggles, about what this means, for example, for religious organizations with religious convictions about the meaning of sex and sexuality."[85]

Conservatives were soon reassured when the 5–4 court handed down a decision in the Montana case, striking down the state's constitutional provision that forbade public support for private education. Writing for the majority, Chief Justice John Roberts used the ruling to rehabilitate public support for private religious schools. "The prohibition before us today burdens not only religious schools but also the families whose children attend or hope to attend them,"

he wrote. "The no-aid provision [of the Montana Constitution] pe-
nalizes that decision by cutting families off from otherwise available
benefits if they choose a religious private school rather than a secular one, and for no other reason." The decision marked the triumph
of the child-benefit theory first put forward by the Catholic church
in the 1940s.[86]

Associate Justice Samuel Alito went further in his concurring
opinion. He noted that the desire to keep public money out of sectarian schools had originated in the Protestant suspicion of Catholicism.
That anti-Catholic animus had been, Alito alleged, reproduced in the
jurisprudence of the court that proclaimed a wall of separation between church and state. The anti-Catholic impulse of church–state
separatism made it into a form of antireligious discrimination that
the court ought to strike down in all its forms. Large portions of the
opinion drew on the recent academic literature critical of secularism,
especially the work of Philip Hamburger, and the entire thrust of Alito's reasoning showed how far he was willing to revitalize religious
bodies with public money.[87]

Yet the majority's reasoning had tensions that the opinion did not
resolve. It alleged discrimination that it never showed. The opposite
was the case: the court's reasoning displayed both a special favoring
and a discrimination against the nonreligious. In allowing for the
public subsidization of private religious education, as the columnist
Linda Greenhouse pointed out, "parents of religious-school students
ended up with a privilege that no other parents in the state enjoyed,
all in the name of preventing discrimination against religion."[88]

One week later, on July 8, the court handed down its decision on
the Obamacare contraception mandate. In a 7–2 opinion the court
upheld the Trump administration's decision to free employers who
had moral and religious objections to birth control from the obligation to provide coverage for their employees. In essence, religious
conservatives declared that indirect support for birth control paid
for by insurers, if it ran against an organization's avowed religious
principles, abridged religious freedom. But direct state support of
private religious institutions raised no constitutional issues.[89]

That same day the court handed down another decision, also
7–2, that affirmed a ministerial exception for religious schools from
otherwise applicable discrimination laws. The *New York Times* legal

reporter Adam Liptak called the two decisions "part of a broad examination of the relationship between church and state over the 15-year tenure of Chief Justice John G. Roberts Jr. in which the court's conservative majority has almost always sided with religious groups."[90]

Others had more sympathetic analyses. The conservative legal scholar Michael McConnell, who had long championed religious freedom as an essential constitutional value, asserted in an op-ed that the court was not protecting religion per se. It was protecting pluralism. As McConnell put it, the combined decisions of the final weeks of the 2020 term showed a solicitousness to "the right of individuals and institutions to be different, to teach different doctrines, to dissent from dominant cultural norms and to practice what they preach." This was the real rationale behind the court's decision to protect gay and transgender rights as well as the decisions protecting religious institutions. "Very roughly speaking," McConnell explained, "the court seems to side with the party defending the right to live in accordance with one's identity: whether that is the right of a gay person to be free from discrimination in the workplace, or the right of a religious order to decline insurance coverage for contraceptive drugs that violate its teachings, or the right of religious schools to be free of government interference with their choice of people to teach religious doctrine or practice to their children."[91]

McConnell failed to point out these identities conflicted, as both Christian conservatives and gay activists realized. The court protected gay and transgender people from discrimination, yet it also allowed religious organizations, even for-profit corporations, wide exceptions to law, which potentially allowed them to discriminate as they wished. In effect, as Linda Greenhouse put it, the Roberts court has been "insisting on organized religion's entitlement to public benefits as a matter of equal treatment while at the same time according religion special treatment in the form of relief from the regulations that everyone else must live by. Benefits without burdens, equal treatment morphing into special treatment."[92]

Taken together these cases reveal the partial unraveling of American secularism under the banner of religious freedom. In the 1930s the concept was a mechanism to eliminate the de facto Christian establishment by allowing for alternative religious expressions frowned upon by the Christian majority. In the 1960s religious liberty was a right of private faith that required public equality, nondiscrimination, and the cultural disestablishment of American Christianity. In the early twenty-first century religious freedom has become a rhetoric that justifies the projection of private religious sensibilities into the public realm and the appropriation of public money to private religious ends. The rules of public reason have slowly broken down, and all that remains is an agonistic fight in a bitterly divided political context.

Afterword

This much ought to be clear: The origins of the contemporary disagreement about secularism lie deep in the past. They began with the construction of the First Amendment, which was not carefully drawn and which was coursed with ambiguities, if not contradictions. The amendment's special protection of religion has been especially difficult to uphold. The framers offered no definition of religion or a limit on its protection, save that a religion must not be established, which they also failed to define. The wording was already vague in the eighteenth century. Given the vastly disparate, expanded horizons of the present, with its massive diversity and epistemic uncertainties, the amendment has become a source of social, political, and legal instability.

Other piers of secularism have likewise proven unsteady. At the beginning of the twentieth century the vocabulary of secularism took its meaning from the relative dominance of Christianity in American governance. The privatization of religion and the language of privacy itself were a response to that dominance and also its solution. But privacy has become uncertain in value and volatile in valence. Although the privatization of religion was essential to the creation of a secular settlement, now the declaration that something is private shields religious ideas and bodies from the reach of public scrutiny. The shield holds even when private groups are using public funds.

The layered social conflict of the middle of the twentieth century has also begun to shift. The earlier dispute saw multiple religious and nonreligious people turn to the state and the courts for protection. There was no obvious partisan divide, and the groups relied on somewhat surprising alliances such as that between the ACLU and the Jehovah's Witnesses. As claimants came before the court, the contradictory and overlapping religious interests on display left it with no choice but to erect a secular political order in an attempt to preserve the peace.

In the twenty-first century the demographic decline of liberal Christianity and the union of conservative Protestants and Catholics have led to a more straightforward dispute that aligns neatly with the political parties. Republicans are the religious party, with few exceptions. There are intimations of a conservative ecumenical movement encompassing more than just Christians—the Trump photo op with orthodox Jews and a Sikh leader alongside Protestants and Catholics is one such instance. But photo ops aside, in almost every case the religion championed by Republican partisans is a somewhat strict form of Christianity. Democrats, with their much broader political coalition, often look to a form of secularism to overcome their division. They continue to use a mid-twentieth-century vocabulary in much the same way it was used then, which has put them at a disadvantage and continually off balance.

The conservative Christian mobilization has been profoundly effective. Earlier generations presumed majority status in American political life. They were accordingly indifferent or hostile to the language of civil liberties. But the loss of social, cultural, and, to some extent, political power has more recently made them reconsider what they see as the selective view that has underwritten the American secular order. They have complained that the secularism of an intolerant Left undermines such foundational liberties as the right of association, property, and free exercise.

None of these developments should come as a surprise. The political scientist Stephen Skowronek has pointed out that "a political tradition is not a coherent set of political ambitions but a common grammar through which ambitions are manipulated and redefined." American secularists in the early twentieth century appropriated the language and the grammar of earlier generations to build the secular arrangement. Given secularism's dominance at the middle of the twentieth century, the leaders of the Christian Right turned to the only strategy available to them, appropriating parts of the secular political vocabulary to prevent alternative uses. The result has been a destabilization, if not a rejection, of the American secular order.[1]

The United States is now entering a political moment in which there appears to be no agreed-upon basis of politics, no collective set of commitments to help resolve debate. It has become clear that even the negative secularism of the mid-twentieth century had meaningful substantive components, many of which have been lost. It relied on a dedication to inclusiveness and a commitment to what John Rawls called civic friendship, a seeking out of commonalities necessary to achieve political stability and peace. The resulting constitutional politics involved a set of positive virtues and habits that were, to be sure, usually honored in the breach but that in some sense formed the basis for debate. The rejection of these virtues and norms has left even the negative secularism of the mid-twentieth century in a parlous position and the nation itself not much better.

If American political culture continues down the same path, the nation will have entered a state in which the politics of preemption becomes semipermanent. Much that used to be assumed is up for grabs. But that does not mean that all the rules are gone, that the American political tradition is suddenly no longer relevant, and that the past has no operative hold on the present. So long as Americans live in a constitutional democracy and so long as their disputes take part in the wider constitutional politics of American life, there is no escaping the requirement to articulate from within, from using American political words for contested ends.[2]

The discursive continuities between past and present then offer a lesson. Secularists have decried the actions and the rhetoric of the Christian Right, but they might instead learn from them. The strategy of preemption, so integral to conservative success, is still available to any and all. It could be that secularists decide that the language of pluralism, which led to the embrace of diversity during the first part of the twentieth century, has reached its limits given the centrifugal force of postsixties politics. If so, they might decide that the language of equality is now the more relevant or controlling vocabulary. Or it could be, as Rawls said, that the language of public and private needs to be reaffirmed and reimagined, that political self-discipline and the public norms of debate need to be considered anew. In that case the identity politics of the New Left might have to be modified or discarded. Or it could be that liberal secularists decide that the language of religious freedom has become antithetical to secular governance, that the only choice is a positive secularism on the French model.

In any case, political mobilization requires a searching examination of how words function in debate, how they relate to one another in a constellation of concepts, and how they are substituted for other words over time. The point is not merely academic. As the recent endeavors of the Christian Right have shown, to take account of the political tradition, to learn its language and its uses, is a first step in trying to shape the tradition or in attempting to overcome it.

Acknowledgments

This is the third of three loosely related books I have written about American history. The first, *The Myth of American Religious Freedom*, offers a comprehensive history of Christian coercion in the law, culture, and politics of the United States. The second, *The Jefferson Rule*, probes the quasi-religious mythmaking in American political debate that has often used the Founding Fathers as American apostles. The third book, this one, depicts the rise of modern American secularism and the tensions within the resulting secular order. Taken together, these books offer an extended examination, through different lenses, of religion and the American political tradition—the animating notions, the recurrent pathologies, the past and future possibilities.

Because this book is a culmination of sorts, my list of acknowledgments is long. I began thinking about secularism as a graduate student. Early versions of my prospectus promised a large history on the subject. That promise remained unfulfilled as my first book changed into something else. In 2014 I was asked to join a conference session at a meeting of the Organization of American Historians (OAH). The purpose was to assess the work of David Hollinger. For that paper I returned to the topic of secularism. I am grateful to David Engerman for conceiving of the panel and for inviting me to take part. The paper that I wrote for the OAH session eventually became an essay entitled "Political Atheism: The Secularization and Liberalization of American Public Life" (*Modern Intellectual History* 17 [March 2020]: 249–77). Marni Davis, Isaac Weiner, and Charlie Capper sharpened my thinking at that point. Small parts of that essay are reproduced here in disparate paragraphs. They are reprinted with the permission of Cambridge University Press.

The book began in earnest during the 2017–18 academic year, when I had the immense fortune of serving as the John G. Winant Visiting Professor of American Government at the Rothermere American Institute (RAI) and Balliol College, Oxford. At the RAI, Sally Bayley, Kris Collins, Huw David, Gareth Davis, Pekka Hämäläinen, Mandy Izadi, Hal Jones, Alice Kelly, Des King, Karen O'Brien, Jane Rawson, Tessa Roynon, Tara Stubbs, Stephen Tuck, and Elliott West made up a wonderful community. I also received helpful criticism from the American Politics Graduate Seminar at the RAI and the American History Seminar at the University of Edinburgh. Thanks to David Silkenat for the invitation to Edinburgh.

As anyone who has spent time at either Oxford or Cambridge will tell you, the colleges are where much of the social life is found. For me, Balliol was what I thought the university would be when I first decided to become a professor. On any given day I found myself talking to philosophers, political scientists, biologists, and physicians over lunch and dinner. I am grateful to the fellows who welcomed me and made me feel that I belonged to the fellowship, especially William Barford, Diana Berruezo-Sanchez, Martin Burton, Martin Conway, John-Paul Ghobrial, Phil Howard, Bruce Kinsey, Rachel Quarrell, Seb Shimeld, Simon Skinner, Adam Smyth, Nicky Trott, Gijsbert Werner, and Stefano Zacchetti.

My colleagues at Georgia State (GSU) have been very supportive. Jake Selwood and Jared Poley critiqued an early draft of my introduction. Nick Wilding and Julia Gaffield gave me helpful feedback on several fellowship proposals. Michelle Brattain worked to get me time off to allow me to go to Oxford, as did Associate Dean Mary Ann Romski.

I am hugely thankful to my friend and law school colleague Tim Lytton, who began inviting me to his manuscript workshops a few years ago and then proposed to do a workshop for this book. Funding came from the University Research Services Administration at Georgia State and from Wendy F. Hensel, then dean of the GSU College of Law. I was honored and astounded by the scholars who took the time to read my manuscript and who came to Atlanta to tell me what they thought: Elesha Coffman, John Corrigan, Healan

Gaston, Fred Gedicks, Steve Green, Alison Greene, Leslie Griffin, Sarah Igo, Neil Kinkopf, Paul Lombardo, Monica Miller, Ed Rubin, Don Seeman, Eric Segall, Isaac Weiner, and Jack Williams. Given the number of disciplines and the divergent lines of criticism, I have not done justice to all their suggestions. But the book is far, far better for their efforts.

Many other people read the manuscript in part or whole, which also made it better. I am thankful to Andrew Hartman, Mike Lienesch, Larry Moore, Leigh Schmidt, Matt Sutton, and Molly Worthen for their criticism. Jennifer Banks, my editor at Yale, made a number of crucial interventions. Lawrence Kenney, my copy editor, helped me to curb my stylistic errors and infelicities. The insights from five external reviewers markedly improved the final book and reminded me once again of the efficaciousness of peer review.

A more personal kind of thanks goes to my wife, Connie, and my son, Thomas, who listened and offered suggestions as I talked through intellectual problems. But mostly they did other things: they came to Oxford with me, they picked me up when I was down, and they supported and loved me.

Because this book brings to conclusion several lines of thought that I have been developing since graduate school, I am grateful to the professors who let me embark on this long endeavor, even though it did not at the time have manageable proportions or obvious temporal boundaries or the normal markers of a good research project. My advisor, John Kasson, and my committee members, Peter Filene, Fitz Brundage, Grant Wacker, and Mike Lienesch, all gave me advice then that has finally been put to use. If faced with a similar proposal from a student, I would have grave doubts about giving it my approval. But I am thankful that they trusted me and that it has finally come to fruition.

This book is dedicated to two of my teachers who have helped me for some time. The late Thomas Haskell was my advisor when I entered graduate school in history at Rice University. After I received the acceptance letter into the program, he asked me over to his house for a late afternoon meeting because I was already living in Houston. I arrived to find a tall, smiling man who ushered me in, invited me to sit on a low couch facing an Eames lounge chair, and offered me a beer. I was nervous. I turned down the beer. He faltered a moment, then he came back holding a glass of juice for me and a beer for himself. Over the next two years I would occasionally think about that beer as we sat in seminar, or after I read an amazing book that he assigned, or after a conversation in his office. He showed me the power of ideas and introduced me to the practice of intellectual history. I am grateful to him for taking a chance on me. I still wish I could have that beer.

David Hollinger has been an informal mentor to me for fifteen years. I first read his essay "Jews and the De-Christianization of American Public Culture" in a graduate seminar. It was so remarkable that I soon sought out everything else he had written. After graduate school, while working toward a publishing contract, I mentioned to a friend that I wished I could get Hollinger to read my proposal. She said, "You should just send it to him." I thought that was unlikely to work. I had spent the better part of a year in Cambridge, Massachusetts, trying with little effect to get busy academics to sit down with me. A random email from some unknown postdoc wanting time and attention did not seem to have a high probability of success.

"I think he'll do it," she said. "He's just like that."

She was right. I sent David my proposal, which he immediately read. He then read the manuscript as a whole, recommended the book for publication, and provided a blurb. He has been reading my work and writing recommendations for me ever since. I do not know of a more generous scholar or one that I respect more, and I am enormously grateful for his support.

Notes

Introduction

1. Robert G. Ingersoll, "Individuality," in Ingersoll, *Works of Robert G. Ingersoll* (New York: C. P. Farrell, 1900), 1:199.

2. For examples of writers who assert the secularity of the United States at the nation's birth, see Steven K. Green, *Inventing a Christian America: The Myth of the Religious Founding* (New York: Oxford University Press, 2015); Frank Lambert, *The Founding Fathers and the Place of Religion in America* (Princeton: Princeton University Press, 2003); Isaac Kramnick and R. Laurence Moore, *The Godless Constitution: A Moral Defense of the Secular State*, rev. ed. (New York: Norton, 2005); Kevin M. Kruse, *One Nation under God: How Corporate America Invented Christian America* (New York: Basic Books, 2015).

3. See R. Laurence Moore and Isaac Kramnick, *Godless Citizens in a Godly Republic: Atheists in American Public Life* (New York: Norton, 2018); Leigh Eric Schmidt, *Village Atheists: How America's Unbelievers Made Their Way in a Godly Nation* (Princeton: Princeton University Press, 2016); Susan Jacoby, *Freethinkers: A History of American Secularism* (New York: Metropolitan, 2004); Christian Smith, "Rethinking the Secularization of American Public Life," in Christian Smith, ed., *The Secular Revolution: Power, Interests, and Conflict in the Secularization of American Public Life* (Berkeley: University of California Press, 2003), 1–96.

4. Jacoby, *Freethinkers*, 3.

5. Wilfred M. McClay, "Two Concepts of Secularism," *Wilson Quarterly* 24 (Summer 2000): 67.

6. Talal Asad, *Formations of the Secular: Christianity, Islam, Modernity* (Stanford: Stanford University Press, 2003), 8 (second quotation), 25 (first quotation). For writers engaged in a similar interrogation, see Philip Hamburger, *Liberal Suppression: Section 501 (c) (3) and the Taxation of*

Speech (Chicago: University of Chicago Press, 2018); Saba Mahmood, *Religious Difference in a Secular Age: A Minority Report* (Princeton: Princeton University Press, 2016); George Marsden, *The Twilight of the American Enlightenment: The 1950s and the Crisis of Liberal Belief* (New York: Basic Books, 2014); John Lardas Modern, *Secularism in Antebellum America* (Chicago: University of Chicago Press, 2011).

7. McClay, "Two Concepts of Secularism," 67.

8. For examples of works that point to the essentially or latently Protestant character of American secularism, see Tracy Fessenden, *Culture and Redemption: Religion, the Secular, and American Literature* (Princeton: Princeton University Press, 2007); Philip Hamburger, *Separation of Church and State* (Cambridge: Harvard University Press, 2002). A similar argument, from a slightly different angle, can be found in James E. Block, *A Nation of Agents: The American Path to a Modern Self and Society* (Cambridge: Harvard University Press, 2002). For books that speak more generally of the long-term effect of Protestantism as a move to secularization, see Brad S. Gregory, *The Unintended Reformation: How a Religious Revolution Secularized Society* (Cambridge: Harvard University Press, 2012); Charles Taylor, *A Secular Age* (Cambridge: Harvard University Press, 2007). For a helpful, if somewhat polemical, analysis of these overlapping historiographical trends, see Jacques Berlinerblau, "The Crisis in Secular Studies," *Chronicle Review*, September 8, 2014, https://www.chronicle.com/article /the-Crisis-in-Secular-Studies/.

9. Walter Lippmann, *Drift and Mastery: An Attempt to Diagnose the Current Unrest* (New York: Mitchell Kennerley, 1914), 270. For examples of foundational texts in social science that reject ideas and culture in favor of individual or group interests, see, for example, V. O. Key, *Politics, Parties and Pressure Groups* (New York: Thomas Y. Crowell, 1942); David Easton, *The Political System: An Inquiry into the State of Political Science* (New York: Knopf, 1953); Heinz Eulau, *The Behavioral Persuasion in Politics* (New York: Random House, 1963); Heinz Eulau, ed., *Behavioralism in Political Science* (New York: Atherton Press, 1969). The rise of institutionalist theories challenged but did not displace the basic behavioralist orientation within American social science. For an explanation of those institutionalist theories, see James G. March and Johan P. Olsen, "The New Institutionalism: Organizational Factors in Political Life," *American Political Science Review* 78 (September 1984): 734–49; Peter A. Hall and Rosemary C. R. Taylor, "Political Science and the Three New Institutionalisms," *Political Studies* 44 (1996): 936–57; and especially Vivien A. Schmidt, "Reconciling Ideas and Institutions through Discursive Institutionalism," in Daniel Béland and Robert Henry Cox, eds., *Ideas and Politics in Social Science Research* (New York: Oxford University Press, 2010), 47–64. My book could be seen as an extended analysis using the conceptual frame of discursive institutionalism. It could be seen also as a study in "critical

ideational development," to use the phrasing of Desmond S. King and Rogers M. Smith. See King and Smith, " 'Without Regard to Race': Critical Ideational Development in Modern American Politics," *Journal of Politics* 76 (October 2014): 958–71.

10. Rush Welter, "On Studying the National Mind," in John Higham and Paul K. Conkin, eds., *New Directions in American Intellectual History* (Baltimore: Johns Hopkins University Press, 1979), 65 (first quotation), 65–66 (second quotation).

11. Jack N. Rakove, *The Beginnings of National Politics: An Interpretive History of the Continental Congress* (New York: Knopf, 1979); Daniel T. Rodgers, *Contested Truths: Keywords in American Politics Since Independence* (New York: Basic Books, 1987). On the Constitution as civic scripture, see Jack N. Balkin, *Living Originalism* (Cambridge: Harvard University Press, 2011), 74–99.

12. Alasdair MacIntyre, *After Virtue: A Study in Moral Theory* (Notre Dame: University of Notre Dame Press, 1981), 222. MacIntyre's definition of a tradition was first pointed out to me by Elesha Coffman. See Elesha J. Coffman, *The Christian Century and the Rise of the Protestant Mainline* (New York: Oxford University Press, 2013), 6.

13. David A. Hollinger and Charles Capper, *The American Intellectual Tradition: 1865 to the Present*, 7th ed. (New York: Oxford University Press, 2016), 2:xiii.

Chapter One. An Enlightenment Settlement

1. Thomas Jefferson to the Citizens of Albemarle, February 12, 1790, in Thomas Jefferson, *The Papers of Thomas Jefferson*, ed. Julian P. Boyd (Princeton: Princeton University Press, 1950–), 16:179. On Jefferson's wider concern for liberty and how it affected the political process, see David Sehat, *The Jefferson Rule: How the Founding Fathers Became Infallible and Our Politics Inflexible* (New York: Simon and Schuster, 2015), 3–38. On the contradictory political thought bound up in the slogan "new order of the ages," see Michael Lienesch, *New Order of the Ages: Time, the Constitution, and the Making of Modern American Political Thought* (Princeton: Princeton University Press, 1988).

2. Jefferson to Isaac Story, December 5, 1801, in Jefferson, *Papers*, 36:30.

3. Joseph Canning, *Ideas of Power in the Late Middle Ages, 1296–1417* (New York: Cambridge University Press, 2011); Steven Ozment, *The Age of Reform, 1250–1550: An Intellectual and Religious History of Late Medieval and Reformation Europe* (New Haven: Yale University Press, 1980), 135–81; Michael Wilks, *The Problem of Sovereignty in the Later Middle Ages: The Papal Monarchy with Augustinus Triumphus and the Publicists* (New York: Cambridge University Press, 1963); Ernst H. Kantorowicz, *The King's Two Bodies: A Study in Mediaeval Political Theology* (Princeton: Princeton University Press, 1957).

4. Morton Borden, *Jews, Turks, and Infidels* (Chapel Hill: University of North Carolina Press, 1984).

5. On the Massachusetts Bay Charter, see Bobby Wright, " 'For the Children of Infidels'?: American Indian Education in the Colonial Colleges," *American Indian Culture and Research Journal* 12 (January 1988): 2. On the colonial connection between slavery and heathenism, including the quotation from the colonial court, see David Sehat, *The Myth of American Religious Freedom*, updated ed. (New York: Oxford University Press, 2015), 73–74 (quotation on 73).

6. On Jefferson's religious beliefs and especially his notion that religion was a private matter, see Dumas Malone, *Jefferson and His Time* (Boston: Little, Brown, 1948), 1:106–9.

7. On the religious arrangements prior to the U.S. Constitution, see Sehat, *The Myth of American Religious Freedom*, 13–29.

8. Virginia Constitution of 1776, Declaration of Rights, sec. 16.

9. See editorial note in Jefferson, *Papers*, 2:547.

10. "A Bill for Establishing Religious Freedom," in Jefferson, *Papers*, 2:545–46 (first quotation), 546 (second quotation).

11. Richard Henry Lee to James Madison, November 26, 1784, in James Madison, *The Papers of James Madison*, ed. William T. Hutchison and William M. E. Rachal (Chicago: University of Chicago Press, 1962–91), 8:149.

12. Petition quoted in Thomas E. Buckley, *Church and State in Revolutionary Virginia, 1776–1787* (Charlottesville: University Press of Virginia, 1977), 74. On the legislative history of the bill in 1779, see editorial note in Jefferson, *Papers*, 2:547–48.

13. Madison, "Outline A," in Madison, *Papers*, 8:197.

14. Madison, "Outline B," in ibid., 8:198. See also Madison to the Marquis de Lafayette, March 20, 1785, where Madison discusses "the Act for the corrupting Religious system." Ibid., 8:254.

15. On Madison's parliamentary moves, see Buckley, *Church and State*, 107–12.

16. Madison to Jefferson, January 9, 1785, in Madison, *Papers*, 8:229.

17. Madison, "Memorial and Remonstrance Against Religious Assessments," in ibid., 8:295–306.

18. On rights in the Whig political tradition, see Jack N. Rakove, *Original Meanings: Political Ideas and the Making of the Constitution* (New York: Knopf, 1996), 310–16.

19. Madison, "Memorial and Remonstrance," 8:299.

20. Ibid., 8:300.

21. Ibid., 8:304.

22. Madison to Jefferson, January 22, 1786, in ibid., 8:473.

23. Ibid. For the legislative emendations to Jefferson's original bill and an account of its passage, see Jefferson, *Papers*, 2:545–53 (second quotation on 546).

24. Madison, "Vices of the Political System of the United States," in Madison, *Papers*, 9:356.
25. On the concerns over the godlessness of the Constitution, see Isaac Kramnick and R. Laurence Moore, *The Godless Constitution: A Moral Defense of the Secular State*, rev. ed. (New York: Norton, 2005), 26–45 (quotation on 33–34).
26. Quoted by ibid., 33.
27. Madison to Jefferson, October 17, 1788, in Madison, *Papers*, 11:297.
28. On Madison's change of mind, see Sehat, *The Myth of American Religious Freedom*, 42–45.
29. Joseph Gales, ed., *Debates and Proceedings of the Congress of the United States* (Washington: Gales and Seaton, 1834–56), 1:451. This source is commonly called the *Annals of Congress*.
30. Ibid., 1:452.
31. Ibid., 1:757.
32. Ibid., 1:757 (first quotation), 758 (remaining quotations).
33. Ibid., 1:796.
34. *Journal of the First Session of the Senate of the United States* (Washington: Gales and Seaton, 1820), 77.
35. Ibid., 1:796 (first quotation), 948 (second quotation).
36. Sidney E. Mead, *The Lively Experiment: The Shaping of Christianity in America* (New York: Harper & Row, 1963), 57. For a more extended discussion of the drafting process, see Sehat, *The Myth of American Religious Freedom*, 31–50.
37. On the expansion of evangelicalism and evangelical authority, see Jon Butler, *Awash in a Sea of Faith: Christianizing the American People* (Cambridge: Harvard University Press, 1990), 257–88, particularly 282–84; Christine Leigh Heyrman, *Southern Cross: The Beginnings of the Bible Belt* (New York: Knopf, 1997). For an excellent explanation of how the broad Protestant consensus promoted "nonsectarianism" as the source of its cohesion, see Noah Feldman, *Divided by God: America's Church–State Problem—And What We Should Do About It* (New York: Farrar, Straus, and Giroux, 2005), 61–64. On the shared general characteristics of the Protestant denominations, see Robert T. Handy, *Undermined Establishment: Church–State Relations in America, 1880–1920* (Princeton: Princeton University Press, 1991), 8–12. On the decline of the Enlightenment with the expansion of Protestantism, see Henry F. May, *The Enlightenment in America* (New York: Oxford University Press, 1976), 307–62. On the interlocking connection of Protestant social thought with the institutional structure of the Protestant establishment, see William R. Hutchison, *Religious Pluralism in America: The Contentious History of a Founding Ideal* (New Haven: Yale University Press, 2003), 60–65.
38. On the explosive growth of evangelicalism, see Roger Finke and Rodney Stark, *The Churching of America, 1776–2005: Winners and Losers in Our*

Religious Economy, 2nd ed. (New Brunswick: Rutgers University Press, 2005), 22–24.

39. Sehat, *The Myth of American Religious Freedom*, 53–59.

40. For discussion about this coalition, see the reference to "the Physicians & [the] Dissenting Clergy," in Gideon Granger to Jefferson, October 18, 1800, in Jefferson, *Papers*, 32:228.

41. Jefferson to the Danbury Baptist Association, January 1, 1802, in Jefferson, *Papers*, 36:258. See also the editorial comments and his more expansive first draft of the letter in ibid., 253–56.

42. Charles I. Foster, *An Errand of Mercy: The Evangelical United Front, 1790–1837* (Chapel Hill: University of North Carolina Press, 1960), 275–79. See also Ronald G. Walters, *American Reformers, 1815–1860*, rev. ed. (New York: Hill & Wang, 1997); Paul S. Boyer, *Urban Masses and Moral Order in America, 1820–1920* (Cambridge: Harvard University Press, 1978); Clifford S. Griffin, *Their Brothers' Keepers: Moral Stewardship in the United States, 1800–1865* (New Brunswick: Rutgers University Press, 1960).

43. Lyman Beecher, *A Reformation of Morals Practical and Indispensable* (Andover, Mass.: Flagg and Gould, 1814), 18.

44. Foster, *Errand of Mercy*, xi.

45. Madison, "A Proclamation," July 9, 1812, in James D. Richardson, ed., *A Compilation of the Messages and Papers of the Presidents, 1789–1897* (New York: Bureau of National Literature, 1897), 1:498.

46. For more on blasphemy, obscenity, and Sabbath laws, see Sehat, *The Myth of American Religious Freedom*, 59–69 (quotation on 62).

47. *Permoli v. New Orleans*, 44 U.S. 589 (1845).

48. Sehat, *The Myth of American Religious Freedom*, 155–80.

49. Ibid., 73–154.

50. Robert Ingersoll, "Interview with *Mail and Express*," January 12, 1885, in Robert G. Ingersoll, *The Works of Robert G. Ingersoll* (New York: C. P. Farrell, 1900), 8:227.

51. Quoted in Sehat, *The Myth of American Religious Freedom*, 62. Chris Beneke has argued that the relative scarcity of blasphemy prosecution in the nineteenth century means that I have overstated the Christian power and influence in public life. See Chris Beneke, "The Myth of American Religious Coercion," *Commonplace: The journal of early American life*, accessed February 4, 2021, http://commonplace.online/article/the-myth -of-american-religious-coercion. It is true that there were fairly few recorded trials for blasphemy, particularly on the appellate level, though Beneke still notes that by his reckoning there was one a year for the first fifty years of the nineteenth century. But the notion that blasphemy was not therefore an enforceable (and enforced) crime is inaccurate. Leigh Eric Schmidt points out that in the 1870s, well after blasphemy prosecutions went into decline, there were frequent instances of blasphemy in the annual jail statistics in Connecticut counties: 2 in 1877, 3 in 1878, 4 in

1879 in New Haven County alone. These are the kinds of records that will not show up in reviews of jurisprudence, but they reveal the kind of state- and local-level coercion that was fairly common, if unevenly exerted, in the nineteenth century. Schmidt also points out that blasphemy was often prosecuted as obscenity, which critics complained was an obscurement of the religious underpinning of the law's enforcement. See Leigh Eric Schmidt, *Village Atheists: How America's Unbelievers Made Their Way in a Godly Nation* (Princeton: Princeton University Press, 2016), 197–98.

Chapter Two. The Sociology of Law

1. Adolph Brandeis quoted by Josephine Goldmark, *Pilgrims of '48: One Man's Part in the Austrian Revolution of 1848, and a Family Migration to America* (New Haven: Yale University Press, 1930), 202.

2. Frederika Brandeis quoted by Alpheus Thomas Mason, *Brandeis: A Free Man's Life* (New York: Viking, 1946), 28.

3. Dorothy Ross, ed., *Modernist Impulses in the Human Sciences, 1870–1930* (Baltimore: Johns Hopkins University Press, 1994). On the fight in the European, and especially German, context between secularists and their religious opponents, see Todd H. Weir, *Secularism and Religion in Nineteenth-Century Germany: The Rise of the Fourth Confession* (New York: Cambridge University Press, 2014); Helmut Walser Smith, ed., *Protestants, Catholics, and Jews in Germany, 1800–1914* (New York: Berg, 2001); Christopher Clark and Wolfram Kaiser, eds., *Culture Wars: Secular–Catholic Conflict in Nineteenth-Century Europe* (New York: Cambridge University Press, 2003); Mark Lilla, *The Stillborn God: Religion, Politics, and the Modern West* (New York: Knopf, 2007).

4. Freund quoted by Mason, *Brandeis*, 31.

5. Brandeis quoted by ibid., 69.

6. Yuri Slezkine, *The Jewish Century* (Princeton: Princeton University Press, 2004), 63. See also John Murray Cuddihy, *The Ordeal of Civility: Freud, Marx, Lévi-Strauss, and the Jewish Struggle with Modernity* (New York: Basic Books, 1974), 8–13.

7. Ernest Poole, "Brandeis," *American Magazine* 71 (February 1911): 481.

8. George M. Marsden, *The Soul of the American University: From Protestant Establishment to Established Nonbelief* (New York: Oxford University Press, 1994).

9. Grant Wacker, "The Demise of Biblical Civilization," in *The Bible in America: Essays in Cultural History*, ed. Nathan O. Hatch and Mark A. Noll (New York: Oxford University Press, 1982), 121–38; David Mislin, *Saving Faith: Making Religious Pluralism an American Value at the Dawn of the Secular Age* (Ithaca: Cornell University Press, 2015), 14–33.

10. Charles W. Eliot, "The New Education," *Atlantic Monthly*, February 1869, https://www.theatlantic.com/magazine/archive/1869/02/the-new-education /309049/. See also Laurence Veysey, *The Emergence of the American University* (Chicago: University of Chicago Press, 1965).

11. On the Langdellian revolution, see Anthony Chase, "The Birth of the Modern Law School," *American Journal of Legal History* 23 (October 1979): 329–48; Louis D. Brandeis, "The Harvard Law School," *Green Bag* 1 (January 1889): 10–25, esp. 18–22.

12. David Sehat, *The Myth of American Religious Freedom*, updated ed. (New York: Oxford University Press, 2015), 60–69.

13. *Vidal v. Girard's Executors*, 43 U.S. 127 (1844), at 198.

14. *Latter-Day Saints v. United States*, 136 U.S. 1 (1890), at 49 (first quotation); *Holy Trinity v. United States*, 143 U.S. 457 (1892), at 471 (second quotation); *Hennington v. Georgia*, 163 U.S. 299 (1896), at 304 (third quotation). For more in this vein and for a penetrating discussion of "general religion" in law, see David Sikkink, "From Christian Civilization to Individual Civil Liberties: Framing Religion in the Legal Field, 1880–1949," in Christian Smith, ed., *The Secular Revolution: Power, Interests, and Conflict in the Secularization of American Public Life* (Berkeley: University of California Press, 2003), 311–20.

15. Oliver Wendell Holmes Jr., "Book Notices," *American Law Review* 14 (March 1880): 234. See also Anthony J. Sebok, *Legal Positivism in American Jurisprudence* (New York: Cambridge University Press, 1998), who argues that Langdell saw law as a natural science and that legal realists saw his position as creedal rather than scientific.

16. Brandeis, "The Harvard Law School," 21.

17. Melvin I. Urofsky, *Louis D. Brandeis: A Life* (New York: Pantheon, 2009), 49.

18. Louis Menand, *The Metaphysical Club* (New York: Farrar, Straus and Giroux, 2001), 3–69.

19. Oliver Wendell Holmes Jr., "Ideals and Doubts," in *Collected Legal Papers* (New York: Harcourt, Brace and Howe, 1920), 304 (first quotation), 304–5 (second quotation).

20. Sehat, *The Myth of American Religious Freedom*, 61, 64–67, 178. Sikkink first pointed out that conservatives' view of the common law mirrored their conception of God. See Sikkink, "From Christian Civilization to Individual Liberties," 326–27.

21. *Southern Pacific v. Jensen*, 244 U.S. 205 (1917), at 222.

22. Holmes, *The Common Law* (London: Macmillan, 1882), 1.

23. Ibid.

24. Holmes, "The Path of the Law," *Harvard Law Review* 10 (March 25, 1897): 469.

25. Ibid.

26. Ibid., 474.

27. Samuel D. Warren and Louis D. Brandeis, "The Right to Privacy," *Harvard Law Review* 4 (December 15, 1890): 193–220.

28. Sarah E. Igo, *The Known Citizen: A History of Privacy in Modern America* (Cambridge: Harvard University Press, 2018), 8.

29. Warren and Brandeis, "The Right to Privacy," 193.

30. Ibid., 205.

31. On the property/contract framework of American law before the 1930s, see Bruce Ackerman, *We the People: Foundations* (Cambridge: Harvard University Press, 1991), 119–30, especially 123–24.

32. On the transformation from property to personality, see Igo, *The Known Citizen*, 19–22. See also Roscoe Pound, "Interests of Personality," *Harvard Law Review* 28 (February 1915): 343–51.

33. Brandeis to Alice Goldmark, February 26, 1891, in Melvin I. Urofsky and David W. Levy, eds., *Letters of Louis D. Brandeis* (Albany: State University of New York Press, 1971–78), 1.100. He eventually wrote this other article, in which he delivered his famous aphorism, "Sunlight is said to be the best of disinfectants; electric light the most efficient policeman." See Brandeis, "What Publicity Can Do," *Other People's Money, and How Bankers Use It* (New York: Frederick A. Stokes, 1914), 92.

34. Roscoe Pound, *Social Justice and Legal Justice* (Pittsburgh, 1912), 18.

35. This definition of classical liberalism comes from Mike O'Connor, *A Commercial Republic: America's Enduring Debate over Democratic Capitalism* (Lawrence: University Press of Kansas, 2014), 26.

36. Gary Gerstle, "The Protean Character of American Liberalism," *American Historical Review* 99 (October 1994): 1043–73, especially 1046–49.

37. See Christopher Cameron, *Black Freethinkers: A History of African American Secularism* (Evanston: Northwestern University Press, 2019), 109–18. Cameron defines secularism as a personal rejection of God.

38. On the American bohemians, see Christine Stansell, *American Moderns: Bohemian New York and the Creation of a New Century* (Princeton: Princeton University Press, 2010); Russell Jacoby, *The Last Intellectuals: American Culture in the Age of Academe* (New York: Basic Books, 1987), 27–40.

39. Paul Buhle, *Marxism in the United States: A History of the American Left*, 3rd ed. (London: Verso, 2013), 46–49, 84 (quotation). On the Jewish component of free thought and political radicalism, see Susan Jacoby, *Freethinkers: A History of American Secularism* (New York: Metropolitan, 2004), 233–38; David A. Hollinger, "Jewish Intellectuals and the De-Christianization of American Public Culture in the Twentieth Century," in *Science, Jews, and Secular Culture: Studies in Mid-Twentieth-Century American Intellectual History* (Princeton: Princeton University Press, 1996), 17–41.

40. David A. Hollinger, "Ethnic Diversity, Cosmopolitanism, and the Emergence of the American Liberal Intelligentsia," in Hollinger, *In the American Province: Studies in the History and Historiography of Ideas* (Bloomington: Indiana University Press, 1985), 56–73.

41. Walter Lippmann, *A Preface to Politics* (New York: M. Kennerley, 1913); Walter E. Weyl, *The New Democracy: An Essay on Certain Political and Economic Tendencies in the United States* (New York: Macmillan, 1912), 1; Floyd Dell, *Intellectual Vagabondage: An Apology for the Intelligentsia* (New York: George H. Doran, 1926), 107. For a wider exploration of the role of modernism in a variety of domains, see William R. Hutchison, *The Modernist Impulse in American Protestantism* (Cambridge: Harvard University Press, 1976); Daniel Joseph Singal, "Towards a Definition of American Modernism," *American Quarterly* 39 (Spring 1987): 7–26; Dorothy Ross, "Modernism Reconsidered," in Dorothy Ross, ed., *Modernist Impulses in the Human Sciences, 1870–1930* (Baltimore: Johns Hopkins University Press, 1994), 1–9.

42. Lippmann, *Drift and Mastery: An Attempt to Diagnose the Current Unrest* (New York: M. Kennerley, 1914), 203.

43. See Menand, *The Metaphysical Club.*

44. Ann Douglas, *Terrible Honesty: Mongrel Manhattan in the 1920s* (New York: Farrar, Straus and Giroux, 1995), 6; Horace M. Kallen, "Democracy versus the Melting Pot," *The Nation,* February 18, 1915, 190–94, February 25, 1915, 217–20; Randolph Bourne, "Trans-national America," *Atlantic Monthly* 118 (July 1916), 86–97; Alain Locke, *Race Contacts and Interracial Relations,* quoted in Louis Menand, *Metaphysical Club,* 398.

45. James T. Kloppenberg, *Uncertain Victory: Social Democracy and Progressivism in European and American Thought, 1870–1920* (New York: Oxford University Press, 1986).

46. On Brandeis's shift from assimilationism to cultural pluralism, see Jeffrey Rosen, *Louis D. Brandeis: American Prophet* (New Haven: Yale University Press, 2016), 146–51.

47. *Leo M. Frank v. C. Wheeler Mangum,* 237 U.S. 309 (1915), at 349 (first quotation), 350 (second and third quotations). For Brandeis's opinion of the case, see Brandeis to Roscoe Pound, November 27, 1914, in *Letters,* 3:373–74.

48. On Leo Frank and his lynching, see Steve Oney, *And the Dead Shall Rise: The Murder of Mary Phagan and the Lynching of Leo Frank* (New York: Pantheon, 2003); Nancy Maclean, "The Leo Frank Case Reconsidered: Gender and Sexual Politics in the Making of Reactionary Populism," *Journal of American History* 78 (December 1991), 917–48.

49. On the second Klan and its relationship to Protestantism, see Kelly J. Baker, *Gospel According to the Klan: The KKK's Appeal to Protestant America, 1915–1930* (Lawrence: University Press of Kansas, 2011); Matthew Avery Sutton, *American Apocalypse: A History of Modern Evangelicalism* (Cambridge: Harvard University Press, 2014), 128–30; Steven K. Green, *The Third Disestablishment: Church, State, and American Culture, 1940–1975* (New York: Oxford University Press, 2019), 24–25, 32.

50. Brandeis, "The Jewish Problem: How to Solve It," *Brandeis on Zionism* (Washington D.C.: Zionist Organization of America, 1942), 12–35.

51. Ibid., 15.
52. Brandeis, "True Americanism," *Brandeis on Zionism*, 5 (first quotation), 11 (second and third quotations).
53. Philippa Levine, *Eugenics: A Very Short Introduction* (New York: Oxford University Press, 2017), 55–58.
54. For examples of Brandeis's behind-the-scenes maneuvering and coordination of responses, see Brandeis to Norman Hapgood, March 14, 1916, in *Letters*, 4:118–19, and Brandeis to Edward Francis McLennen, April 3, 1916, in ibid., 4:143–44. For a good summary of the entire episode, see Urofsky, *Louis D. Brandeis*, 430–59.
55. Felix Frankfurter, "Mr. Justice Brandeis and the Constitution," in Felix Frankfurter, ed., *Mr. Justice Brandeis* (New Haven: Yale University Press, 1932), 50.

Chapter Three. Piers of American Secularism

1. A. H. Macmillan, *Faith on the March* (Englewood Cliffs, N.J.: Prentice-Hall, 1957), 42–44, 47 (quotations). Macmillan was one of the leaders among the first generation of the Bible Students.
2. Ibid., 48–57, 71–73.
3. David M. Kennedy, *Over Here: The First World War and American Society* (New York: Oxford University Press, 1980), 3–14.
4. Wilson quoted by Cara Lea Burnidge, *A Peaceful Conquest: Woodrow Wilson, Religion, and the New World Order* (Chicago: University of Chicago Press, 2016), 66.
5. Ibid., 68 (quotations); Andrew Preston, *Sword of the Spirit, Shield of Faith: Religion in American War and Diplomacy* (New York: Knopf, 2012), 233–74.
6. See Leah Weinryb Grohsgal, "Reinventing Civil Liberties: Religious Groups, Organized Litigation, and the Rights Revolution" (PhD diss.: Emory University, 2011), 6–7. In this chapter and the next, I have relied heavily on Grohsgal's excellent dissertation. I hope it will be published as a book at some point soon.
7. John Reed, *Ten Days That Shook the World* (New York: Boni and Liveright, 1919); Vladimir I. Lenin, "Socialism and Religion," in Lenin, *Collected Works*, trans. and ed. by Andrew Rothstein (Moscow: Progress Publications, 1965), 10:83–84.
8. On the fear about labor and atheist agitators, see Susan Jacoby, *Freethinkers: A History of American Secularism* (New York: Metropolitan, 2004), 227–45. Heath Carter describes how many workers objected to the notion that they had no religion or the wrong religion and began to push Christian leaders to embrace a more social form of Christianity. See Heath W. Carter, *Union Made: Working People and the Rise of Social Christianity in Chicago* (New York: Oxford University Press, 2015).

9. William R. Hutchison, ed., *Between the Times: The Travail of the Protestant Establishment in America, 1900–1960* (New York: Cambridge University Press, 1989).

10. Kennedy, *Over Here*, 79–80.

11. Rutherford, quoted by Macmillan, *Faith on the March*, 85–86. For an extended articulation of the Bible Students' rejection of existing church–state arrangements, see Charles T. Russell, *The Finished Mystery* (Brooklyn: International Bible Students Association, 1917), preface, 247–53, 406–7, 469.

12. For a compelling analysis of the Witnesses' attraction to the down and out, see James A. Beckford, *The Trumpet of Prophecy: A Sociological Study of the Jehovah's Witnesses* (New York: Wiley, 1975).

13. Macmillan, *Faith on the March*, 86–90.

14. Ibid., 95–99.

15. Ibid., 84–85, 99 (quotations).

16. *Schenck v. United States*, 249 U.S. 47 (1919).

17. Ibid., at 52.

18. *Debs v. United States*, 249 U.S. 211 (1919), at 214. See also *Frohwerk v. United States*, 249 U.S. 204 (1919).

19. Eugene Debs, "Statement to the Court," *Writings and Speeches of Eugene V. Debs*, ed. Arthur M. Schlesinger Jr. (New York: Hermitage Press, 1948), 437.

20. *Debs v. United States*, 249 U.S. 211 (1919).

21. John Dewey, "In Explanation of Our Lapse" (1917), in John Dewey, *The Middle Works, 1899–1924*, ed. Jo Ann Boydston (Carbondale: Southern Illinois University Press, 1976–83), 10:292.

22. On the bad tendency test, see David M. Rabban, *Free Speech in Its Forgotten Years* (New York: Cambridge University Press, 1997). On Holmes's initial articulation of the limits of speech, see Samuel Konefsky, *The Legacy of Holmes and Brandeis: A Study in the Influence of Ideas* (New York: Macmillan, 1956), 192–94.

23. Ernst Freund, "The Debs Case and Freedom of Speech," *New Republic*, May 3, 1919, 14.

24. Brandeis–Frankfurter Conversations, Brandeis Papers, quoted by Robert Cover, "The Left, the Right, and the First Amendment, 1918–1928," *Maryland Law Review* 40:3 (1981): 374. On the history of working-class radicalism and the fight over free speech, see Laura Weinrib, *The Taming of Free Speech: America's Civil Liberties Compromise* (Cambridge: Harvard University Press, 2016).

25. On free speech as a public right, see Bruce Ackerman, *We the People: Foundations* (Cambridge: Harvard University Press, 1991), 124–27.

26. Macmillan, *Faith on the March*, 100–101.

27. Grohsgal, "Reinventing Civil Liberties," 80–81.

28. Zechariah Chafee Jr., "Freedom of Speech in Wartime," *Harvard Law Review* 32 (June 1919): 957.

29. Ibid.; Oliver Wendell Holmes Jr., "The Path of the Law," *Harvard Law Review* 10 (March 25, 1897): 469.

30. Chafee, "Freedom of Speech," 934 (second quotation), 956 (first quotation).

31. Ibid., 960–63.

32. Rabban, *Free Speech in Its Forgotten Years*, 7.

33. *Abrams v. United States*, 250 U.S. 616 (1919).

34. Ibid., at 621.

35. Ibid., at 628.

36. Ibid., at 630.

37. Ibid.

38. Brandeis to Holmes, April 23, 1919, in *Letters*, 4.390.

39. *Schaefer v. United States*, 251 U.S. 466 (1920).

40. Ibid., at 495.

41. *Pierce v. United States*, 252 U.S. 239 (1920), at 273.

42. *Gilbert v. Minnesota*, 254 U.S. 325 (1920).

43. Ibid., at 338.

44. On the ACLU, see Samuel Walker, *In Defense of American Liberties: A History of the ACLU*, 2nd ed. (Carbondale: University of Illinois Press, 1999).

45. Ibid., 30–34, 52.

46. Paul L. Murphy, *World War I and the Origin of Civil Liberties in the United States* (New York: Norton, 1979), 153–56.

47. Walker, *In Defense of American Liberties*, 37–40.

48. Ibid., 40.

49. Ibid., 52–54; Laura M. Weinrib, "Civil Liberties Outside the Courts," *Supreme Court Review* (2014): 315–16.

50. Weinrib calls this positive view of government the "progressive vision," which she contrasts with the "radical vision." See Weinrib, "Civil Liberties Outside the Courts," 316–18.

51. Walker, *In Defense of American Liberties*, 60.

52. On the Protestant fundamentalism of the KKK, see Kelly J. Baker, *The Gospel According to the Klan: The KKK's Appeal to Protestant America, 1915–1930* (Lawrenceville: University Press of Kansas, 2011). On the NAACP's response, see Walker, *In Defense of American Liberties*, 62.

53. DeSilver quoted by Walker, *In Defense of American Liberties*, 62.

54. Ibid., 61.

55. Grohsgal, "Reinventing Civil Liberties," 87–88; Macmillan, *Faith on the March*, 120–21.

56. Green, *Third Disestablishment*, 62; Grohsgal, "Reinventing Civil Liberties," 14.

57. For an example of the rhetoric, see "Church–State Destroys Religious Liberty," *The Golden Age*, September 29, 1920, 711–12 (quotation on 711).

58. "Dry Law is the Scheme of the Devil," *Washington Post*, July 22, 1924, p. 3; Grohsgal, "Reinventing Civil Liberties," 92–101.

59. Grohsgal, "Reinventing Civil Liberties, 14–15, 110.
60. Roger Baldwin, Unpublished Biography (Galley Proofs), Roger Baldwin Papers, quoted by ibid., 178.
61. Ibid., 178–79.
62. *Gitlow v. New York*, 268 U.S. 652 (1925).
63. Ibid., at 656 footnote 2.
64. Ibid., at 654.
65. Gitlow quoted in Richard C. Cortner, *The Supreme Court and the Second Bill of Rights: The Fourteenth Amendment and the Nationalization of Civil Liberties* (Madison: University of Wisconsin Press, 1981), 50.
66. "Gitlow's Trial," in Alfred Fried, ed. *Communism in America: A History in Documents* (New York: Columbia University Press, 1997), 52 (first quotation), 53 (second quotation). For the early history of American communism and its connection to the Soviet Union, see Theodore Draper, *The Roots of American Communism* (New York: Viking, 1957); Theodore Draper, *American Communism and Soviet Russia* (New York: Viking Press, 1960).
67. Appeals court quoted by Cortner, *The Second Bill of Rights*, 54.
68. *Gitlow v. New York*, at 667.
69. Cortner, *The Supreme Court and the Second Bill of Rights*, 3–11, 38–62.
70. Chafee quoted by Walker, *In Defense of American Liberties*, 80.
71. These biographical details come from Neil Richards, *Intellectual Privacy: Rethinking Civil Liberties in the Digital Age* (New York: Oxford University Press, 2015), 27–28.
72. Ibid., 28–29.
73. *St. Louis Post-Dispatch*, July 19, 1927, quoted by Konefsky, *Legacy of Holmes and Brandeis*, 94.
74. *Whitney v. California*, 274 U.S. 357 (1927).
75. Ibid., at 376.
76. Ibid., 375 (first quotation), 377 (second and third quotations).
77. *Olmstead v. United States*, 277 U.S. 438 (1928).
78. Ibid., at 478.
79. On this point, see Richards, *Intellectual Privacy*, 6–8.
80. Harlan Fisk Stone, "The Conscientious Objector," *Columbia University Quarterly* 21 (October 1919): 253–72 (quotations on 263). On Stone's religious views and training, see Alpheus Thomas Mason, *Harlan Fiske Stone: Pillar of the Law* (New York: Viking, 1956), 42–61. On Stone's work with conscientious objectors, see Mason, *Harlan Fiske Stone*, 100–114.
81. Mason, *Harlan Fiske Stone*, 114–25, 251–62.
82. Brandeis to Harold Joseph Laski, February 28, 1932, in *Letters*, 5:497.
83. Holmes quoted by Konefsky, *Legacy*, 169. For his exploration of what he called the sociological method in jurisprudence, see Benjamin N. Cardozo, *The Nature of the Judicial Process* (New Haven: Yale University Press, 1921), 98–141.
84. Brandeis to Harold Joseph Laski, February 28, 1932, in *Letters*, 5:497.

85. Walter Lippmann, *A Preface to Politics* (New York: M. Kennerley, 1913), 31.
86. Roosevelt, "The Governor Accepts the Nomination for the Presidency," July 2, 1932, in Franklin Delano Roosevelt, *The Public Papers and Addresses of Franklin D. Roosevelt*, ed. Samuel I. Rosenman (New York: Random House, 1938–50) 1:649 (second quotation), 659 (first and third quotations).
87. Brandeis to Fannie Brandeis, July 11, 1932, in *Letters*, 5:505.
88. See David Schat, *The Jefferson Rule: How the Founding Fathers Became Infallible and Our Politics Inflexible* (New York: Simon and Schuster, 2015), 131–34.
89. Robert H. Jackson, *The Struggle for Judicial Supremacy: A Study of a Crisis in American Power Politics* (New York: Knopf, 1941), v.
90. *West Coast Hotel v. Parrish*, 300 U.S. 379 (1937); *National Labor Relations Board v. Jones and Laughlin Steel Corp.*, 301 U.S. 1 (1937).
91. *United States v. Carolene Products Co.*, 304 U.S. 144 (1938), at 152 note 4. On the importance of the footnote as a marker for future synthesis, see Ackerman, *We the People*, 119–21.

Chapter Four. The Difficulties of Diversity

1. Joseph F. Rutherford, *Liberty: Explained in Seven Bible Treatises* (Brooklyn: Watchtower Bible and Tract Society, 1932), 6.
2. Joseph F. Rutherford, "Liberty to Preach," *The Golden Age*, March 20, 1929, 387–92.
3. Ibid., 392.
4. Leah Weinryb Grohsgal, "Reinventing Civil Liberties: Religious Groups, Organized Litigation, and the Rights Revolution," (PhD diss.: Emory University, 2011), 133.
5. A. H. Macmillan, *Faith on the March* (Englewood Cliffs, NJ: Prentice-Hall, 1957), 162.
6. "The Empire and the Courts," *The Golden Age*, June 22–July 6, 1921, 570.
7. Grohsgal, "Rethinking Civil Liberties," 186.
8. *Boston Post*, September 21, 1935, reprinted in *The Golden Age*, October 9, 1935, 40.
9. Baldwin to Carleton Nichols Sr., October 4, 1935, quoted by Grohsgal, "Rethinking Civil Liberties," 198.
10. Grohsgal, "Rethinking Civil Liberties," 198–203.
11. Moyle to ACLU, October 22, 1935, quoted by ibid., 204.
12. Baldwin quoted by ibid., 182.
13. "Model Brief for Flag Salute Cases" (1936), quoted by ibid., 206.
14. Baldwin quoted by ibid., 213.
15. ACLU Press Release, June 1, 1936, in ibid., 206.
16. Quoted by ibid., 217.
17. Ibid.

18. *Reynolds v. United States*, 98 U.S. 145 (1878).
19. *Davis v. Beason*, 133 U.S. 333 (1890).
20. *Latter-day Saints v. United States*, 136 U.S. 1 (1890), at 49. For more on the struggle over Mormonism in the nineteenth century, see David Sehat, *The Myth of American Religious Freedom*, updated ed. (New York: Oxford University Press, 2015), 168–73; Sarah Barringer Gordon, *The Mormon Question: Polygamy and Constitutional Conflict in Nineteenth-Century America* (Chapel Hill: University of North Carolina Press, 2002).
21. Moyle to Rutherford, February 7, 1938, quoted by Grohsgal, "Rethinking Civil Liberties," 229.
22. *Lovell v. City of Griffin*, 303 U.S. 444 (1938).
23. Moyle to Rutherford, April 7, 1938, quoted by Grohsgal, "Rethinking Civil Liberties," 231.
24. Moyle to Rutherford, May 2, 1938, quoted by ibid., 240.
25. Moyle to Rutherford (undated but possibly May 1938), quoted by ibid., 244.
26. Richard C. Cortner, *The Supreme Court and the Second Bill of Rights: The Fourteenth Amendment and the Nationalization of Civil Liberties* (Madison: University of Wisconsin Press, 1981), 103–4.
27. "Hughes in a Clash on Religious Right," *New York Times*, March 29, 1940, 12.
28. Del Dickson, *The Supreme Court in Conference (1940–1985): The Private Discussions Behind Nearly 300 Court Decisions* (New York: Oxford University Press, 2001), 392.
29. *United States v. Carolene Products Co.*, 304 U.S. 144 (1938), at 152 note 4.
30. *Cantwell v. Connecticut*, 310 U.S. 296 (1940), at 310.
31. Ibid.
32. Grohsgal, "Rethinking Civil Liberties," 254–55.
33. Ibid.
34. Dickson, *Supreme Court in Conference*, 430 (first quotation), 431 (second quotation).
35. Grohsgal, "Rethinking Civil Liberties," 252.
36. *Minersville School District v. Gobitis*, 310 U.S. 586 (1940), 593 (first quotation), 594 (second and third quotations).
37. Ibid., at 601.
38. Ibid., at 604.
39. "The Flag Salute Case," *Christian Century*, June 19, 1940, 791 (first quotation), 792 (second and third quotations).
40. Dickson, *The Supreme Court in Conference*, 431.
41. Grohsgal, "Rethinking Civil Liberties," 264–67.
42. Dickson, *The Supreme Court in Conference*, 431.
43. Franklin Delano Roosevelt, "The Annual Message to Congress," January 6, 1941, in Franklin Delano Roosevelt, *The Public Papers and Addresses of Franklin D. Roosevelt*, ed. Samuel I. Rosenman (New York: Random House, 1938–50), 9:672.

44. *Jones v. Opelika*, 316 U.S. 584 (1942), at 597.
45. Ibid., at 610.
46. Ibid., at 611–23.
47. *Murdock v. Pennsylvania*, 319 U.S. 105 (1943), at 111.
48. Ibid., at 130.
49. Ibid., at 140.
50. Jackson articulated his dissent in a separate case decided at the same time. See *Douglas v. City of Jeannette*, 319 U.S. 517 (1943), at 181.
51. *West Virginia Board of Education v. Barnette*, 319 U.S. 624 (1943), at 634.
52. Ibid., at 641.
53. Ibid., at 646.
54. Ibid., at 653.
55. Joan Wallach Scott, *The Politics of the Veil* (Princeton: Princeton University Press, 2007), 15 (quotation), 91–100. On the formation of *laïcité* during the Third Republic, see Eugen Weber, *Peasants into Frenchmen: The Modernization of Rural France, 1870–1914* (Stanford: Stanford University Press, 1976).
56. *West Virginia Board of Education v. Barnette*, at 654.
57. Ibid., at 658.

Chapter Five. Stumbling toward Secularism

1. Franklin Delano Roosevelt quoted by Kevin M. Schultz, *Tri-Faith America: How Catholics and Jews Held Postwar America to Its Protestant Promise* (New York: Oxford University Press, 2011), 10.
2. David Sehat, "A Mainline Moment: The American Protestant Establishment Revisited," *Modern Intellectual History* 11 (November 2014): 740–41.
3. Leigh E. Schmidt, "The Parameters and Problematics of American Religious Liberalism," in Leigh E. Schmidt and Sally M. Promey, eds., *American Religious Liberalism* (Bloomington: Indiana University Press, 2012), 7; William R. Hutchison, *Religious Pluralism in America: The Contentious History of a Founding Ideal* (New Haven: Yale University Press, 2003), 111–38. See also Schmidt, *Restless Souls: The Making of American Spirituality*, 2nd ed. (Berkeley: University of California Press, 2012).
4. David Mislin, *Saving Faith: Making Religious Pluralism an American Value at the Dawn of the Secular Age* (Ithaca: Cornell University Press, 2015), 63–89; David Sehat, *The Myth of American Religious Freedom*, updated ed. (New York: Oxford University Press, 2015), 155–68; John T. McGreevy, *Catholicism and American Freedom: A History* (New York: Norton, 2003), 91–150.
5. Mislin, *Saving Faith*, 33–38; Matthew S. Hedstrom, "Reading Across the Divide of Faith: Liberal Protestant Book Culture and Interfaith Encounters in Print, 1921–1948," in Schmidt and Promey, eds., *American Religious Liberalism*, 222; Ann Taves, *Fits, Visions, Trances: Experiencing Religion*

and Explaining Difference from Wesley to James (Princeton: Princeton University Press, 1999), 253–307.

6. David A. Hollinger, "After Cloven Tongues of Fire: Ecumenical Protestantism and the Modern Encounter with Diversity," in *After Cloven Tongues of Fire: Protestant Liberalism in Modern American History* (Princeton: Princeton University Press, 2013), 18–55.

7. George Marsden, *Fundamentalism and American Culture*, 2d ed. (New York: Oxford University Press, 2006).

8. David A. Hollinger, *Protestants Abroad: How Missionaries Tried to Change the World but Changed America* (Princeton: Princeton University Press, 2017), 90.

9. Lyman Beecher, *Lectures on Political Atheism and Kindred Subjects* (Boston: John P. Jewett, 1852).

10. On the loss of religious authority as the *sine qua non* of secularization, see Mark Chaves, "Secularization as Declining Religious Authority," *Social Forces* 72 (March 1994), 749–74.

11. Charles Clayton Morrison, "Can Protestantism Win America? 3: Protestantism and the Public School," *Christian Century*, April 17, 1946, 490. See also Morrison, "Can Protestantism Win America? 2: The Protestant Situation," *Christian Century*, April 10, 1946, 458–60; Arnold Nash, "The End of the Protestant Era," *Christian Century*, October 30, 1946, 1306–8.

12. On the claim of nonsectarianism, see Sehat, *The Myth of American Religious Freedom*, 155–58.

13. Ibid., 158–59.

14. For Decree 426 and its translation, see Bernard Julius Meiring, *Educational Aspects of the Legislation of the Councils of Baltimore, 1829–1884* (New York: Arno, 1878), 278.

15. Sehat, *The Myth of American Religious Freedom*, 159–68.

16. *Longinqua* (1895), in Claudia Carlen, ed., *The Papal Encyclicals* (Wilmington, NC: McGrath, 1981), 2:363–70.

17. *Pascendi Dominici Gregis* (1907), in ibid., 5:71 (first quotation), 89 (second quotation). On Pius XI and the American bishops, see Schultz, *Tri-Faith America*, 33.

18. Stanislaus Woywood, "The Teaching Authority of the Church," in *The New Canon Law: A Commentary on and Summary of the New Code of Canon Law*, 7th ed. (New York: Joseph F. Wagner, 1940), 272–92 (especially canons 1322, 1325, 1372, 1382, 1384, 1399, 1401–5).

19. Steven K. Green, *The Third Disestablishment: Church, State, and American Culture, 1940–1975* (New York: Oxford University Press, 2019), 37–41; Hollinger, *Protestants Abroad*, 99.

20. Green, *Third Disestablishment*, 42–57 (quotation on 51); Hollinger, *Protestants Abroad*, 99; Samuel Moyn, "Religious Freedom Between Truth and Tactic," in Winifred Fallers Sullivan et al., eds., *Politics of Religious Freedom* (Chicago: University of Chicago Press, 2015), 137–38.

21. Benjamin Fine, "Catholic Schools Raise Enrollment to 4,000,000 Peak," *New York Times*, May 30, 1952, 1, 75.

22. On the child-benefit theory and the general Catholic argument for public subsidy, see Richard C. Cortner, *The Supreme Court and the Second Bill of Rights: The Fourteenth Amendment and the Nationalization of Civil Liberties* (Madison: University of Wisconsin Press, 1980), 108–9.

23. Gregg Ivers, *To Build a Wall: American Jews and the Separation of Church and State* (Charlottesville: University Press of Virginia, 1995), 17.

24. For an example of handwringing about being caught between two opposing forces, see Morrison, "Protestantism and the Public School," 492–93. For Protestant distrust of the child-benefit theory, see "The Wisconsin Bus Bill," *Christian Century*, October 30, 1946, 1302–3.

25. John Dewey, "Implications of S.2499," (1947), in John Dewey, *The Later Works, 1925–1953*, ed. Jo Ann Boydston (Carbondale: Southern Illinois University Press, 1989), 15:284; Horace Kallen, *The Education of Free Men: An Essay Toward a Philosophy of Education for Americans* (New York: Farrar, Straus, 1949), 213. For a discussion of the liberal intellectual suspicion of Catholic power and purposes, see McGreevy, *Catholicism and American Freedom*, 166–88.

26. Samuel Krislov, "The Amicus Curiae Brief: From Friendship to Advocacy," *Yale Law Journal* 72 (March 1963): 694–721; Frank J. Sorauf, *The Wall of Separation: The Constitutional Politics of Church and State* (Princeton: Princeton University Press, 1976), 205–57.

27. *Everson v. Board of Education*, 330 U.S. 1 (1947). On the Catholic church's support, see Green, *Third Disestablishment*, 107–8.

28. *Everson v. Board of Education*, at 18.

29. Ibid., at 46–47.

30. Ibid., 23 (first quotation), 23–34 (second quotation).

31. Gladwin Hill, "Methodist Bishops Attack Catholics," *New York Times*, May 8, 1947, 26.

32. "Baptists Warned on Liberty Test," *New York Times*, May 8, 1947, 22.

33. "Now Will Protestants Awake?" *Christian Century*, February 26, 1947, 262–64 (quotations on 262).

34. "Supreme Court Decision on Bus Transportation," *America*, February 22, 1947, 561. For a more extended theoretical treatment that supports the notion of "Protestant secularism," see Ann Pellegrini, "Everson's Children," in Sullivan et al., eds., *Politics of Religious Freedom*, 259.

35. "Spellman Charges Protestant Bias," *New York Times*, June 12, 1947, 22.

36. Frank L. Kluckhohn, "Cushing Stresses Parents' Rights," *New York Times*, April 10, 1947, 18.

37. Robert C. Hartnett, "Religion and American Democracy," *America*, August 23, 1947, 569 (first two quotations), 571 (last quotation). For Catholic criticism of public educators and for their response, see Frank L. Kluckhohn, "N.E.A. Is Assailed before Catholics," *New York Times*, April

11, 1947, 18; Benjamin Fine, "Religious Attack Stirs Educators," *New York Times*, March 6, 1947, 27, 35.

38. Protestants and Other Americans United, "Separation of Church and State: A Manifesto," *Christian Century*, January 21, 1948, 79.

39. Ibid. See also "Protestants United Issue Manifesto," *Christian Century*, January 21, 1948, 68; "New Body Demands Church Separation," *New York Times*, January 12, 1948, 1, 12.

40. Protestants and Other Americans United, "Separation of Church and State," 79–82.

41. "K. of C. Criticizes Separation Drive," *New York Times*, January 13, 1948, 1, 13 (quotation).

42. "Denies Catholics Oppose Separation," *New York Times*, January 26, 1948, 17.

43. "Oxnam Says Cushing Attempted 'Smear,' " *New York Times*, February 16, 1948, 5 (first quotation); "Indecent Controversy," *Christian Century*, February 18, 1948, 199 (subsequent quotations). For the POAU response, see "Indecent Controversy," 198–200.

44. Sorauf, *Wall of Separation*, 29–47, 169–70.

45. Ivers, *To Build a Wall*, 2–3.

46. Leo Pfeffer, "An Autobiographical Sketch," in *Religion and the State: Essays in Honor of Leo Pfeffer*, ed. James E. Wood Jr. (Waco: Baylor University Press, 1985), 487.

47. Sorauf, *Wall of Separation*, 161.

48. *McCollum v. Board of Education*, 333 U.S. 203 (1948).

49. Rob Boston, "Vashti's Victory: How a Valiant Illinois Woman and Her Family Won the First Supreme Court Verdict on Religion and the Public Schools Fifty Years Ago," *Church & State*, April 1998, 83.

50. Ibid.

51. Ibid., 83–84.

52. *McCollum v. Board of Education*, 333 U.S. 203 (1948).

53. Pfeffer, "An Autobiographical Sketch," 493; Ivers, *To Build a Wall*, 70–78.

54. Ivers, 79–80 (quotation on 79).

55. Ibid., 73.

56. *McCollum v. Board of Education*, at 212.

57. Ibid., at 231.

58. Ibid., at 239.

59. "Releasing the Time," *Commonweal*, March 26, 1948, 581 (first quotation), 582 (second and third quotations).

60. Ibid., 582.

61. "Statement by Catholic Bishops Attacking Secularism as an Evil," *New York Times*, November 21, 1948, 63.

62. Wilfred Parsons, *The First Freedom: Considerations on Church and State in the United States* (New York: McMullen, 1948), 141 (first quotation), 155 (second and third quotations); James M. O'Neill, *Religion and Education under the Constitution* (New York: Harper, 1949); Robert C. Harnett, "The McCollum Case," *America*, April 24, 1948, 49–52.

63. "The Champaign Case," *Christian Century*, April 7, 1948, 309. On the cultural effect of *McCollum* and its threat to both Catholics and Protestants, see Ivers, *To Build a Wall*, 81–83.

64. "Statement on Church and State," June 17, 1948, reprinted in *First Things* 26 (October 1992): 32. See also "Church's Teaching Held Endangered," *New York Times*, June 13, 1948, 50.

65. John Courtney Murray, "A Common Enemy, A Common Cause" (1948), in *First Things* 26 (October 1992): 29–37 (quotation on 32). See also Murray, "Law or Prepossessions," *Law and Contemporary Problems* 14 (Winter 1949): 23–43; Murray, "A Statement by Fr. Murray," *American Mercury* 69 (November 1949): 637–39, in *Bridging the Sacred and the Secular: Selected Writings of John Courtney Murray*, ed. J. Leon Hooper (Washington: Georgetown University Press, 1994), 306–8.

66. McGreevy, *Catholicism and American Freedom*, 191–206 (quotation on 206).

67. On the Catholic and liberal Protestant concerns about secularism, see K. Healan Gaston, "Demarcating Democracy: Liberal Catholics, Protestants, and the Discourse of Secularism," in Schmidt and Promey, eds., *American Religious Liberalism*, 337–58, esp. 343–47, 351–54. On the National Council of Churches, see Martin E. Marty, *Modern American Religion: Under God, Indivisible, 1941–1960* (Chicago: University of Chicago Press, 1996): 3:272 (quotations). On the resulting sectarian conflict, see Will Herberg, "The Sectarian Conflict over Church and State: A Divisive Threat to Our Democracy?" *Commentary* 14 (November 1952): 450–62.

68. "Pluralism—National Menace," *Christian Century*, June 13, 1951, 701–3.

69. "Poison Three Ways," *Time*, May 5, 1952, 57.

70. Sorauf, *Wall of Separation*, 64–68.

71. Ivers, *To Build a Wall*, 86–87.

72. ACLU quoted in Sorauf, *Wall of Separation*, 108.

73. Pfeffer, "Autobiographical Sketch," 498–99.

74. Ibid., 500 (quotations); Sorauf, *The Wall of Separation*, 119–20.

75. Sorauf, *Wall of Separation*, 88–89.

76. "Court Told of Need for Bible Training," *New York Times*, February 2, 1952, 9.

77. Del Dickson, *The Supreme Court in Conference (1940–1985): The Private Discussions Behind Nearly 300 Court Decisions* (New York: Oxford University Press, 2001), 404–5.

78. *Zorach v. Clauson*, 343 U.S. 306 (1952), at 312 (first and second quotations), 313 (third and fourth quotations).

79. Ibid., 324 (first quotation), 325 (second quotation).

80. Pfeffer, "Autobiographical Sketch," 500; Ivers, *To Build a Wall*, 98–99.

81. *Humani generis* (1950), in Carlen, ed., *The Papal Encyclicals*, 4:175–84.

82. Ibid., 176, 182 (quotation).

83. Joseph A. Komonchak, " 'The Crisis of Church–State Relationships in the U.S.A.': A Recently Discovered Text by John Courtney Murray," *Review of Politics* 61 (Autumn 1999): 689.

84. Ibid., 687.
85. Joseph McCarthy, "Enemies Within," in Robert Torricelli and Andrew Carroll, eds., *In Our Own Words: Extraordinary Speeches of the American Century* (New York: Washington Square Press, 1999), 173.
86. For the sectarian dimension of McCarthyism, see Green, *Third Disestablishment,* 199–200.
87. C. P. Trussell, "3 on McCarthy Panel Assail Aide for 'Shocking Attack' on Clergy," *New York Times,* July 3, 1953, 1 (first quotation), 6 (second quotation).
88. "Church Groups Hit Red Clergy Charge," *New York Times,* July 5, 1953, 18 (first quotation); Green, *Third Disestablishment,* 204 (second quotation), 205 (third quotation).
89. Oxnam quoted in "Church Groups Hit Red Clergy Charge," 18.
90. C. P. Trussell, "Motion on Oxnam Splits House Unit," *New York Times,* July 23, 1953, 7.
91. Ibid.
92. Ibid.
93. "Spellman Rebukes Inquiries' Critics," *New York Times,* October 25, 1953, 20.
94. "Church Men Decry M'Carthy' Inquiries," *New York Times,* October 27, 1953, 17.
95. Peter Kihss, "City Police Cheer Talk by M'Carthy," *New York Times,* April 5, 1954, 12.
96. Green, *The Third Disestablishment,* 205–6.
97. Komonchak, "A Recently Discovered Text," 703. On his relativizing moves toward Leo XIII, see ibid., 692–93.
98. Ibid., 683–84 (quotation on 683).
99. Ibid., 684–85.
100. Ibid. On the recollections of Murray's friend, see McGreevy, *Catholicism and American Freedom,* 208. On the wider effort to open up the church and the embrace of what was called the Nouvelle Théologie, see ibid., 189–215.
101. Paul Hutchinson, "The President's Religious Faith," *Christian Century,* March 24, 1954, 362–67.
102. "President-Elect Says Soviet Demoted Zukhov Because of Their Friendship," *New York Times,* December 23, 1952, 16.
103. Ibid.
104. Dwight D. Eisenhower, "Inaugural Address," January 20, 1953, in *Public Papers of the Presidents of the United States: Dwight D. Eisenhower* (Washington: Government Printing Office, 1958–61), 1953:1.
105. On Eisenhower's religiousness in office, see Andrew Preston, *Sword of the Spirit, Shield of Faith: Religion in American War and Diplomacy* (New York: Knopf, 2012), 441.
106. Oxnam, quoted in ibid., 453.
107. Eisenhower, quoted in Hutchinson, "The President's Religious Faith," 366.

108. Eisenhower, "Statement by the President Upon Signing Bill to Include the Words 'Under God' in the Pledge to the Flag," June 14, 1954, *Public Papers*, 1954:563; Sarah Barringer Gordon, *The Spirit of the Law: Religious Voices and the Constitution in Modern America* (Cambridge: Harvard University Press, 2010), 52–53.

109. Will Herberg, *Protestant–Catholic–Jew: An Essay in American Religious Sociology* (Garden City, NY: Doubleday, 1955), 52.

110. Ibid., 15.

111. Miller quoted in Hutchinson, "The President's Religious Faith," 367; Martin E. Marty, "The New Establishment," *Christian Century*, October 5, 1958, 1177.

112. Marty, "The New Establishment," 1179. See also Martin E. Marty, "The Remnant: Retreat and Renewal," *Christian Century*, November 26, 1958, 1361–65.

113. "Perils of Freedom," *Time*, August 4, 1958, 53.

114. Ibid.

Chapter Six. Religion Is Personal

1. John T. McGreevy, *Catholicism and American Freedom: A History* (New York: Norton, 2003), 213.

2. Joseph A. Komonchak, " 'The Crisis of Church–State Relationships in the U.S.A.': A Recently Discovered Text by John Courtney Murray," *Review of Politics* 61 (Autumn 1999): 686; John Courtney Murray, *We Hold These Truths: Catholic Reflections on the American Proposition* (New York: Sheed and Ward, 1960), 43.

3. Salinger quoted in Andrew Preston, *Sword of the Spirit, Shield of Faith: Religion in American War and Diplomacy* (New York: Knopf, 2012), 502.

4. Fletcher Knebel, "Democratic Forecast: A Catholic in 1960," *LOOK*, March 3, 1959, 17.

5. Timothy J. Sarbaugh, "Champion or Betrayer of His Own Kind: Presidential Politics and John F. Kennedy's 'LOOK' Interview," *Records of the American Catholic Historical Society of Philadelphia* 106 (Spring–Summer 1995): 58.

6. Ibid., 57–59 (quotation on 59).

7. Ibid., 65.

8. "Two Protestants Find '60 Queries Proper," *New York Times*, April 26, 1960, 28.

9. "Test of Religion," *Time*, September 26, 1960, 21.

10. Ibid.

11. "Transcript of Kennedy Talk to Ministers and Questions and Answers," *New York Times*, September 13, 1960, 22.

12. *McGowan v. Maryland*, 366 U.S. 420 (1961).

13. Steven K. Green, *The Third Disestablishment: Church, State, and American Culture, 1940–1975* (New York: Oxford University Press, 2019), 250–51.

14. Del Dickson, ed., *The Supreme Court in Conference (1940–1985): The Private Discussions behind Nearly 300 Supreme Court Decisions* (New York: Oxford University Press, 2001), 393.

15. Ibid., 394.

16. *McGowan v. Maryland*, 366 U.S. 420 (1961).

17. Ibid., at 561.

18. Gregg Ivers, *To Build a Wall: American Jews and the Separation of Church and State* (Charlottesville: University Press of Virginia, 1995), 107–8.

19. Ibid., 108.

20. *Torcaso v. Watkins*, 367 U.S. 488 (1961).

21. "Religious Oath Held Unconstitutional," *Christian Century*, July 5, 1961, 821; *Zorach v. Clauson*, 343 U.S. 306 (1952), at 313.

22. The Board of Regents statement was cited in oral argument by William J. Butler. See *Engel v. Vitale* Oral Argument, April 3, 1962, Oyez, https://www.oyez.org/cases/1961/468. Accessed February 15, 2021.

23. *Engel v. Vitale*, 370 U.S. 421 (1962), at 422.

24. Green, *The Third Disestablishment*, 257.

25. Ibid.

26. Ivers, *To Build a Wall*, 125; Green, *Third Disestablishment*, 257.

27. *Engel v. Vitale* Oral Argument, April 3, 1962, Oyez, https://www.oyez.org/cases/1961/468. Accessed February 15, 2021.

28. Ibid.

29. Ibid. See also Anthony Lewis, "Prayer in School Put to High Court," *New York Times*, April 4, 1962, 45, 86.

30. Dickson, *Supreme Court in Conference*, 424.

31. *Engel v. Vitale*, 370 U.S. 421 (1962), at 435.

32. Ibid., at 437.

33. Ibid., at 445.

34. Anthony Lewis, "Supreme Court Outlaws Official School Prayers in Regents Case Decision; Ruling is 6 to 1," *New York Times*, June 26, 1962, 1 (quotations), 16.

35. Alexander Burnham, "Edict Is Called Setback by Christian Clerics—Rabbis Praise It," *New York Times*, June 26, 1962, 1 (first quotation), 17 (second quotation); "Spellman Renews Attack on Court's Decision," *New York Times*, June 28, 1962, 17 (third and fourth quotations).

36. Burnham, "Edict Is Called Setback," 17 (first through fourth quotations); "Spellman Renews Attack," 17 (fifth quotation); Anthony Lewis, "Both Houses Get Bills to Lift Ban on School Prayer," *New York Times*, June 27, 1962, 20. See also Paul Hofmann, "Vatican Regrets Ruling on Prayer," *New York Times*, July 22, 1962, 36.

37. Burnham, "Edict Is Called Setback," 17.

38. Lewis, "Both Houses Get Bills," 20.

39. Ibid., 1 (first two quotations); "President Urges Court Be Backed on Prayer Issue," *New York Times*, June 28, 1962, 17 (third quotation); Alexander

Burnham, "Court's Decision Stirs Conflicts," *New York Times*, June 27, 1962, 20 (fourth and fifth quotations).

40. Andrews quoted in Ivers, *To Build a Wall*, 244 note 74. All other quotations from "The Court Decision—And the School Prayer Furor," *Newsweek*, July 9, 1962, 44.

41. For the religious affiliations of the justices, see "To Stand as a Guarantee," *Time*, July 6, 1962, 7.

42. John F. Kennedy, "The President's News Conference," June 27, 1962, in *Public Papers of the Presidents of the United States: John F. Kennedy* (Washington: Government Printing Office, 1962–64), 1962:510.

43. Ibid., 511.

44. "The Court Decision—And the School Prayer Furor," 45.

45. "Spellman Scores Ruling on Prayer," *New York Times*, August 3, 1962, 21.

46. "Jewish Congress on Church–State," *America*, January 10, 1953, 386.

47. "To Our Jewish Friends," *America*, September 1, 1962, 665.

48. Ibid., 666.

49. Leo Pfeffer, "An Autobiographical Sketch," in *Religion and the State: Essays in Honor of Leo Pfeffer*, ed. James E. Wood Jr. (Waco: Baylor University Press, 1985), 514–17 (first quotation on 515–16, second and third quotations on 516).

50. "To Our Catholic Friends," *America*, September 8, 1962, 680.

51. "Is *America* Trying to Bully the Jews?" *Christian Century*, September 5, 1962, 1057.

52. "The Main Issue," *America*, September 15, 1962, 713; "P.S.—To Jewish Friends," *America*, September 22, 1962, 768–69. See also "Religion and Pluralism," *Commonweal*, September 1962, 5–6.

53. Sorauf, *Wall of Separation*, 134.

54. Ibid. See also "Bible Reading Is Growing L.I. Controversy," *Newsday*, February 26, 1962, p. 9C.

55. Robert Anton Wilson, "The Passion of Madalyn Murray," *Fact*, January–February 1965, 18; "Playboy Interview: Madalyn Murray," *Playboy*, October 1965, 61–74.

56. Wilson, "The Passion of Madalyn Murray," 18–19; "Playboy Interview," 65.

57. Robert Anton Wilson, "The Most Hated Woman in America," *Fact*, March–April 1964, 12 (first quotation), 14 (second and third quotations).

58. "Is the Supreme Court on Trial?" *Christianity Today*, March 1, 1963, 28.

59. "Court Weighs Religious Exercises," *Christianity Today*, March 15, 1963, 31.

60. Ibid.

61. Ibid.

62. Ibid.

63. Dickson, *Supreme Court in Conference*, 426.

64. Ibid., 427.

65. *School District of Abington Township v. Schempp*, 374 U.S. 203 (1963).

66. Ibid., at 207.

67. Ibid., at 247.
68. Ibid., at 306.
69. Fred M. Hechinger, "Wide Effect Due: Decisions Will Require Change in Majority of State Systems," *New York Times*, June 18, 1963, 1, 27.
70. Sorauf, *Wall of Separation*, 151.
71. The National Association of Evangelicals and Ockenga quoted by Daniel K. Williams, *God's Own Party: The Making of the Christian Right* (New York: Oxford University Press, 2010), 64 (NAE), 65 (Ockenga).
72. James O'Gara, "Religion and the Court," *Commonweal*, July 5, 1963, 391.
73. George Dugan, "Churches Divided, With Most in Favor," *New York Times*, June 18, 1963, 29 (quotations). See also Anthony Lewis, "Public Mood Plays a Big Role in Court Rulings," *New York Times*, June 23, 1963, 148; Anthony Lewis, "New Judges and Doctrines Alter Character of the Supreme Court," *New York Times*, June 23, 1963, 64; "A Tide Reversed," *Time*, June 19, 1964, 61.
74. Green, *The Third Disestablishment*, 293–99.
75. "A Tide Reversed," *Time*, June 19, 1964, 61.
76. Leo Pfeffer, "A Momentous Year in Church and State, 1963," *Journal of Church and State* 6 (Winter 1964): 36 (first quotation), 38 (second quotation).
77. Dickson, *Supreme Court in Conference*, 434.
78. *United States v. Seeger*, 380 U.S. 163 (1965).
79. *Griswold v. Connecticut*, 381 U.S. 479 (1965).
80. Dickson, *Supreme Court in Conference*, 800 (first and second quotations), 801 (subsequent quotations).
81. *Griswold v. Connecticut*, at 484.

Chapter Seven. The Death of God

1. Key quoted by Barry Friedman, *The Will of the People: How Public Opinion Has Influenced the Supreme Court and Shaped the Meaning of the Constitution* (New York: Farrar, Straus and Giroux, 2009), 260.
2. Ibid.
3. *NAACP v. Button*, 371 U.S. 415 (1963), at 429 (second quotation), 430 (third quotation), 452 (first quotation).
4. On custodianship, see Elesha J. Coffmann, *The Christian Century and the Rise of the Protestant Mainline* (New York: Oxford University Press, 2013), 5–6, 218–19.
5. David A. Hollinger, "The Accommodation of Protestant Christianity with the Enlightenment: An Old Drama Still Being Enacted," in Hollinger, *After Cloven Tongues of Fire: Protestant Liberalism in Modern American History* (Princeton: Princeton University Press, 2013), 6–7.
6. Andrew Hartman, *A War for the Soul of America: A History of the Culture Wars* (Chicago: University of Chicago Press, 2015), 21.

7. Ibid., 9–37.
8. Stokely Carmichael and Charles V. Hamilton, *Black Power: The Politics of Liberation* (New York: Random House, 1967), 44. On the split over Christianity among black intellectuals, see Christopher Cameron, *Black Freethinkers: A History of African American Secularism* (Evanston: Northwestern University Press, 2019), especially 119–64; Barbara Dianne Savage, *Your Spirits Walk Beside Us: The Politics of Black Religion* (Cambridge: Harvard University Press, 2008).
9. Garry Wills, *Bare Ruined Choirs: Doubt, Prophecy, and Radical Religion* (Garden City, NY: Doubleday, 1972), 15–37.
10. "Pope John Convokes the Council," in Walter M. Abbott, ed., *The Documents of Vatican II* (New York: America Press, 1966), 703.
11. Joseph A. Komonchak, "What They Said Before the Council: How the U.S. Bishops Envisioned Vatican II," *Commonweal*, December 7, 1990, 715–16. Komonchak tries to modify the common view that the American bishops were unprepared for Vatican II, but the evidence that he offers tends instead to confirm it.
12. Joseph A. Komonchak, "The Silencing of John Courtney Murray," in A. Melloni et al., eds., *Cristianesimo nella Storia* (Bologna: Il Mulino, 1996), 698–701.
13. "Pope John's Opening Speech to the Council," in *Documents of Vatican II*, 715.
14. John Courtney Murray, "Appendix: Toledo Talk," in *Bridging the Sacred and the Secular: Selected Writings of John Courtney Murray*, ed. J. Leon Hooper (Washington: Georgetown University Press, 1994), 335.
15. "Constitution on the Sacred Liturgy," *Documents of Vatican II*, 137–78.
16. "Declaration of the Relationship of the Church to Non-Christian Religions," *Documents of Vatican II*, 660–68 (first quotation on 660, second quotation on 663).
17. Komonchak, "The Silencing of John Courtney Murray," 701.
18. John Courtney Murray, "The Problem of Religious Freedom," *Theological Studies* 25 (December 1964): 512.
19. Ibid., 560.
20. "Declaration of Religious Freedom," in *Documents of Vatican II*, 677.
21. Blanshard and Fletcher quoted in John T. McGreevy, *Catholicism and American Freedom: A History* (New York: Norton, 2003), 214 (Blanshard), 256 (Fletcher).
22. Gabriel Vahanian, *The Death of God: The Culture of Our Post-Christian Era* (New York: G. Braziller, 1961), xxxii.
23. Paul Van Buren, *Secular Meaning of the Gospel, Based on an Analysis of Its Language* (New York: Macmillan, 1963); "Linguistic Analysis: A Way for Some to Affirm Their Faith," *Time*, July 10, 1964, 64.
24. Harvey Cox, *The Secular City: Secularization and Urbanization in Theological Perspective* (New York: Macmillan, 1965), 268.

25. Thomas J. J. Altizer, "Creative Negation in Theology," *Christian Century*, July 7, 1965, 864. See also Thomas J. J. Altizer and William Hamilton, *Radical Theology and the Death of God* (Indianapolis: Bobbs-Merrill, 1966).

26. William Hamilton, "The Shape of a Radical Theology," *Christian Century*, October 6, 1965, 1219–22.

27. "Christian Atheism: The 'God Is Dead' Movement," *Time*, October 22, 1965, 62.

28. Williams quoted in ibid; " 'New' Theologians See Christianity Without God," *New York Times*, October 17, 1965, 85.

29. "A Letter from the Publisher," *Time*, April 8, 1966. For the article, see "Toward a Hidden God," *Time*, April 8, 1966, 82–87.

30. See Letters to the Editor, *Time*, April 15, April 22, and April 29, 1966.

31. Hamilton quoted by Jackson Lee Ice and John J. Carey, eds., *The Death of God Debate* (Philadelphia: Westminster Press, 1967), 12. For the letters, see "Letters to William Hamilton," in ibid., 159–93 (quotations on 161). See also "Letters to Thomas Altizer," ibid., 194–209. The Ice and Carey book has many more elaborate responses and is a quite useful entry into the midcentury discussion.

32. Bartlett quoted in Ice and Carey, eds., *The Death of God Debate*, 168. Paul Vitello, "William Hamilton Dies at 87; Known for 'Death of God,' " *New York Times*, March 10, 2012.

33. For examples of these responses, see the commentary in "Toward a Hidden God" and in Ice and Carey, eds., *The Death of God Debate*.

34. Paul L. Holmer, "Contra the New Theologies," *Christian Century*, March 17, 1965, in *The Death of God Debate*, 138 (second quotation), 141 (first quotation). See also "On Tradition, or What Is Left of It," *Time*, April 22, 1966, 42–43.

35. National Council of Churches, "Separation and Interaction of Church and State," *Journal of Church and State* 6 (Spring 1964): 150.

36. David A. Hollinger, *Protestants Abroad: How Missionaries Tried to Change the World but Changed America* (Princeton: Princeton University Press, 2017), 105–6 (quotation on 105).

37. David A. Hollinger, "After Cloven Tongues of Fire: Ecumenical Protestantism and the Modern American Encounter with Diversity," in Hollinger, *After Cloven Tongues of Fire*, 36–39.

38. "POAU in Crisis," *Newsweek*, October 5, 1964, 102–3 (quotation on 102).

39. See Hartman, *War for the Soul of America*, 14–15 (quotations on 14).

40. John Courtney Murray, "The Problem of Mr. Rawls's Problem," in *Law and Philosophy: A Symposium*, ed. Sidney Hook (New York: NYU Press, 1964), 32.

41. Betty Friedan, *The Feminine Mystique* (New York: Norton, 1963), 309.

42. McGreevy, *Catholicism and American Freedom*, 222–23.

43. George Dugan, "Foes of Abortion Assailed by Rabbi," *New York Times*, February 12, 1967, 61.

44. Gannon quoted by Robert M. Byrn, "The Future in America," *America*, December 9, 1967, 710–13 (quotation on 713).

45. "Foes of Abortion Assailed by Rabbi," 61.

46. "Life in the Dark Age," *Christian Century*, May 31, 1972, 624. For a helpful and concise summary of Protestant positions on abortion, with excerpts from denominational statements, see Robert F. Drinan, "Contemporary Protestant Thinking," *America*, December 9, 1967, 713–15.

47. Robert F. Drinan, "The Morality of Abortion Laws," *Catholic Lawyer* 14 (Summer 1968): 190–98, 264; Drinan, "Contemporary Protestant Thinking," 715.

48. "The Connecticut Decision," *Commonweal*, June 25, 1965, 427–28 (quotation on 427); William F. Buckley Jr., "The Catholic Church and Abortion," *National Review*, April 5, 1966, 308.

49. McGreevy, *Catholicism and American Freedom*, 245–46, 268; Sorauf, *Wall of Separation*, 17. See also "A Protestant Affirmation on the Control of Human Reproduction," *Christianity Today*, November 8, 1968, 18–19.

50. Sorauf, *Wall of Separation*, 17.

51. Del Dickson, ed., *The Supreme Court in Conference (1940–1985): The Private Discussions behind Nearly 300 Supreme Court Decisions* (New York: Oxford University Press, 2001), 804–13.

52. *Roe v. Wade*, 410 U.S. 113 (1973).

53. Laurence II. Tribe, "The Supreme Court, 1972 Term: Foreword: Toward a Model of Roles in the Due Process of Life and Law," *Harvard Law Review* 87 (November 1973): 11.

Chapter Eight. The Personal Is Political

1. On the Leftist disdain for liberalism, see Richard J. Ellis, *The Dark Side of the Left: Illiberal Egalitarianism in America* (Lawrence: University Press of Kansas, 1998); Maurice Isserman, *The Other American: The Life of Michael Harrington* (New York: PublicAffairs, 2000), 276–77.

2. C. Wright Mills quoted in Andrew Hartman, *A War for the Soul of America: A History of the Culture Wars* (Chicago: University of Chicago Press, 2015), 29; Brian Balogh, "Making Pluralism 'Great': Beyond a Recycled History of the Great Society," in Sidney M. Milkis and Jerome M. Mileur, eds., *The Great Society and the High Tide of Liberalism* (Amherst: University of Massachusetts Press, 2005), 159–60.

3. Tom Hayden, *The Port Huron Statement: The Visionary Call of the 1960s Revolution* (1962; New York: Thunder's Mouth Press, 2005), 52.

4. MacKinnon quoted in Sarah E. Igo, *The Known Citizen: A History of Privacy in Modern America* (Cambridge: Harvard University Press, 2018), 295; see also Hartman, *A War for the Soul of America*, 11–14, 29–30; Carol Hanisch, "The Personal Is Political" (1969), in Shulamith Firestone and Anne Koedt, eds., *Notes from the Second Year: Women's Liberation* (n.p.; Redstockings, 1970).

5. Igo, *Known Citizen*, 267–76; Peter Clecak, *America's Quest for the Ideal Self: Dissent and Fulfillment in the 60s and 70s* (New York: Oxford University Press, 1983), 211–26.

6. *Stanley v. Georgia*, 394 U.S. 557 (1969), at 565.

7. Leigh Ann Wheeler, *How Sex Became a Civil Liberty* (New York: Oxford University Press, 2014), 7–8 (quotations on 7).

8. Robert Wuthnow, *The Restructuring of American Religion: Society and Faith Since World War II* (Princeton: Princeton University Press, 1988).

9. Ibid., 147–48. For the conservative evangelical opposition to civil rights, see Matthew Avery Sutton, *American Apocalypse: A History of Modern Evangelicalism* (Cambridge: Harvard University Press, 2014), 306–7, 333–41; Daniel K. Williams, *God's Own Party: The Making of the Christian Right* (New York: Oxford University Press, 2010), 69–78. On liberal Christian support of the civil rights movement, see Steven K. Green, *The Third Disestablishment: Church, State, and American Culture, 1940–1975* (New York: Oxford University Press, 2019), 320–21; David A. Hollinger, *Protestants Abroad: How Missionaries Tried to Change the World but Changed America* (Princeton: Princeton University Press, 2017), 104, 266–87; Lilian Calles Barger, *The World Come of Age: An Intellectual History of Liberation Theology* (New York: Oxford University Press, 2018).

10. On this overlap, see Anthony Lewis, "Court Again Under Fire," *New York Times*, July 1, 1962, 114.

11. Joseph Crespino, "Civil Rights and the Religious Right," in Bruce J. Schulman and Julian E. Zelizer, *Rightward Bound: Making America Conservative in the 1970s* (Cambridge: Harvard University Press, 2008), 93.

12. George Dugan, "Churches Divided, With Most in Favor," *New York Times*, June 18, 1963, 29. Crespino, "Civil Rights and the Religious Right," 90–91; Crespino, *In Search of Another Country: Mississippi and the Conservative Counter Revolution* (Princeton: Princeton University Press, 2007), 249–50.

13. Crespino, "Civil Rights and the Religious Right," 92–93.

14. *Green v. Kennedy*, 309 F. Supp. 1127 (D.D.C. 1970); *Green v. Connally*, 330 F. Supp. 1150 (D.D.C. 1971). The lower court's decision was affirmed in *Coit v. Green*, 404 U.S. 997 (1971).

15. Jonathan Spivak and Tom Herman, "New Policy on Taxes May Not End All-White School Problem in South," *Wall Street Journal*, July 13, 1970, 24.

16. *Walz v. Tax Commission*, 397 U.S. 664 (1970), at 701.

17. Spivak and Herman, "New Policy on Taxes," 24.

18. On their sense of estrangement from a cultural consensus, see Neil J. Young, *We Gather Together: The Religious Right and the Problem of Interfaith Politics* (New York: Oxford University Press, 2016), 2–3.

19. Williams, *God's Own Party*, 116–20 (first three quotations on 117, last three on 119). See also R. Marie Griffith, *Moral Combat: How Sex Divided American Christians and Fractured American Politics* (New York: Basic Books, 2017), 201–39.

20. Sara Dubow, " 'A Constitutional Right Rendered Utterly Meaningless': Religious Exemptions and Reproductive Politics, 1973–2014," *Journal of Policy History* 27 (January 2015): 7.

21. Ibid., 4–5 (quotation on 5).

22. Stephen Skowronek, *The Politics Presidents Make: Leadership from John Adams to Bill Clinton* (Cambridge: Harvard University Press, 1997), 43–45. See also Stephen Skowronek, "The Reassociation of Ideas and Purposes: Racism, Liberalism, and the American Political Tradition," *American Political Science Review* 100 (August 2006): 385–401.

23. On Murray's suspicion of freedom of conscience, see John T. McGreevy, *Catholicism and American Freedom: A History* (New York: Norton, 2003), 265. On this "Catholic pivot" toward freedom of conscience, see Samuel Moyn, "Religious Freedom between Truth and Tactic," in Winnifred Fallers Sullivan et al., *Politics of Religious Freedom* (Chicago: University of Chicago Press, 2015), 135–41.

24. Dubow, "A Constitutional Right," 10–11.

25. Ibid., 15.

26. Ibid., 12–14.

27. Ibid., 1. See also David Sehat, *The Myth of American Religious Freedom*, updated ed. (New York: Oxford University Press, 2015), 268–69.

28. Crespino, "Civil Rights and the Religious Right," 98–99 (quotation on 99).

29. Ibid., 99.

30. Ibid., 99–100.

31. A. O. Sulzberger Jr., "Private Academics Protest Tax Plan," *New York Times*, December 11, 1978, A20. See also Crespino, "Civil Rights and the Religious Right," 100–103.

32. Crespino, "Civil Rights and the Religious Right," 91 (first and third quotations); Williams, *God's Own Party*, 164 (second quotation).

33. Williams, *God's Own Party*, 162–64.

34. Falwell quoted in Sehat, *The Myth of American Religious Freedom*, 265 (first quotation), 265 66 (second quotation), Young, *We Gather Together*, 3 (third quotation).

35. Robertson quoted in Williams, *God's Own Party*, 159.

36. Ibid., 188.

37. On Reagan's jeremiad, see David Sehat, *The Jefferson Rule: How the Founding Fathers Became Infallible and Our Politics Inflexible* (New York: Simon and Schuster, 2015), 157–78.

38. *Bob Jones University v. United States*, 461 U.S. 574 (1983).

39. Ibid.

40. *Bob Jones University v. United States*, 468 F. Supp. 890 (D.S.C. 1978).

41. Robert Lindsay, "Reagan to Debate His G.O.P. Rivals in South Carolina," *New York Times*, January 31, 1980, B8; Crespino, "Civil Rights and the Religious Right," 104.

42. Crespino, "Civil Rights and the Religious Right," 103 (first quotation); Williams, *God's Own Party*, 189 (second quotation), 190 (third quotation).

43. Howell Raines, "Reagan Backs Evangelicals in Their Political Activities," *New York Times*, August 23, 1980, 8.

44. Ibid.
45. Anthony Lewis, "Religion and Politics," *New York Times*, September 18, 1980, A31.
46. Ibid.
47. Howell Raines, "Reagan Is Balancing 2 Different Stances," *New York Times*, October 4, 1980, 9.
48. Kenneth A. Briggs, "Dispute on Religion Raised by Campaign," *New York Times*, November 9, 1980, 31.
49. Ibid.; Williams, *God's Own Party*, 192.
50. Ronald Reagan, "Inaugural Address," January 20, 1981, in *Public Papers of the Presidents of the United States: Ronald Reagan* (Washington: U.S. Government Printing Office, 1981–89), 1981:2 (second quotation), 3 (first quotation).
51. *Bob Jones University v. United States*, 639 F2d 147 (4th Cir. 1981).
52. Bob Jones University petition for a writ of certiorari, October 1981.
53. Amicus Brief of the National Association of Evangelicals (NAE), 3; Amicus Brief of the Church of Jesus Christ of Latter-day Saints, 2.
54. Amicus Brief of the Center for Law and Religious Freedom of the Christian Legal Society, 5; Amicus Brief of the NAE, 9.
55. *Bob Jones University v. United States*, 461 U.S. 574 (1983), at 583; Genesis 9:22 (RSV).
56. Amicus Brief of Congressman Trent Lott; David Whitman, "Ronald Reagan and Tax Exemptions for Discriminatory Schools," in *How the Press Affects Federal Policymaking: Six Case Studies*, Martin Linsky et al., eds. (New York: Norton, 1986), 271 (quotation); Crespino, *In Search of Another Country*, 258–60.
57. Whitman, "Ronald Reagan and Tax Exemptions," 271–78 (first quotation on 272, second quotation on 275).
58. *Bob Jones University v. United States*, 461 U.S. 574 (1983), at 585 note 9.
59. Amicus Brief of the National Association for the Advancement of Colored People, 40 (first quotation), 41 (second quotation).
60. Del Dickson, ed., *The Supreme Court in Conference (1940–1985): The Private Discussions behind Nearly 300 Supreme Court Decisions* (New York: Oxford University Press, 2001), 417–21.
61. *Bob Jones University v. United States*, at 591 (first quotation), 592 (second through fourth quotations).
62. Beverly LaHaye, *Who But a Woman?* (Nashville: Thomas Nelson, 1984), 109–11 (quotation on 109).
63. Robert M. Cover, "The Supreme Court, 1982 Term: Foreword: Nomos and Narrative," *Harvard Law Review* 97 (November 1983): 4–68.
64. Igo, *Known Citizen*, 294–98 (quotation on 297).
65. Larry Gross, *Contested Closets: The Politics and Ethics of Outing* (Minneapolis: University of Minnesota Press, 1993), 146.
66. William M. Eskridge Jr., *Dishonorable Passions: Sodomy Laws in America, 1861–2003* (New York: Viking, 2008), 230–36.

67. Oral argument in *Bowers v. Hardwick,* Oyez, https://www.oyez.org/cases/1985/85–140. Accessed February 18, 2021.

68. Dickson, *The Supreme Court in Conference,* 821–25 (quotation on 824).

69. *Bowers v. Hardwick,* 478 U.S. 186 (1986), at 191.

70. Ibid., at 211 (first quotation), 211-212 (second quotation).

71. Igo, *Known Citizen,* 299; Deborah Nelson, *Pursuing Privacy in Cold War America* (New York: Columbia University Press, 2002), 158.

72. James Davison Hunter, *Culture Wars: The Struggle to Define America* (New York: Basic Books, 1991), 42.

73. Hartman, *War for the Soul of America,* 15–16.

74. Dickson, *Supreme Court in Conference,* 427.

75. David T. Courtwright, *Forces of Habit: Drugs and the Making of the Modern World* (Cambridge: Harvard University Press, 2001).

76. Carolyn N. Long, "*Employment Division, Department of Human Resources of Oregon v. Smith:* The Battle for Religious Freedom," in Leslie C. Griffin, ed., *Law and Religion: Cases in Context* (New York: Aspen, 2010), 108–9.

77. Ibid., 110–11 (quotation on 111).

78. Ibid., 113.

79. Ibid., 114.

80. *Employment Division v. Smith,* 494 U.S. 872 (1990).

81. Ibid., at 888 (first quotation), 889 (second quotation).

82. Ibid., at 879.

83. Ibid., at 890. On Scalia's defense of monotheism, see his dissent in *Mc-Creary County v. ACLU,* 545 U.S. 844 (2005).

84. Gustav Niebuhr, "Disparate Group Unite Behind Civil Rights Bill on Religious Freedom," *Washington Post,* October 16, 1993, A7.

85. Religious Freedom Restoration Act (1993), sec. 2.

86. Robert T. Drinan and Jennifer I. Huffmann, "The Religious Freedom Restoration Act: A Legislative History," *Journal of Law and Religion* 10:2 (1994): 531–41 (Solarz quotation on 534).

87. Clinton quoted in Adam Serwer and Irin Carmon, "The Law That Could Sink Birth Control Coverage," MSNBC, March 21, 2014, http://www.msnbc.com/msnbc/birth-control-coverage-stake; Long, "*Employment Division,*" 123. The court soon voided the federal law as it applied to state and local governments in *City of Boerne v. Flores,* 521 U.S. 507 (1997).

Chapter Nine. Religious Freedom

1. "Evangelicals & Catholics Together," *First Things,* May 1994, 15–22 (quotations on 18).

2. Ibid., 20.

3. John Rawls, "Outline of a Decision Procedure for Ethics," in Samuel Freeman, ed., *John Rawls: Collected Papers* (Cambridge: Harvard University Press, 1999), 1–19; John Rawls, *A Theory of Justice* (Cambridge:

Harvard University Press, 1971); P. Mackenzie Bok, "To the Mountain-top Again: The Early Rawls and Post-Protestant Ethics in Postwar America," *Modern Intellectual History* 14 (April 2017): 153–85.

4. William A. Galston, "Pluralism and Social Unity," in Chandran Kukathas, ed., *John Rawls: Critical Assessments of Leading Philosophers* (London: Routledge, 2003), 4:124.

5. See Burton Dreben, "On Rawls and Political Liberalism," in Samuel Freeman, *The Cambridge Companion to Rawls* (New York: Cambridge University Press, 2003), 316–25.

6. Rawls, "The Domain of the Political and Overlapping Consensus" (1989), in *Collected Papers*, 473–96.

7. John Rawls, *Political Liberalism* (New York: Columbia University Press, 1993). See also John Rawls, "The Idea of an Overlapping Consensus" (1987), in *Collected Papers*, 421–48; Charles Larmore, "Public Reason," in Freeman, ed., *Cambridge Companion to Rawls*, 368–93.

8. "Evangelicals & Catholics Together," 18.

9. "*Commonweal* Interview with John Rawls" (1998), in Rawls, *Collected Papers*, 619 (first and second quotations); "The Idea of Public Reason Revisited" (1997), in Rawls, *Collected Papers*, 573–615 (third quotation on 579).

10. "*Commonweal* Interview," in Rawls, *Collected Papers*, 622.

11. Richard Rorty, *Contingency, Irony, and Solidarity* (New York: Cambridge University Press, 1989), 12. Richard Rorty, *Achieving Our Country: Leftist Thought in Twentieth-Century America* (Cambridge: Harvard University Press, 1998).

12. Adam Liptak, "John Lawrence, Plaintiff in Gay Rights Case, Dies," *New York Times*, December 23, 2011, D8.

13. Oral argument in *Lawrence v. Texas*, Oyez, March 26, 2003, https://www.oyez.org/cases/2002/02-102. Accessed February 18, 2021.

14. *Lawrence v. Texas*, 539 U.S. 558 (2003).

15. Ibid., 590 (first quotation), 591 (second quotation).

16. Katherine Q. Seelye, "Conservatives Mobilize against Ruling on Gay Marriage," *New York Times*, November 20, 2003, A29.

17. Ibid.

18. David D. Kirkpatrick, "Conservatives Using Issue of Gay Unions as a Rallying Tool," *New York Times*, February 8, 2004, 16.

19. Ibid.

20. David Grann, "Where W. Got Compassion," *New York Times Magazine*, September 12, 1999, 62–65. For the deeper history of animosity toward state-based welfare, see Alison Collis Greene, *No Depression in Heaven: The Great Depression, the New Deal, and the Transformation of Religion in the Delta* (New York: Oxford University Press, 2015), 2–3, 7.

21. Grann, "Where W. Got His Compassion," 65.

22. "Bush Would Back Constitutional Ban on Same-Sex Marriage," CNN.com, December 17, 2003, http://www.cnn.com/2003/ALLPOLITICS/12/17/bush.gay.marriage/.

23. Adam Nagourney, " 'Moral Values' Carried Bush, Rove Says," *New York Times*, November 10, 2004, A20; Daniel K. Williams, *God's Own Party: The Making of the Christian Right* (New York: Oxford University Press, 2010), 261.

24. Daniel Cox and Robert P. Jones, "America's Changing Religious Identity," PRRI, September 6, 2017, https://www.prri.org/research/american-religious-landscape-christian-religiously-unaffiliated/; "America's Changing Religious Landscape," *Pew Research Center*, May 12, 2015, https://www.pewforum.org/2015/05/12/americas-changing-religious-landscape; " 'Nones' on the Rise," *Pew Research Center*, October 9, 2012, http://www.pewforum.org/2012/10/09/nones-on-the-rise/; "7.5 Million Americans Have 'Lost Their Religion' Since 2012," *Huffington Post*, March 13, 2015, http://www.huffingtonpost.com/2015/03/13/americans-no-religion _n_6864536. Accessed February 18, 2021.

25. "Understanding Religion's Role in the 2006 Election," *Pew Research Center*, December 5, 2006, https://www.pewforum.org/2006/12/05/understanding -religions-role-in-the-2006-election/. Accessed February 18, 2021.

26. "Changing Attitudes on Same-Sex Marriage," *Pew Research Center*, May 14, 2019, https://www.pewforum.org/fact-sheet/changing-attitudes-on -gay-marriage/. Accessed February 18, 2021.

27. Diana B. Henriques, "As Exemptions Grow, Religion Outweighs Regulation," *New York Times*, October 8, 2006, https://www.nytimes.com/2006 /10/08/business/08religious.html.

28. Charles Taylor, *A Secular Age* (Cambridge: Harvard University Press, 2007).

29. Susan Jacoby, *Freethinkers: A History of American Secularism* (New York: Metropolitan, 2004); Sam Harris, *The End of Faith: Religion, Terror, and the Future of Reason* (New York: Norton, 2004); Daniel Dennett, *Breaking the Spell: Religion as a Natural Phenomenon* (New York: Viking, 2006); Sam Harris, *Letter to a Christian Nation* (New York: Knopf, 2006); Richard Dawkins, *The God Delusion* (New York: Houghton Mifflin, 2006); Christopher Hitchens, *God Is Not Great: How Religion Poisons Everything* (New York: Twelve, 2007).

30. Taylor, *A Secular Age*, 22.

31. Ibid., 38.

32. Ibid., 145 (first quotation), 376 (third quotation), 506 (second quotation).

33. Charles Larmore, "How Much Can We Stand?" *New Republic*, April 9, 2008; John Patrick Diggins, "The Godless Delusion," *New York Times*, December 16, 2007, https://www.nytimes.com/2007/12/16/books/review /Diggins-t.html.

34. Templeton Prize biography, Templeton Foundation, http://www .templetonprize.org/laureate-sub/taylor-press-release/. Accessed February 18, 2021.

35. Charles Taylor, Templeton Prize Press Conference, http://www .templetonprize.org/laureate-sub/taylor-press-conference-statement/. Accessed on February 18. 2021.

36. *A Secular Age* Book Forum, *The Immanent Frame*, https://tif.ssrc.org /category/book-blog/book forums/secular_age/. Accessed February 18, 2021.

37. Talal Asad, *Formations of the Secular: Christianity, Islam, Modernity* (Stanford: Stanford University Press, 2003), 1–17.

38. Saba Mahmood, *Religious Difference in a Secular Age: A Minority Report* (Princeton: Princeton University Press, 2016), 1–22. See also Saba Mahmood, "Can Secularism Be Other-wise?" in Michael Warner et al., eds., *Varieties of Secularism in a Secular Age* (Cambridge: Harvard University Press, 2010), 282–99.

39. Peter G. Danchin, "Religious Freedom in the Panopticon of Enlightenment Rationality," in Sullivan et al., eds., *The Politics of Religious Freedom* (Chicago: University of Chicago Press, 2015), 240–52 (quotation on 243).

40. Philip Hamburger, *The Separation of Church and State* (Cambridge: Harvard University Press, 2002). See also his *Liberal Suppression: Section 501(c)(3) and the Taxation of Speech* (Chicago: University of Chicago Press, 2018).

41. Jon Meacham, "The Decline and Fall of Christian America," *Newsweek*, April 13, 2009.

42. *Hosanna-Tabor Evangelical Lutheran Church and School v. Equal Employment Opportunity Commission*, 565 U.S. 171 (2012).

43. Ibid.

44. Ibid.

45. Ibid., at 189.

46. Ibid., at 193–94.

47. Ibid., at 195.

48. "The Ministerial Exception," *New York Times*, January 12, 2012, https:// www.nytimes.com/2012/01/13/opinion/the-ministerial-exception.html.

49. Robert Pear, "Obama Reaffirms that Insurers Must Cover Contraception," January 20, 2012, https://www.nytimes.com/2012/01/21/health /policy/administration-rules-insurers-must-cover-contraceptives.html.

50. Dolan quoted in ibid.; United States Conference of Catholic Bishops Ad Hoc Committee for Religious Liberty, "Our First, Most Cherished Liberty: A Statement on Religious Liberty," March 2012, https://www.usccb .org/committees/religious-liberty/our-first-most-cherished-liberty. Accessed February 18, 2021. See also Samuel Moyn, "Religious Freedom between Truth and Tactic," in Sullivan et al., *Politics of Religious Freedom*, 138–40.

51. National Association of Evangelicals quoted in Pear, "Obama Reaffirms that Insurers Must Cover Contraception"; Evangelicals and Catholics Together, "In Defense of Religious Freedom," *First Things*, March 2012, https://www.firstthings.com/article/2012/03/in-defense-of-religious-freedom.

52. Evangelicals and Catholics Together, "In Defense of Religious Freedom."

53. Elizabeth A. Castelli, "The Bishops, the Sisters, and Religious Freedom," in Sullivan et al., *Politics of Religious Freedom*, 228.

54. Sullivan, "The World That *Smith* Made," in Sullivan et al., *Politics of Religious Freedom*, 235.

55. Laurie Goodstein, "Obama Shift on Providing Contraception Splits Critics," *New York Times*, February 14, 2012, https://www.nytimes.com/2012 /02/15/us/obama-shift-on-contraception-splits-catholics.html.

56. Adam Serwer and Irin Carmon, "The Law That Could Sink Birth Control Coverage," MSNBC, March 21, 2014, http://www.msnbc.com/msnbc /birth-control-coverage-stake. Accessed February 18, 2021; "Hobby Lobby Should Not Be Subject to Religious Liberty Protections," Press Release, March 25, 2014, https://nadler.house.gov/news/documentsingle. aspx?DocumentID=391250. Accessed February 18, 2021.

57. Serwer and Carmon, "The Law That Could Sink Birth Control Coverage."

58. *Burwell v. Hobby Lobby Stores Inc.*, 573 U.S. 682 (2014).

59. Micah Schwartzman, Richard C. Schragger, and Nelson Tebbe, "The New Law of Religion: Hobby Lobby rewrites religious-freedom law in ways that ignore everything that came before," *Slate*, July 3, 2014, https:// slate.com/news-and-politics/2014/07/after-hobby-lobby-there-is-only -rfra-and-thats-all-you-need.html.

60. *Burwell v. Hobby Lobby Stores Inc.*, at 702, 739 (quotation), 757 note 19.

61. Ibid., at 739–40.

62. Serwer and Carmon, "The Law That Could Sink Birth Control Coverage."

63. Rorty, *Contingency, Irony, and Solidarity*, 12.

64. Dana Liebelson, "Inside the Conservative Campaign to Launch 'Jim Crow-Style' Bills Against Gay Americans," *Mother Jones*, February 20, 2014, https://www.motherjones.com/politics/2014/02/gay-discrimination -bills-religious-freedom-jim-crow/.

65. Ponnuru quoted in Valerie Bauerlein and Jon Kamp, "Social Conservatives Try New Tack with State-Level Efforts on Religious Freedom," *Wall Street Journal*, April 13, 2016, https://www.wsj.com/articles/social-conservatives- try-new-tack-with-state-level-efforts-on-religious-freedom-1460504840; *Obergefell v. Hodges*, 576 U.S. 644 (2015).

66. "Presidential Candidate Donald Trump Rally in Mount Pleasant, South Carolina," C-SPAN, December 7, 2015, https://www.c-span.org/video /?401762-1/presidential-candidate-donald-trump-rally-mount-pleasant -south-carolina. Accessed February 18, 2021.

67. Elizabeth Dias, "'Christianity Will Have Power,'" *New York Times*, September 8, 2020, https://www.nytimes.com/2020/08/09/us/evangelicals -trump-christianity.html.

68. Erik Ortiz, "What Is the Johnson Amendment that Trump Wants to 'Destroy'?" NBC News, February 2, 2017, https://www.nbcnews.com /politics/donald-trump/what-johnson-amendment-trump-wants-destroy -n716046.

69. Amanda Taub and Max Fisher, "Trump's Immigration Order Tests Limits of Law and Executive Power," *New York Times*, January 30, 2017, https://www.nytimes.com/2017/01/30/us/politics/trump-immigration-muslim-ban.html.

70. Ali Vitali, "Trump Signs 'Religious Liberty' Executive Order Allowing for Broad Exemptions," NBC News, May 4, 2017, https://www.nbcnews.com/news/us-news/trump-signs-religious-liberty-executive-order-allowing-broad-exemptions-n754786.

71. Ibid.

72. "President Donald J. Trump Stands Up for Religious Freedom," May 3, 2018, https://trumpwhitehouse.archives.gov/briefings-statements/president-donald-j-trump-stands-religious-freedom-united-states/. Accessed February 18, 2021. See also Emma Green, "Health and Human Services and the Religious Liberty War," *The Atlantic*, May 7, 2019, https://www.theatlantic.com/politics/archive/2019/05/hhs-trump-religious-freedom/588697/.

73. *Trump v. Hawaii*, 585 U.S. ____ (2018), https://www.supremecourt.gov/opinions/17pdf/17-965_h315.pdf.

74. Ibid.

75. "Attorney General William Barr on Religious Liberty," de Nicola Center for Ethics and Culture, https://www.youtube.com/watch?v=IM87WMsrCWM. Accessed February 18, 2021.

76. Ibid.

77. Ibid.

78. Ibid.

79. Ibid.

80. Phillip Shenon, " 'A Threat to Democracy': William Barr's Speech on Religious Freedom Alarms Liberal Catholics," *The Guardian*, October 20, 2019, https://www.theguardian.com/us-news/2019/oct/19/william-barr-attorney-general-catholic-conservative-speech.

81. Katherine Stewart and Caroline Fredrickson, "Bill Barr Thinks America Is Going to Hell," *New York Times*, December 29, 2019, https://www.nytimes.com/2019/12/29/opinion/william-barr-trump.html.

82. Adam Liptak, "Supreme Court to Consider Limits on Contraception Coverage," *New York Times*, January 17, 2020, https://www.nytimes.com/2020/01/17/us/supreme-court-contraception-coverage.html.

83. Erica L. Green, "Religious School Choice Case May Yield Landmark Supreme Court Decision," *New York Times*, January 21, 2020, https://www.nytimes.com/2020/01/21/us/politics/supreme-court-religion-school-vouchers.html.

84. Adam Liptak, "Civil Rights Law Protects Gay and Transgender Workers, Supreme Court Rules," *New York Times*, June 15, 2020, https://www.nytimes.com/2020/06/15/us/gay-transgender-workers-supreme-court.html.

85. Sarah Pulliam Bailey, "Christian Conservatives Rattled after Supreme Court Rules against LBGT Discrimination," *Washington Post*, June 15, 2020, https://www.washingtonpost.com/religion/2020/06/15/bostock-court -faith-conservatives-lgbt/.

86. *Espinoza v. Montana Department of Revenue*, 591 U. S. ____ (2020).

87. Ibid.

88. Linda Greenhouse, "The Supreme Court Upheld Trump's Muslim Ban. Let's Not Forget That," *New York Times*, January 28, 2021, https://www .nytimes.com/2021/01/28/opinion/supreme-court-muslim-ban.html.

89. Adam Liptak, "Supreme Court Upholds Trump Administration Regula- tion Letting Employers Opt Out of Birth Control Coverage," *New York Times*, July 8, 2020, https://www.nytimes.com/2020/07/08/us/supreme -court-birth-control-obamacare.html.

90. Ibid.

91. Michael W. McConnell, "On Religion, the Supreme Court Protects the Right to Be Different," *New York Times*, July 9, 2020, https://www .nytimes.com/2020/07/09/opinion/supreme-court-religion.html.

92. Linda Greenhouse, "The Many Dimensions of the Chief Justice's Trium- phant Term," *New York Times*, July 16, 2020, https://www.nytimes.com /2020/07/16/opinion/supreme court-roberts-religion.html.

Afterword

1. Stephen Skowronek, "The Reassociation of Ideas and Purposes: Racism, Liberalism, and the American Political Tradition," *American Political Sci- ence Review* 100 (August 2006): 400.

2. Skowronek was the first to make the point that American politics was en- tering a semipermanent state of preemption. See Stephen Skowronck, *The Politics Presidents Make: Leadership from John Adams to Bill Clinton* (New Haven: Yale University Press, 1997), 442–46.

Index

abortion issue, 186–91, 299n46;
Catholic position on, 186–87, 190;
Hyde Amendment (1977), 206;
politicizing of, 210; Protestant
conservatives uniting with
Catholics over, 203–4; Rawlsian
approach to, 231; *Roe* and, 189–91
Abrams v. United States (1919), 62
Ahzug, Bella, 106
ACLU. *See* American Civil Liberties
Union
Adams, John, 26
ADL. *See* Anti-Defamation League
African Americans, 20, 297n8. *See also*
civil rights movement; race and
racism
agnosticism, 3, 27–28, 42–43, 68, 122
AJC. *See* American Jewish Congress
AJ Committee. *See* American Jewish
Committee
Alito, Samuel: *Bostock* and, 259;
Espinoza and, 260; *Hobby Lobby* and,
250–51
Altizer, Thomas J. J., 180
America (Jesuit magazine), 120, 121,
127–28, 136, 147, 158–60
American Bible Society, 25
American Board of Commissioners for
Foreign Missions, 25

American Civil Liberties Union
(ACLU): Bible Students' speech,
defense of, 70–71; civil liberties
and, 82–83; conscientious
exemption from draft and, 205; flag
salute cases, 90–93, 98; founding of,
65, 67; frequency of Supreme
Court appearances by, 87; gay
rights and, 218; *Gitlow* and, 72–73,
Jehovah's Witnesses and, 70–71,
90–95, 98, 264; Klan and, 67–68;
NAACP and, 67; prayer and
religious instruction in public
schools and, 131, 152–53; public-
school fund, defense against
religious use of, 123; Reproductive
Freedom Project, 205, 258;
responsibility for transition to
secularism, 159; tax exemption for
racially discriminatory, private
religious schools and, 214–15;
Women's Rights Project, 205
Americanization of immigrants, 45
American Jewish Committee (AJ
Committee), 123, 125, 131, 134,
160
American Jewish Congress (AJC), 67,
123, 124, 153, 158–59, 215
American Revolution, 13, 15

Weyrich, Paul, 207
Wheeler, Lee Ann, 199
Whig political theory, 17–18, 274n18
white supremacy: demographic
    diversification as challenge to, 173,
    239–40; Klan and, 47; NAACP and,
    68; private decisions to exclude based
    on race and, 197; rejection of white
    Christian privilege, effect of, 175
Whitney, Anita, 74–75
Whitney v. California (1927), 75–76
Williams, Daniel Day, 181
Williams, John Bell, 157
Wilson, Thomas, 20
Wilson, Woodrow, 48, 51

witnesses, theistic oaths of, 27
women: feminism, 185–86, 197–98,
    217; privacy, right to, 190. *See also*
    abortion issue; birth control
World's Parliament of Religions
    (1893), 110
World War I, 46, 50–60, 66
Wuthnow, Robert, 199

Zhukov, Georgi, 140
Zimmermann telegram (1917), 51
Zionism, 45–47
Zorach, Tessim, 131
Zorach v. Clauson (1952), 131–34, 136,
    150, 151, 153, 158